Guidelines for a One-Day Fast

The fast we recommend as the best and most effective form of regular fasting is a 36-hour (or one-day) weekly fast. Here are some guidelines for a successful fast:

◆ The night before: Eat a light dinner consisting of plant foods like vegetable soup, salad, and whole grains. Keep portions small and avoid animal products, including dairy products.

◆ The morning of your fast: Take a long, relaxing shower as soon as you wake up.

◆ For "breakfast," drink 16 ounces of water with a little lemon juice and 8 ounces of freshly squeezed juice, preferably organic.

◆ Throughout the day, have at least two quarts of purified or filtered water, 32 ounces of fresh fruit and/or vegetable juice, 32 ounces of vegetable broth (boil vegetables in purified water, strain the broth, and drink), and as much herbal tea as desired.

◆ Be sure to drink at least 8 ounces of fluid at least every two hours.

◆ Stick by the bathroom because drinking all that fluid means you'll have to use it frequently.

◆ Spend at least 30 and preferably 60 minutes during the day doing some kind of gentle exercise such as walking in the fresh air or doing yoga. Moderate exercise will feel very good.

◆ Spend some time meditating on your spiritual side during the day.

◆ Be prepared to experience mood swings. One minute you may feel irritable, and the next minute, euphoric.

◆ Be prepared to feel light, buoyant, and full of energy by midafternoon.

◆ Avoid contact with food or places where you will smell food. Food can be difficult to resist on the first day of a fast, but you'll feel great when you make it through the whole day!

◆ In the evening, take a long soak in the bathtub or a long shower and gently scrub your skin to help its natural elimination process.

◆ Be prepared to feel very energized at night. You might need a little less sleep than usual.

◆ Be prepared to feel less hungry than usual the following morning. Have a light breakfast of fresh fruit and juice.

ALPHA

Fasting Inspiration

Sometimes fasting can be tough when you smell something tempting or when someone else tries to get you to eat. Just remember that fasting is a holistic practice that helps to rest and heal your physical body, clarify your mental process, release blocked emotions, and free your spirit. During your fasting day, make a point of noticing how you feel inside. Pay attention to the way your inner self is shifting and balancing, how your emotions and spirit are becoming more expansive, how your physical body feels lighter and less attached to the material aspects of life. Continue to remind yourself that you are worth this kind of special self-care. Your whole self craves this peaceful, restful nurturing. You deserve it!

Need a fasting guru to help you? These people understood the power of fasting and made fasting an integral part of their lives. Choose the person who resonates with *your* spirit, and meditate on that person whenever you need some extra inspiration to hold your fast. Some who have made fasting a part of their life include ...

- ◆ Gandhi
- ◆ Mother Teresa
- ◆ Buddha
- ◆ Jesus Christ
- ◆ Moses
- ◆ Muhammad
- ◆ St. Francis of Assisi
- ◆ Socrates
- ◆ Aristotle
- ◆ Pythagoras
- ◆ His Holiness the Dalai Lama
- ◆ Vietnamese Buddhist monk and peace activist Thich Nhat Hahn

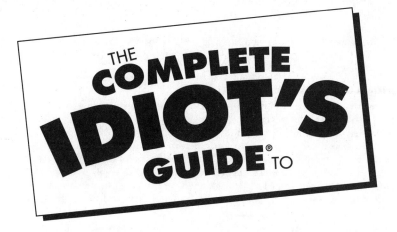

Fasting

by Eve Adamson and Linda Horning, R.D.

ALPHA

A Pearson Education Company

We dedicate this book to everyone who has ever struggled and failed to nourish the whole self. May fasting be your key.

Publisher: *Marie Butler-Knight*
Book Producer: *Lee Ann Chearney/Amaranth*
Product Manager: *Phil Kitchel*
Managing Editor: *Jennifer Chisholm*
Acquisitions Editor: *Randy Ladenheim-Gil*
Development Editor: *Lynn Northrup*
Production Editor: *Billy Fields*
Copy Editor: *Susan Aufheimer*
Illustrator: *Jody Schaeffer*
Cover/Book Designer: *Trina Wurst*
Indexer: *Angie Bess*
Layout/Proofreading: *Mary Hunt, Ayanna Lacey, Kimberly Tucker*

Contents at a Glance

Contents

Appendixes

Foreword

My first experience with fasting happened unintentionally. A serious illness when I was 13 put me in bed for two months. I couldn't eat a thing and could tolerate (that is, keep down!) only sips of water or diluted apple juice. My body, in its innate wisdom, knew that fasting would help me heal. Little did I realize that this episode would shape the course of my life.

As a teenager in the 1960s I struggled with weight gain and yo-yo dieting. The only guidance I got was a prescription for diet pills and a program for counting calories. This regime created much frustration (it didn't work) and resulted in allergies, chronic fatigue, and other imbalances.

I began exploring natural foods and healing in my 20s. I became curious about fasting "on purpose." At first I tried fasting as yet another method of weight loss. I found that although the weight loss was mostly temporary, I experienced dramatic shifts on other levels: My mind cleared, my vitality increased, and my sense of confidence and spirit soared. I found a powerful key to vibrant energy and joy!

Since then, my relationship with food and fasting has taken me on a profound 25-year quest for a life that promotes and sustains this wonderful sense of well-being. A lifestyle approach to healthy diet, yoga, meditation, and especially periodic fasting with live juices all have transformed me—at 50 I have more vitality, clarity, and enthusiasm for life than ever before. My journey has shown me that not only diet but all aspects of my self—body, mind, heart, and soul—need to be honored and nourished.

With *The Complete Idiot's Guide to Fasting*, the authors offer a delightful journey into fasting as a vehicle for transforming one's whole self. In all my years of research, I have never found a book on fasting so comprehensive, inspiring, and enjoyable to read. From the physiology of purification to the fasting stories of spiritual leaders to a complete do-it-yourself retreat, this book is an engaging, sensible, holistic guide to fasting. The authors present clear scientific information interwoven with instruction, humor, and obvious care. An idiot could read this book, but the authors never make the reader feel like one.

I highly recommend *The Complete Idiot's Guide to Fasting* to fasting novices as well as those of us who have long incorporated this profound practice as a path to vibrant health and self-actualization.

Alison Shore Gaines

Alison Shore Gaines leads conscious eating and spiritual fasting retreats at Kripalu Center in Massachusetts, Omega Institute in New York, and Tree of Life Rejuvenation Center in Arizona. She has been training health professionals and leading psycho-spiritual workshops since 1985. A Certified Holistic Lifestyle Educator, Coach, and Kripalu Yoga Teacher, Alison's training includes Ayurveda, Macrobiotics, Lifestyle Counseling, Gestalt Therapy, and Vipassana Meditation. She lives on a llama farm in Massachusetts.

Introduction

Life is complicated. So much to do, so much to plan, so much to accomplish, so much to … eat? Unfortunately for our good health, the grocery lists of twenty-first century Americans tend to be even longer than our to-do lists. Food is widely, prodigiously, dramatically, incessantly available to us, from super-sized value meals to super-sized grocery stores with floor-to-ceiling warehouse-style stacks and rows and columns and piles and bins and cases and giant refrigerators full of food.

And we love our food, too. So much so that over half of Americans are overweight and over 25 percent of us are obese. Chronic disease afflicts over 90 million Americans today, much of it controllable by diet, and we are only beginning to see the effects of processed, chemical-laden food on health, welfare, and longevity. Add to that the typical American obsession with food, the resultant eating disorders such as the newly named but frighteningly common binge-eating disorder, and you've got a quick-and-easy, conveniently packaged, American-style disaster.

How do we stop the madness? Food obsession is only part of the big picture. We are obsessed with the things we can buy, the pleasures we can enjoy, and the stimulation of our five senses. This excessive focus on the material world has led us astray in more ways than down a path towards ill health. It has robbed us of balance, of emotional well-being, of mental clarity, and of a mature spiritual life. Our physical selves, our hungers and instincts and desires, are only a small part of the big picture that makes a human being, and our emotional, mental, and spiritual selves have suffered right along with our waistlines.

The problem is that when our energy pours into the foods we eat, the stuff we buy, the things we have, the way we look, we have precious little in reserve for cultivating emotional, mental, and spiritual health. We are left with full (and bulging) stomachs, and empty hearts. We keep thinking we must be missing something, and as we try to fill that empty space with food, the space grows bigger and bigger.

But then again, how good it is to eat something delicious. Yes … we agree! Eating well is one of the most important things you can do for your health. But so is eating moderately and, every once in awhile, not eating at all. Fasting, especially on water and fresh juice, gives overtaxed digestive systems a much-needed rest while diverting energy to healing of the body, mind, and spirit. Short, regular fasts of one day per week or two to three days per month fine-tune the body's healing power, maximize the mental processes, and unleash spiritual potential. Such short fasts encourage self-discipline and are of immense physical, psychological, emotional, intellectual, and spiritual benefit.

But most people misunderstand what fasting is, what it isn't, what it can do for you, and what it won't do to you if you do it correctly. That's where *The Complete Idiot's Guide to Fasting* comes in. In this book you'll find everything you always wondered about fasting, and more, from the history of fasting in cultures all over the world to the many different ways you can incorporate fasts and fasting variations into your own life.

Fasting can make a big difference in your health, your mental clarity, and your spiritual development, and reading this book is just the beginning. Welcome to a world of better whole-self health. You are on your way to maximizing your potential!

How to Use This Book

The Complete Idiot's Guide to Fasting is divided into five parts that introduce you to fasting in a way that can help you integrate it into your life as a care system for your body, mind, and spirit. Each part of the book has a different purpose, and each part can help you in different ways to understand fasting and to create and manage your own fasting program.

Part 1, "All About Fasting," broaches the question most people first ask when they hear about fasting: Why would anyone want to fast? Food is good, so why avoid it? You will learn how fasting has impacted cultural traditions all over the world and throughout time. You'll learn how your own anatomy works, and what happens to your body when you take a short break from food. You'll also read about how your spirit is affected and nourished by fasting, and how spirit can be your ally as you summon up the willpower, resolution, and commitment to try a fast.

Part 2, "Fasting for Greater Spiritual Awareness," explores the link between fasting and meditation and shows you how to nurture your spirit by focusing away from food and other material pleasures. You'll also learn about your life force energy or chi, how to use your chakras or energy centers to improve your health and enhance your fast, and understanding your aura. This part also includes short profiles on some of the great spiritual leaders in history and how they used fasting to encourage their own spiritual paths.

Part 3, "Fasting to Live Better," helps you to integrate a fasting practice into your life. You'll learn to recognize your mind-body, rather than your physical body alone, as your whole self. You'll read about how to eat and drink well when you aren't fasting, whether you should try using fasting for weight loss, and how to fit fasting into your everyday schedule.

Part 4, "Fasting to Heal the Body," uncovers the healing power of fasting by examining how fasting can help reverse chronic disease, improve immune system health, and facilitate your digestion, which many believe is the core of good physical health.

Part 5, "Four Fasts and How to Do Them Right, Plus Fast Variations," goes into detail about how to get ready for an actual fast. We'll tell you how to conduct a 16-hour or half-day fast; a 36-hour or full-day fast; a two-day fast based on the lunar cycle; a modified three-day fast based on the changing of the seasons; and all kinds of different fasting variations, from potato fasts to raw-food fasts to fasts from spending money, talking, and even watching TV! Each chapter provides specific instructions, step-by-step directions, and inspiration to keep you motivated.

At the end of the book, Appendix A, "How to Feast Beyond Your Fast," gives you hints and help for eating well when you aren't fasting, including a week-long meal plan. Appendix B, "Fasting Resources," lists lots of great websites and books about fasting and fasting-related issues. Appendix C, "Fasting Glossary," defines the terms used in this book.

Use this book well, and in good physical, mental, and spiritual health!

Fasting Knowledge in a Box

Throughout each chapter in this book, we'll add four types of extra information, neatly packaged in boxes, to add to your practical knowledge or give you inspiration to help increase your whole-self health and improve the effectiveness and enjoyment of your fasting experience.

Finer Fasting

These boxes offer you tips, techniques, cautions, and other practical how-to or why-to information about fasting and other related aspects of your healthy lifestyle.

Fast Facts

Looking for statistics, tidbits, or factoids about fasting? These Fast Facts boxes will inform you.

Fasting Wisdom

Plenty of wise people have spoken wise words about fasting in particular or about how to live a full, healthy, holistic existence in general. Here's where we'll quote some of them, for your further enlightenment and inspiration.

Fast Talk

Any words we use that somebody might not have heard before will be clearly defined in these boxes, so if you are wondering exactly what, where, and how long the digestive tract is or what the heck a chakra could be, you'll find the answers here.

Acknowledgments

Eve Adamson: Thanks to my children, Angus and Emmett, for inspiring me to be a good role model in my health habits. Thanks to Nikki, for unwavering emotional support and for keeping my goals lofty. And thanks to Jim, for helping me to find my inner balance and for showing me that I don't have to do it all myself.

Linda Horning, R.D.: Thanks to my son, Neil, for allowing me to see things from his perspective; and to Phil, for broadening my perspective to include all people, all beliefs, and all ideas.

Special Thanks to the Technical Reviewer

The Complete Idiot's Guide to Fasting was reviewed by an expert who double-checked the accuracy of what you'll learn here, to help us ensure that this book gives you everything you need to know about a safe practice of fasting for spiritual, emotional, and physical well-being. Special thanks to **Dr. Glenn Rothfeld**.

Glenn Rothfeld, M.D., MAc, has been at the forefront of the complementary medicine movement for the past 25 years. A former Clinical Fellow of Harvard University School of Medicine's Channing Laboratory, he is currently Clinical Assistant Professor of family medicine at Tufts University School of Medicine, where he developed one of the nation's first courses on alternative medicine. Dr. Rothfeld is a licensed acupuncturist, a frequent lecturer, and the author of several books on complementary medicine topics, most recently, *The Acupuncture Response*. He is currently medical director of WholeHealth New England, a complementary medicine center in Arlington, Massachusetts.

Trademarks

All terms mentioned in this book that are known to be or are suspected of being trademarks or service marks have been appropriately capitalized. Alpha Books and Pearson Education, Inc., cannot attest to the accuracy of this information. Use of a term in this book should not be regarded as affecting the validity of any trademark or service mark.

Part 1

All About Fasting

Fasting is one of the most misunderstood of preventive health care techniques, mainly because people don't understand exactly what it is, how it works, and how much it can boost physical, mental, emotional, and spiritual health and well-being. In this part we address what fasting is, and we also explain why fasting is vastly different from starvation. A brief history of fasting in different cultural traditions is followed by a user-friendly guide to digestion and the benefits of giving the body a rest from digestion, as well as a brief discussion of some common variations to strict water fasting. This section ends with a look at willpower and the physical, psychological, and spiritual challenges fasting presents to the whole self.

Chapter 1

Food Is Good, So Why Fast?

In This Chapter

◆ The benefits of fasting

◆ Why food isn't always good for you

◆ Your fasting misconceptions debunked

◆ Different fasts for different needs

Everybody likes food, right? Food is good. It tastes good, it looks good, and it satisfies your hunger. We need food to function, for energy, to keep our muscles strong. And everybody knows starvation is a bad thing. So why on earth would anybody stop eating on purpose? And if they did, how could it possibly be healthy?

Actually, for people who are sick, suffering from chronic health problems, feeling depressed, or for those who want to focus more closely on a spiritual path, fasting—even for one day, even for *half* a day—is supremely healthy. Fasting refocuses the body, so often distracted and diverted by the energy-intensive process of digesting too much food, on healing, on clarity of thought, and on a heightened awareness. Fasting allows the body and mind, those close neighbors so often separated by the distractions of modern existence and the physical demands of our overindulgent lifestyles, to come together in a quiet place, and that feels really good.

But fasting is more than a feel-good practice. Fasting has immense physical, mental, and spiritual benefits. Fasting is the oldest medical therapy known to humankind. Thousands of years ago, long before the invention of processed food, people knew that when they were sick, they shouldn't eat. Our bodies give us this signal by taking away our hunger. Animals do it, too. When the body requires extra energy for healing, it redirects energy away from the digestive system.

Fasting is also one of the oldest spiritual tools known to humankind. Spiritual seekers, medicine men, monks, nuns, yogis, shamans, people such as Jesus Christ, Moses, and the Buddha, and the rest of us ordinary people seeking spiritual enlightenment have made fasting a part of life for thousands of years, probably ever since the beginning of human-kind. In some cultures and in many religions, fasting was and still is an expected, regular practice, often coinciding with certain religious occasions, festivals, or events like Passover or Ramadan or Lent.

With that much history and so many health benefits behind it, you would think that everyone would fast. While plenty of people still practice periodic fasts to maintain their physical, mental, and spiritual health, most of us don't. Maybe you are reading this book because the idea of fasting interests you. Maybe you've heard a little bit about it but you just aren't sure you want to try something so drastic. Or maybe you didn't know anything about fasting until you saw this title. You always thought fasting was something you did if you were all out of food. But here in America, there's plenty to eat, right? We don't *have* to fast.

Food Is Good, But Not Always

In many ways, we are very lucky. We live in an abundant time. Food is readily available and so well preserved that it can sit on our shelves for months, even years, and still be edi-ble. But we have paid a dangerous price for our abundance and the technological advances we've applied to our food supply. Much of what we eat today bears little resemblance to what our ancestors called food.

The standard American diet is much higher in fat, protein, and salt than it needs to be for good health. It is also lacking in fiber and many important vitamins and minerals, not to mention the phytochemicals from plant foods that can help our bodies stay healthy.

Fasting Wisdom

Natural forces within us are the true healers of disease.

—Hippocrates, Greek physician (460–359 B.C.E)

We have so much, but we aren't healthier. Chronic diseases such as heart disease, cancer, and diabetes are the leading killers of people in the United States, and more people are obese than ever before. Some doctors have dared to step forward and suggest that the health issues plaguing

Americans with increasing frequency just might have something to do with our super-abundant, high-fat, chemical-laden diets. A few go one step further and suggest that perhaps the ancient wisdom still applies. Perhaps fasting can help to reverse the degradation of health precipitated by too much food.

What Exactly Is Fasting?

Fasting is the intentional abstinence from food for a productive purpose. To some, fasting means drinking only purified water (bottled water from the grocery store, distilled water, water filtered through a reverse-osmosis system, or water filtered water from the tap). Others advocate fasting with fresh juices, herbal teas, and vegetable broths but no solid food or animal products. Usually, fasting means going without any drugs, medications (but only with the prior consent of your doctor—never stop taking your medication without being very sure it is safe to do so), or supplements, but some fasts might include fiber supplements, vitamin and mineral supplements, or other herbal supplements designed to help the body's internal cleansing mechanisms. Some people also advocate some kind of colon cleanser such as an enema to hasten and aid the body's cleansing process. Others don't find this necessary, or even view it as harmful.

Even though it has many guises, fasting is not self-starvation, as a person suffering from anorexia nervosa or another form of disordered eating might practice. Fasting is not involuntary starvation due to the inability to get food. Fasting is, instead, practiced for the purpose of improving physical, mental, and/or spiritual health.

Fasting on purpose, with the right mindset and the proper pre- and postfasting eating plan, is a healthy practice. Fasting has amazing effects on the body and the mind. It cleanses the body, efficiently and quickly ridding the body of accumulated waste including excess fat. It clears the mind and makes thinking easier and more efficient. It even facilitates meditation, prayer, and spiritual practices.

When the body isn't using its energy for digestion, it can redirect that energy elsewhere, for the purposes of self-healing, mental focus, and spiritual fulfillment. You won't believe how much energy you have for the other things in your life that deserve attention, the other things besides food.

Fast Talk

Fasting is the practice of abstaining from food for the purpose of improving physical, mental, and/or spiritual health. There are many different kinds of fasts but the most common kinds are water fasts and juice fasts.

A Break from Digestion

Eat a sandwich, chew it up, swallow it, and it moves through your digestive tract as your body slowly digests it, extracting the nutrients it needs and processing the rest to be eliminated as waste. It takes a lot of energy to digest one bite of food. It takes a lot more energy to digest those four slices of pizza you just ate, the breadsticks, the caffeinated cola, the buffalo chicken wings, and the bowl of ice cream you just had to eat because you craved something sweet. Sure, you feel full after an indulgent meal like that, but once you are finished eating, your body's work has just begun.

Finer Fasting

If you are very overweight, shorter fasts are easier to tolerate than very long fasts. Rapid fat loss can be dangerous. Many toxins that have accumulated in your body, such as pesticides, are stored in fat. Melting away large amounts of fat too quickly can result in adverse reactions from too many toxins suddenly released into the bloodstream for processing.

One of the basic effects of fasting is the break it gives your body from the incessant and draining process of digestion. Of course, our bodies are designed to digest food. Food is our external energy source. But we tend to overburden our digestive systems with too much food, food that is difficult to digest, food and drink that tax the organs of elimination (the kidneys, the liver) with toxins such as alcohol and chemical additives.

During a fast, digestion stops. As soon as your body realizes no food is coming along to digest, it turns to itself for energy, and begins using its own stores of energy to keep you going. After a few days (the toughest part of an extended fast is the first three days), hunger ceases. While the body turns inward for energy, it can begin to cleanse toxins and unwanted substances it was too busy to get rid of while you were still eating.

An Internal Housecleaning

Have you ever cleaned out a closet, garage, or basement that hasn't been used for months or years, except for storage? Encountering the built-up dust, mildew, cobwebs, dead bugs, live bugs, water stains, rust, mineral deposits, and plain old clutter can be overwhelming. How do you go about cleaning a mess like that?

A little at a time.

If you don't eat well, don't exercise very much, don't get enough sleep, and generally neglect your health, your body ends up a lot like that old, moldy basement. The house with the moldy basement still functions, may even look pretty good from the outside, but inside, it is filled with all the junk you don't need. Dead cells, damaged cells, extra fat. All the accumulated junk you've been carrying around for years.

Fasting is like decluttering for your body. You help your body to detoxify so it can do its job. Short fasts clean out your system a little at a time. Long fasts do more, and more quickly, but should be practiced only under medical supervision. But any fast will initiate the internal cleansing process by getting rid of what you don't need.

When digestion stops and the body turns inward for energy, it also eliminates what you don't want or need until all the waste is gone. After that, you must begin to eat again so your body doesn't have to burn what you do need, like too much healthy muscle and too large a proportion of fat (yes, we all need some fat on us).

These days, it's trendy to declutter your house, but decluttering your body is even more important. A clean, well-kept body will reflect outward and make it easier to get the rest of your life in order. A body clogged by excess fat and waste can't work or think well, and if your body and mind are not working well, probably much of the rest of your life will gradually go out of order, too.

> **Fast Facts**
>
> According to the National Center for Chronic Disease Prevention and Health Promotion, a subdivision of the Centers of Disease Control in Atlanta, Georgia, poor diet and physical inactivity are associated with 300,000 deaths each year, second only to tobacco use.

A Healing Opportunity

As your body slowly turns inward and begins flushing out all the junk you don't need, you'll enjoy some seemingly miraculous side effects. Those headaches you always get in the afternoons … gone. That morning joint pain … vanished. Some people tell stories of disappearing cysts, rashes, and skin problems that cleared up without any other treatment, or colitis and other digestive complaints cured. Fasting has even been shown to halt asthma attacks and allergic reactions such as hay fever.

Doctors and other healers have prescribed fasting for centuries as a treatment for almost any kind of disease, from the common cold to crippling rheumatoid arthritis, and that's because it really does work in many cases. Why? Because fasting allows the body, with its powerful healing capabilities, to stop fretting about digestion. When your body is free to focus on curing itself, it does a pretty good job. Hippocrates, the famous Greek physician who, in many ways, shaped modern medicine and gave it its ethical framework, often proclaimed that humans have a doctor within, and we need only to get out of the way and let him do his work. Fasting is getting out of the way.

> **Fasting Wisdom**
>
> To lengthen thy days, lessen thy meals.
>
> —Benjamin Franklin, American statesman, scientist, and inventor (1706–1790)

A Window of Mental Clarity

In the past, fasting has often been prescribed for many different mental disorders, from depression to psychosis, but you don't need to have a diagnosable mental condition to enjoy the mental benefits of fasting. As the body gets clean from the inside out, the brain is able to work better, too. Have you ever experienced that lazy, dulled, almost drugged feeling of eating way too much food (think Thanksgiving!)? Fasting results in the opposite feeling: a sharp mental acuity, faster response time, quicker comprehension. Fasting gives you a definite mental edge.

That fasting can help you to think better may seem counterintuitive. Doesn't starvation dull the thinking? Yes, but remember, fasting is not starvation. Fasting is the purposeful, conscious act of abstaining from food. Your body and your mind have a reason to fast. They aren't clouded by the fear of being unable to eat. When fasting, you don't need to worry that you can't feed your children or that food won't be there when your fast is over. Starvation often goes hand in hand with poverty or tragedy, and these conditions carry with them extreme stress that overburdens the mind and body.

But fasting only means not eating. You are still sleeping enough, taking care of yourself, drinking lots of fluids, exercising moderately, going along with your regular life.

Finer Fasting

Drinking plenty of purified or distilled water, at least two quarts per day, during a fast is important to keep the body well hydrated. Dehydration is a common cause of discomfort during a fast.

Fasting is also a mental curative because it so dramatically counteracts the effects of *too much food*. It's one thing to eat a nice, light, healthy supper and feel good. But too much food with too much fat over too many meals in a row is poison to the body and the mind. Give yourself a break, literally, from the dulling effects of overeating and you'll be amazed at how great it feels. You'll wonder how on earth you could have ever eaten so much at one time. You'll wonder what ever possessed you to say, "Sure, go ahead and supersize it."

A Fountain of Youth

Fasting feels good and it's good for you, but it has even more benefits. One of the best for those of us who are worried about aging (isn't that most of us?) is that fasting really does make you younger. Studies have already shown that caloric restriction can extend the life span of laboratory animals (mice, rats, roundworms) and slow down the development of disease and tumors. Many scientists believe these benefits may extend to humans. No, it doesn't literally turn back the clock, but because fasting clears out your system and cleans out your body, all your internal organs start to work a little better. You'll start to feel like you felt 10 years ago. You'll also start to look younger. No, you 50-somethings won't suddenly look 18, but you might very well pass for 40. And you 30-somethings might just start getting carded the next time you buy a bottle of wine.

Fasting makes your skin firmer and clearer, your eyes brighter, and gives you an inner glow. During a long fast (of a week or more), toward the end of the fast, you may actually look older. Your body is purging and all those toxins are coming out, some of them right through your pores. Lots of showers and dry brush scrubs on your skin as well as gentle cleansing and exfoliating on your face will help to remove these toxins.

But after a fast, and most particularly, for those who fast according to a regular schedule (like one day a week or three days each month), the body begins to look younger and younger, shedding excess bulk, processing food more efficiently, imbuing you with vital energy. Some people fast for no other reason than for its youth-inducing effects. It's not the only benefit, but it's a pretty compelling one.

Fast Facts

Fasting is used most often in the United States as a treatment for obesity, often in the guise of liquid diet drinks. However, without the proper transitional diet before and after a fast to discourage subsequent overeating, and without changes in lifestyle that caused obesity, fasting will be only a temporary fix, and may contribute to health problems overweight people have, such as hypertension and diabetes. However, fasting can make lifestyle changes easier. Fresh, whole, organic plant foods seem more appealing after a fast, and heavy, fatty, processed foods taste less like good food.

A Tool for Greater Spirituality

Fasting is an important part of many religious traditions around the world. Many Christians fast as a religious observance, as a way to feel more removed from the material world and closer to God, and as a way of praising God. Some Christians do 40-day fasts, as Jesus and Moses are said to have practiced. Others fast just on days or for short periods during which they want to be particularly focused on their spiritual selves or feel humbled before God. These are some of the same reasons Jews fast during important Jewish holidays such as Yom Kippur. Muslims fast during the Islamic holiday of Ramadan. Buddhists and Hindus fast as a spiritual practice. Many Buddhist and Christian monks and nuns make fasting an important part of their lives.

You certainly don't have to be religious to fast, however. Many people fast when their religion doesn't require it, and many more, who don't consider themselves a subscriber to any particular religion, fast for spiritual reasons above all others.

Fasting can be a part of a spiritual retreat, or a periodic practice for spiritual maintenance. Whatever your reasons, fasting does indeed redirect your body's energy and your attention away from the sensual pleasure of eating, and once you get past that initial hunger (this becomes easier and easier the more often you fast), you'll find it much easier to meditate, pray, or simply practice contemplation of your own spirituality. You won't feel quite so attached to material pleasures.

> **Fasting Wisdom**
>
> To attain enlightenment, the legend says, the Buddha sat beneath a fig tree, fasting and meditating, until he was finally enlightened. On his deathbed, the Buddha, also known as Siddhartha Gautama, advised his followers, "Be a light unto yourself." Throughout his life, he encouraged his followers to engage in an inner search for spiritual meaning and self-knowledge. Fasting and a vegetarian diet are important factors in the spiritual lives of many Buddhists, even today.

The Ultimate Approach to Mind-Body Integration

"Mind-body" is a popular concept you hear a lot about these days. But that's a good thing because it means people are becoming increasingly aware of the link between body and mind. Our old friend Hippocrates understood the link between body and mind, and so did the old-time doctors who made house calls, knew whole families throughout their lives, and saw where and how people lived. Hippocrates also once said that it was more important to see *who* had a disease than what disease a person had.

But modern medical practitioners often don't get a chance to see how people live. Because of insurance company changes, frequent job changes, or frequent geographical shifts, people often switch doctors multiple times in a lifetime, and a doctor sometimes sees an individual patient only once or twice. Doctors are often so overscheduled that they don't have the time, or haven't had the training, to ask about anything other than symptoms specifically related to a condition. These days, most doctors stick to some version of "Where does it hurt? For how long?"

But more and more doctors are rediscovering how intricately mind and body are related. Illness can cause depression, depression can cause illness. A stressful life can result in a depressed immune system, and chronic illness can cause stress. Feeling blue could be caused by the body's natural cycles of cleansing and renewing. Some holistic health practitioners believe the body goes through cycles of cleaning out and building up. During the cleaning-out stage, you'll have less energy, be more susceptible to minor illnesses, and feel a little bit down. During the building-up cycle, when the body is refreshed and renewed, you'll feel high on energy and in a really good mood.

When the mind and body are integrated, they can help each other make the most of these stages. The person whose mind and body are in close communication will get through the low cycles with greater awareness and sensitivity, perhaps choosing to fast to help the body along. During the feel-good cycles, the person who pays attention to both mind and body will be able to take full advantage of the high energy and good moods he or she is experiencing. This is the time to make more social connections, exercise more vigorously, and even eat a little bit more, as long as what you eat is healthful, wholesome, and life bestowing.

Some people get stuck in the "down" cycle. They hardly ever feel energetic and rarely experience moods they could call good. These people are in need of a more drastic cleansing, which is exactly what you can induce through a fast. Fasting, again, boosts your body's natural abilities, and you can fast right along with your body's needs if you recognize your low cycles, when you need fasting the most. When fasting becomes a part of your life's cycle, your entire self will naturally work together better. You'll be more self-aware. How you feel will make more sense to you, and you'll probably feel a lot better than you did before.

What Fasting Isn't

People have a lot of false impressions about fasting. Fasting isn't weird or marginal or something practiced only by monks. It doesn't cause anorexia nervosa and it is completely different from starving yourself. It isn't bad for you if you do it the right way. You can still do all the things you normally do when fasting, and plenty of doctors do it, too. You'll feel better, not worse, during and after a fast. And if you do it with the right mindset and surround it with a healthy diet, it can cure compulsive eating, addictions, and even depression.

But fasting isn't a miracle, either. It isn't a cure-all or a panacea that will solve all your problems. Fasting is, simply, a proven method for giving your body the space and energy it needs to work the way it is supposed to work. Nothing mysterious about it.

Fasting Isn't Starvation

People often assume there is a link between fasting and the potentially fatal eating disorder, *anorexia nervosa*. Actually, there doesn't seem to be any connection. People with anorexia nervosa don't fast; they starve themselves. They have an emotional or mental disorder that compels them to refuse food. A fast, by contrast, is for a

Fast Talk

Anorexia nervosa is a serious eating disorder associated with a distorted body image, severe calorie restriction, and loss of 25 percent or more of normal body weight.

predetermined amount of time, after which eating resumes. Fasting isn't a low-calorie diet. It's a therapy, not a disease.

As we explained earlier in this chapter, fasting is also different from starvation because it doesn't carry with it all the accompanying trauma and stress that poverty-induced or trauma-induced starvation usually includes. People who fast do it to help themselves feel better, become healthier, and/or as part of a spiritual practice.

Fasting Doesn't Make You Weak

If food is energy and fasting means going without food, certainly fasting will make you feel weak. Doesn't that make sense? You might think so, but actually, fasting is incredibly energizing.

Finer Fasting

Fasting can even restore a lagging sex drive, and some people swear that they have had the most energetic, aware, and sensual sex of their lives during a fast. Just one more perk!

Yes, fasting can be challenging. At first it can be very hard to withstand the hunger (most of which is psychological) that accompanies the beginning of a fast. But energy won't be your problem because fasting allows your body's energy to be released. When you aren't digesting, your energy is free for other things. If your body needs healing, it will work on that. If you are exercising, working, or doing anything else that needs physical and mental effort, fasting will help you to direct your entire body and mind toward the task at hand.

Fasting Isn't Weird (Doctors Do It!)

A lot of people still think fasting is kind of weird, or cultlike, or unnatural, or is sure to make you act a little loopy. Nonsense! Fasting is health maintenance and should be practiced to help the body regain its equilibrium, and/or to help retrain the focus on things above and beyond the material world. Fasting because a cult leader tells you to or being forced to fast isn't really fasting. That's being starved and it has nothing to do with legitimate, healthy fasting.

Some people think fasting is bad for your body because it induces hallucinations. Native Americans fasted during certain rituals or observances, and fasting, some say, was the cause of their visions or hallucinations. During Jesus Christ's 40-day fast in the desert, according to the Bible, he was visited by the devil and tempted. Another hallucination from fasting?

Actually, according to the wisdom of many ancient cultures, fasting merely helps to prepare the body to be more open to visions and revelations. It doesn't cause them. People who fast for reasons other than spiritual ones don't see visions or have divine revelations.

They aren't fasting for that purpose. If fasting caused these things, if they were really due to a physical reaction in response to lack of food, then dieters who fast in clinics for long periods would report these, too. They don't.

No, fasting provides your body with the opportunity to do what it needs to do, and what you want it to do. It keeps you healthy, thinking clearly, and getting the most out of your days. What's so weird about that?

If fasting were dangerous or hokey or weird, you also wouldn't see so many health care professionals practicing it. The health benefits of fasting are so profound that a lot of doctors do it, and some of the best and most solid information on fasting has been written by medical doctors. While some of them disagree on some of the minor points of fasting—whether fasting should involve only water or whether juice and broth can also be consumed, for example—they have all seen hundreds of their own patients regain their health through fasting. Sensible is a much better word to describe fasting.

Fasting Isn't Dangerous (If You Do It Right)

Probably the most common reaction to fasting by people who don't know much about it is that it's dangerous. Surely, if we need food, then going without it is harmful to health, or so the reasoning goes. But our reaction is based on very recent historical conditions. Not so very long ago, when humans relied heavily on the land for their food, fasting was part of the natural cycle. Sometimes we had food, and sometimes we didn't. Sometimes we felt good, and sometimes we didn't. Sometimes we felt hungry, and sometimes we didn't. Food was a necessity, and people were more aware of just how much food they needed, and what kind of food was best for their needs.

We may have lost some of that awareness, at least temporarily, as convenience foods, junk foods, fast foods, and a simple overabundance of foods are so available to us. But these foods pose the real danger, not our abstinence from them. Giving our bodies a chance to clear out the damaging effects of junk foods and too much food from our systems is not only safe but extremely conducive to good health. Also important is changing our diets, especially in the day or two before and after a fast, to contain primarily fresh organic plant foods.

Fasting Wisdom

The human body is designed to fast safely. Certain biochemical changes take place when no food is taken that enable the body to fuel itself by burning up its fat reserves and conserving its vital tissues.

—Joel Fuhrman, M.D., from *Fasting and Eating for Health* (St. Martin's Griffin, 1995)

That being said, some people should never fast. Always check with your doctor first if you are unsure whether fasting is appropriate for you. If you are pregnant, nursing, underweight, have a weak heart, low blood pressure, diabetes, an eating disorder, certain serious mental illnesses, or suffer from nutritional deficiencies, you should not fast. Children shouldn't fast as long as they are still growing, and those who are very elderly and frail should not fast. Also, if your doctor advises you that you should not fast because of a health condition, then please follow your doctor's advice.

Different Fasts for Different Folks

One man's fast is another man's famine, and one man's feast is another man's fast, to rewrite a cliché. There are many, many different ways to fast, and anyone can find a fasting program with personal appeal.

Some of the fasts we've encountered include …

- **Water fasts,** during which you drink only purified water. These fasts work best when the fast is short. We prefer water fasting for half-day or 16-hour fasts only. These short fasts work well to refresh and renew the body.

- **Juice fasts,** during which you drink only diluted freshly made fruit and vegetable juices (preferably organic), and sometimes, herbal teas and/or vegetable broth. You can successfully sustain a juice fast for quite a long time, and this is the kind of fast we recommend if you fast for longer than 24 hours. A one-day juice fast every month does for your body what changing the oil every 3,000 miles does for your car.

- **Partial fasts,** during which you eat a very limited range of foods. These aren't true fasts, but they give your body a similar chance to spend less energy on digestion. Some options are to "fast" on nothing but fresh, raw fruit and vegetables or a milk/grain gruel for a set period of time.

Finer Fasting

Don't be confused by the arguments you might see on the Internet or elsewhere between different proponents of fasting about whether a juice fast is really a fast. Some say fasting means ingesting nothing but water, or even nothing at all! (Because your body can quickly become dehydrated, we would never recommend a fast that doesn't include liquid.) Others insist that fasting means ingesting only clear liquids like water and juice freshly squeezed from organic fruits and vegetables, but no solid food or animal products such as milk. Use your common sense and individual preference to determine what kind of fast you would like to try. We promise we won't argue with you if you say you are on a fresh-fruit-only-for-one-day fast.

Other fasts are designed around the length of time they last. Some options are ...

- **Half-day fasts.** These involve skipping one meal in a day, not eating after 3:00 P.M., not eating until lunchtime, etc.

- **One-day weekly fasts.** Many people choose one day of the week on which they always fast, such as Sunday or Monday.

- **Two-day monthly fasts.** Fasting for two days each month is an excellent way to maintain health. Some people like to fast at the beginning or end of each month, or during the last two days leading up to the new moon, which some believe is the most conducive time to fast.

- **Seasonal fasts.** Some people like to fast on the days or the week preceding the solstices and equinoxes, using the beginning of each season as a time for cleansing and renewal. We recommend a three-day seasonal fast.

- **One long fast every year or decade.** Some people have logged a single very long fast, for 10 days to two weeks, or even for 40 or more days. These fasts are best practiced no more than once a year, and only under medical supervision. Even every five or 10 years is enough for a very long supervised fast.

We'll talk about how to do each of these different types of fasts in subsequent chapters, so stay tuned!

The Least You Need to Know

- Fasting is the intentional abstinence from food for a set period of time for the purpose of improving or maintaining physical, mental, and/or spiritual health.

- Fasting allows your body's healing energy to focus on itself rather than on digestion of food.

- Fasting can precipitate rapid healing, feeling and looking younger, improved concentration, and a more sensitive spiritual awareness.

- Fasting is not starvation, nor, when practiced correctly, is it dangerous. Many medical doctors practice fasting to stay healthy.

- There are many different types of fasts—from half-day fasts to 40-day fasts, from water fasts to juice and vegetable broth fasts—to fit anyone's individual needs.

Body and Soul: A Fast Trip Around the World

In This Chapter

- ◆ Fasting as a global practice
- ◆ How the Native Americans fasted
- ◆ Fasting in the Christian and Jewish traditions
- ◆ Fasting in the Eastern and Islamic traditions
- ◆ Fasting and twenty-first-century spirituality

Fasting has never been an isolated practice. Cultures and religions all over the world have practiced fasting since before recorded history, both for health and as a spiritual practice. Learning about the history of fasting and fasting in other cultures is interesting, but it can also become relevant to you.

In this chapter, we'll take a brief world tour to look at how other cultures and different religions apply the practice of fasting to their needs. Then we'll give you ideas for how to incorporate some of those same ideas and traditions into your own life.

Whether you are a Catholic interested in taking your Lenten fast more seriously or a nonreligious faster who is interested in exploring different traditions, or anyone of any religion who feels the urge to progress along the spiritual path, this chapter will guide you.

Fasting Around the World

Few practices are as widespread throughout time and geography as fasting. From the United States to China, from Africa to India, from the West to the Near East to the Middle East to the Far East, people have used fasting for centuries.

The practice of fasting is less varied in character than the people who practice it, however. Most people around the world and throughout history fast for two reasons: to keep the body healthy (as a part of any of a number of different health systems around the world), and as a part of a spiritual practice.

In North America, the Native Americans have traditionally used fasting as a sacred ritual. Young boys sent off on their vision quests in the wilderness alone would fast, and fasting was a part of other ceremonies and observances. Other native cultures around the globe have also used fasting as a way to purify the body, prepare it for visions, or to honor the creator. Many native cultures fast as a way to honor the creator or the gods, as a ritual to ask for special favors or pacify the forces that be, and for many other reasons. Fasting is sometimes a component of superstition, sometimes a component of organized religion, sometimes a folk remedy, sometimes a remedy specifically prescribed by a doctor.

Becoming aware of the great international practice of fasting can give us a new perspective in our own fasting practice. For example, you can set up your own vision quest, complete with fasting, in the spirit of the Native American culture that practices it. While you probably don't have the time or the inclination to wander around in the wilderness by yourself for a week, you might decide to take a day off work and spend the day fasting and walking through a forest or other natural area. Focus on your own spiritual life, who you are, what you are looking for in life, and whether you are on the path to your goals.

Finer Fasting _____

If you are fasting and spending time in nature on your own personal vision quest, keep an eye out for your totem animal. If you see an unusual animal, or an animal doing something unusual (a squirrel, a deer, a crow, even a frog or a fish), such as stopping and staring at you, consider whether you think the animal could be your spirit guide. What might the animal be trying to tell you or show you about your life?

Fasting and Christianity

Food may be nourishing, but many religious traditions also perceive food, or certain foods, as contrary to spiritual pursuits. Many early Christians believed that Satan entered the body along with food. We like to look at this as a metaphor. Food is a material pleasure, and when consumed in abundance, food can result in gluttony (one of the seven deadly sins!). Food can also represent the material world, the opposite of God. Food ties us to our senses, and we can get a little too attached to sensual pleasures when they are so readily available. Overindulging makes us both less in touch with our own inner spiritual selves, and less able to heal ourselves because we have overburdened our bodies.

Christians have fasted since Christianity began. The early Christians, the Puritans in America, and Christians today fast to feel closer to God, purify the body, feel humbled, or even as a way to practice fellowship with other Christians or to protest things like human rights violations or practices they feel are contrary to their beliefs.

Christian fasting is a fairly widespread practice. Some Christians practice fasting only occasionally, such as during Lent. Others fast on a regular basis, whether that means a weekly fast or an every-decade, 40-day fast. Some Christians like to practice the fasts, or the attitude toward fasting, as described in the Bible, which often mentions fasting in many different contexts in both the Old and the New Testaments.

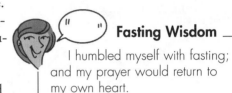

Fasting Wisdom

I humbled myself with fasting; and my prayer would return to my own heart.
—Psalm 35: 13

Biblical Fasts

Fasting is frequently mentioned in the Bible, often in the Old Testament as a way to lament (and often accompanied by the donning of sackcloth and ashes). Moses fasted. Esther fasted. David fasted. And of course Jesus fasted for 40 days and 40 nights before beginning his three-year ministry.

One famous passage in the book of Matthew advises the fasting person to attempt to go about normal life without looking like he or she is fasting because the "hypocrites" fast and look drawn and miserable so everyone knows they are fasting. The person who fasts for God and not to show off to others will be rewarded, the Bible explains, by God rather than the admiration of others.

In another passage, people ask Jesus why the disciples of John the Baptist and others fasted, but not Jesus' disciples, to which Jesus replied that the wedding guests cannot be expected to fast when the bridegroom is among them, but that when he was gone, they would fast again.

Some Christians practice Jesus' 40-day fast every year or every few years, or sometimes just once, to honor and be humbled before God. However, we don't recommend any medically unsupervised fast last longer than three days, and advise that anyone considering undertaking longer fasts do so only under the direct supervision of a qualified medical professional with experience in fasting.

Because the Bible advises that you shouldn't proclaim your fasting, many people continue to believe you shouldn't tell others when you are fasting. However, there is nothing wrong with seeking moral support from others. But beware: Some people feel very threatened by someone who is fasting. They don't know about fasting or can't imagine themselves doing it. They may try to get you to eat. Around such people, the easiest way to resist temptation is to avoid it completely by not mentioning your fast.

The Lenten Fast

The season of *Lent* consists of the approximately 40 days leading up to Easter Sunday. During Lent, many Christians, especially Catholics, choose to make certain sacrifices, from giving up chocolate to eating only one meal a day. Many Catholics choose to eat no meat on any Friday during Lent. Lent is also a time for extra prayer and penance, according to Catholicism.

> **Fast Talk**
>
> **Lent** is the 40 weekdays or eight weeks between Ash Wednesday and Easter Sunday traditionally observed by Christians as a time of penance. Fasting is a common practice during Lent.

The Christian season of Lent coincides with the beginning of spring, or the vernal equinox. Not coincidentally, ancient spring equinox traditions were sometimes incorporated into Lenten traditions when Christianity merged with more ancient religions in Europe. Many people who don't fast for Lent choose to fast as a cleansing ritual around the spring equinox, which is on or about March 20.

Lent is a good time for practicing a fast because so many other people are doing it, or at least are relinquishing something. Whether or not you are Catholic, you can choose to fast during part or all of the Lenten season. Here are some ways you might choose to fast for Lent:

◆ Don't eat after a certain time each day, such as 3:00 P.M. or 4:00 P.M.

◆ Don't eat before a certain time each day, such as noon or 3:00 P.M.

◆ On Sundays or Mondays, drink only juice, herbal tea, and vegetable broth, but abstain from all solid food.

◆ On Sundays or Mondays, eat only fresh fruit and drink only fresh juice, purified water, and herbal tea.

◆ Fast for the week leading up to Easter.

Whatever form of fasting you choose, remember to drink lots of water and, on fasts of more than half a day, juice and broth. Later in this book, we'll go into more detail about how to do different types of fasts. For now, just keep in mind that the Lenten season is a nice time to fast.

Fasting and Judaism

Fasting has always been an important observance in the Jewish religion, but no more so than on the holiest of holy Jewish holidays, *Yom Kippur*, also called the Day of Atonement.

Yom Kippur is the last of 40 days of repentance. On that day, people celebrating the holiday ask for forgiveness for broken promises and refrain from eating and drinking. But fasting from food is only one of the five things that are prohibited on Yom Kippur, which are …

- ◆ Eating and drinking.
- ◆ Putting on perfume or lotion.
- ◆ Engaging in sexual intercourse.
- ◆ Bathing or otherwise washing yourself.
- ◆ Wearing leather shoes.

It is thought that during Yom Kippur, the gates of heaven are open and all who repent and ask forgiveness can enter. Whether or not you are Jewish, you can practice a similar one-day fast, during which you focus on asking forgiveness for the people in your life that you have wronged. Fasting helps to focus the mind inward, rather than outward on the food in front of you.

This kind of one-day "forgiveness fast" can be an excellent time for self-reflection. As your body is purging toxins, you can work on purging your mind and your conscience of those things that burden it.

Fast Talk

Yom Kippur is the most important Jewish holiday. It occurs on the tenth day of the seventh month of the Jewish calendar (usually sometime in mid to late September) and is a day for asking for forgiveness.

Fasting and Islam

Fasting is a solemn and necessary observance during the Islamic holiday of *Ramadan*. Ramadan is the ninth month in the 12-month Islamic calendar. Muslims all over the world fast during the day for the entire month of Ramadan, and eat small meals in the evening. Muslims are also supposed to refrain from sexual relations and immoral and angry behavior, and should engage in acts of compassion toward others.

One of the reasons for fasting during Ramadan is to practice self-control and self-discipline. Fasting for Ramadan is also designed to help the faster focus more directly on God. Fasting is one of the five pillars of Islam:

◆ Faith

◆ Prayer

◆ The "Zakat," a form of charitable giving

◆ Fasting

◆ Pilgrimage to Mecca (for those who are able)

Fast Talk

Ramadan is the ninth month in the Islamic calendar and a time when Muslims fast from sunrise to sunset. Fasting time varies according to day length; each year it's a bit shorter or longer, depending on the season. Because the Islamic calendar is lunar, it is 10 days shorter than our year. Over 10 years, the month has moved 100 days.

You don't have to be Muslim to practice the kind of fast Muslims practice during Ramadan. Choose a day to fast from sunrise to sunset. While the fast of Ramadan doesn't even allow drinking water, we would strongly recommend that you drink plenty of water during your fast, but if your fast lasts only through the hours of daylight, you can drink only water and abstain from juice, tea, and broth, as well.

During your sunrise-to-sunset fast, focus on self-discipline and self-control, as well as your own inner spirituality or your relationship to a higher power.

Fasting and the Far East

Fasting in the Far East takes many forms, as do the religions in the Far East. Hinduism and Buddhism are the primary religions, and both use fasting in different ways and for different purposes.

Buddhism and Fasting

Buddhism has many different branches, but most of them include fasting in their spiritual practices. For some, fasting occurs on full moon days or Buddhist holidays. Traditional Buddhists are always vegetarians, but on fasting days, Buddhists abstain from all solid foods, drinking only certain allowed liquids. Buddhist monks also have certain regimented fasting days.

Buddhists fast for many reasons. For some, it is a purification of the system. Buddhism has many links with Hinduism, including the practice of yoga, and fasting can also be used in concert with a yoga practice. Some Buddhists fast to help free the mind from the world of the senses so it can more easily comprehend ultimate truth. In this way, fasting becomes a partner in meditation.

The Buddha, it is said, fasted during his years as an ascetic, living for several years on one grain of rice a day (please don't try this at home—it is certainly a legend!). After renouncing the ascetic life, the Buddha chose the "Middle Path" as the way to enlightenment, meaning moderation in all things. Many of his ascetic followers then denounced him, but he persisted in his quest for enlightenment.

Hinduism and Fasting

For Hindus, fasting is a common practice on certain holidays, and is also used as an aid to meditation. Many ubiquitous health practices such as *yoga* and *ayurveda* originated in India, along with Hinduism. Today they are often practiced separately from Hinduism, but they all retain similar element.

In yoga, fasting can aid meditation, purify the body, help the body to heal more quickly, and can even make the practice of yoga poses easier. Even today, yoga teachers advise practicing the yoga poses on an empty stomach, but yoga is often much easier during a fast. See Chapter 6, "Fasting and Spiritual Growth," for more information on yoga.

While the practice of ayurveda, one of the oldest health systems in the world, isn't directly related to Hinduism, it comes out of India and influences many of the practices of both Hindus and Buddhists. One of ayurveda's primary motives is to purify and cleanse the system, freeing its internal energy, so the body and mind can work better. Fasting is an integral part of ayurvedic practice, as is the consumption of the correct "pure" foods and many different internal cleansing practices.

> **Fast Talk**
>
> **Yoga** is a 3,000-year-old spiritual practice that includes physical exercises, breathing exercises, and meditation for greater physical, mental, and spiritual health. **Ayurveda** is a life science or ancient system of health designed to maximize longevity and optimize the body and mind through purification practices such as fasting, eating pure foods, and internal and external cleansing techniques.

Fasting in Other Traditions

While fasting is a part of all the major world religions, whether formally or informally, many lesser known religions incorporate fasting as well. According to the excellent and comprehensive website, Beliefnet (www.beliefnet.com), the following religions use fasting for specific purposes:

- **Baha'i.** The Baha'i abstain from food and drink from sunrise to sunset during the 19th month of the Baha'i year, which corresponds to March 2 through 20, in order to focus more closely on their love for God and on their spiritual lives.

- **Eastern Orthodox.** The Eastern Orthodox abstain from meat, dairy products, eggs, and sometimes fish during Lent, the Apostles' Fast, the Dormition Fast, the Nativity Fast, and every Wednesday and Friday, with the exception of certain fast-free weeks during the fall, to waylay tendencies toward gluttony and to help the faster become more open to God.

- **Mormon.** The Mormons fast from food and drink for two consecutive meals and also donate food or money to those in need on the first Sunday of every month, to grow closer to God and concentrate more closely on their religious lives. Individuals or groups sometimes also fast to petition God for help, guidance, or intervention.

- **Pagan.** While fasting isn't a regimented part of the pagan religion, many pagans fast as a cleansing or purification ritual during the spring equinox. These fasts purge the heaviness of winter from the body and prepare it for the new season. Some pagans fast during or around both the fall and spring equinoxes and the winter and summer solstices to feel more in tune to the seasonal vibrations and cycles of the earth.

Fasting and the New Age of Spirituality

The new spirituality, which some call New Age, is a truly global mixture of traditions updated for contemporary life. Many people who wouldn't call themselves "New Age" embrace the philosophy of a more global or even universal spiritual practice.

The religions of the world have much in common, and while they quibble on various points, many of us today believe that each religion is a culture's search for truth. Within each religion, and each culture from which it came, are seeds of wisdom, men and women of uncanny vision, and the common goal of self-actualization or the merging of body and mind with spirit.

Fasting fits perfectly into such a sensibility, and one might even venture to say that fasting could become a significant spiritual unifier in the world today if more people were to practice it. What better way to promote peace, equality, and international unity than to have this one physical, mental, and spiritual practice in common?

The Relevance of Fasting Today

Fasting in the twenty-first century becomes particularly relevant because of the circumstances that have befallen the world around us. Many of us suffer failing health. Environmental impurities are everywhere. Through extensive use of computer networks and the Internet, we experience both simultaneous instant communication with others and total isolation.

We are surrounded by food and by people who are starving. We are surrounded by money and by abject poverty. The loss of our natural resources leaves us feeling poor and spiritually bereft in a land of plenty. Though we have easy access to hiking trails, sidewalks, and exercise facilities, more of us are obese than ever before.

Fasting can put us in touch with an awareness that not everyone around the world has the resources we have. It can give us a taste of "doing without." It can be a spiritual practice that observes and shows respect for our universally *human* nature. In essence, we are all the same.

Fasting also increases physical sensitivity. In a modern world full of overstimulation, we sometimes learn to turn off, losing touch with individual sights, smells, and sounds. Fasting turns us back on. Things look sharper, sound clearer, smell stronger. Fasting can help us to regain our dulled and overwrought senses, just as it helps us to focus our minds on something other than what we want to stuff in our mouths next.

If the twenty-first century doesn't demand that fasting put a halt to the overconsumption and the loss of physical and spiritual energy so many people suffer today, it certainly suggests it. For anyone who is overconsuming—and that means overconsuming anything, whether food, drink, drugs, money, possessions, or other people's attentions—for anyone who feels out of control, has a loss of energy, or suffers from chronic health problems, fasting will feel like a miracle.

Fasting is like pushing an internal "reset" button. Suddenly, things come back into perspective. Self-control and energy return. And so does a lust for life—not food, not material possessions, not money, but life.

Finer Fasting

Fasting doesn't have to be about food. For example, you can set aside one day or several days for a spending fast in which you stop all spending, or limit yourself to necessities only. Just as fasting from food can put a stop to chronic overeating, fasting from spending money can help put a stop to chronic overspending. We'll talk more about this in Chapter 23, "Not-Quite-Fasting Variations."

The Least You Need to Know

◆ Fasting is a part of every major world religion, including Christianity, Judaism, Islam, Buddhism, and Hinduism.

◆ Fasting is also a part of many lesser known religions such as the Baha'i faith, the Eastern Orthodox tradition, the Church of Mormon, and the pagan religions.

◆ Fasting is an important part of New Age spirituality for many, bringing an ancient healing practice into the twenty-first century.

◆ Fasting today is often practiced to increase global awareness, tune up the senses, increase spiritual awareness, and put a stop to chronic overconsumption.

3

The Anatomy of a Fast

In This Chapter

- ◆ How your digestive system works when you eat
- ◆ How your mind and spirit work when you eat
- ◆ How your digestive system works when you fast
- ◆ How your mind and spirit work when you fast
- ◆ A brief description of some fasting variations and how they work

Our digestive systems allow us to survive by transforming the food we eat into the chemicals and energy we require, but what's actually going on down there when you put a bite of something in your mouth? And what happens when we don't put anything in there for awhile?

Our bodies, our minds, our spirits respond to everything we do, think, experience, and that includes, to a dramatic extent, the foods we eat. In this chapter, we'll look briefly at what happens to the whole self during eating and during fasting, and we'll break down a fast for you so you can see how it works.

Take a Trip Through Your Digestive Tract

What do you feel like eating today? A Caesar salad? A tuna salad sandwich? A bowl of soup? Whatever it is, if you eat it, your body will have to digest it, and that means every bite of food you eat will travel through some 30 feet of hollow tubing that makes up your digestive tract. That bite of salad or spoonful of soup will go through some pretty amazing changes as it moves from one end to the other, changes you may have considered only briefly before deciding you didn't really want to know!

Fast Facts

The 20-something feet of small intestine that makes up the largest portion of your digestive tract isn't smooth inside. It is covered with tiny hairlike microvilli that absorb nutrients into your bloodstream. A smooth small intestine would have an absorption surface area of 6 square feet, but because of the microvilli, your small intestine actually has an absorption surface of 4,000 square feet.

But knowing how digestion works, at least in a very basic way, can help you to understand how fasting works, and it can also help you to be more motivated to learn about, understand, and experience your body's relationship with food.

Down the Hatch

Let's say you've got a nice, steaming bowl of fresh vegetable soup in front of you. Imagine a thick, tomato-rich stock, tender chunks of potatoes and celery, carrots and onions, some peas and red peppers, maybe some barley or pasta. Yum!

Take your spoon, dip it in the soup, raise it to your lips, and … down the hatch! Let's follow that spoonful of soup to see exactly where it goes.

♦ **First stop: your mouth.** The digestive process begins when you put something into your mouth and chew it up with your teeth, mixing it with your saliva. Saliva and chewing help to break the food down, the first step in changing the food into usable chemicals and energy. Because this is a chunky soup, you'll have to chew up those vegetables before you swallow.

♦ **Swallowing.** After you chew your food, you swallow it. You control when that first swallow happens, but after that, the involuntary muscles of your digestive tract take over and begin to move the food slowly through your body. Swallowing moves food into your throat and down your *esophagus*. After you swallow, that chewed-up spoonful of soup moves down this passageway of less than a foot long to a one-way valve called the *esophageal sphincter*. This valve lets things in, but doesn't let anything out. Occasional malfunctions of the esophageal sphincter let stomach acid into the esophagus, an uncomfortable feeling people often call heartburn. But for now, your esophageal sphincter is working just fine, and your vegetable soup flows into your stomach.

Fast Talk

Your **esophagus** is the approximately 10-inch section of your digestive system that connects your throat or pharynx with your stomach. The **esophageal sphincter** is the one-way valve at the end of the esophagus that releases food into the stomach.

◆ Once your food is in your stomach, three things happen: first, the stomach lets the food in. Second, the stomach mixes the food with stomach acid or digestive acid to further break it down. The churning motion of the stomach muscles act like a blender. Third, the stomach releases this further-digested food, bit by bit, into the small intestine. The work of digestion is still less than half accomplished.

◆ Bit by bit, that now-unrecognizable bite of soup is funneled into your *small intestine* where the real work of digestion begins. In the small intestine, all the usable nutrients are gradually absorbed through the intestinal walls due to the action of different chemicals produced by different organs in the body such as the pancreas and the liver. The protein, carbohydrates, vitamins, and minerals are all shuttled off to millions of cells in your body where they can promote healthy function, build muscle, and give you energy. The small intestine is about 20 feet long, giving that bite of soup plenty of time to make its nutrients available to your body. The parts of the food that aren't absorbed—namely, the waste products and fiber—continues into the large intestine.

Fast Talk

The **small intestine** is the section of your digestive tract in which nutrients are absorbed into the body from digested food. The small intestine has three sections. The first part is the duodenum; the middle part is the jejunum; and the last part is the ileum. The **large intestine,** or colon, reclaims fluid and processes the remaining indigestible portions of food along with other waste products into feces, to be expelled.

◆ What's left for your *large intestine* to do? This 5-foot section, also called your colon, takes all the water from the food and drink you've taken in but haven't used and helps the body to reabsorb the water into its system as needed. The indigestible fiber and other waste products the body is naturally eliminating become feces, which can then be expelled. While most people don't like to talk about this part of the digestive process, the colon must function properly to maintain health. When we don't eat enough fiber or drink enough water, the colon doesn't work very well. We become constipated or develop one of the many health problems associated with a low-fiber diet. Eating the right kinds of foods helps us with this important function of elimination of waste from the system that keeps the body healthy.

And that's it ... in and out in one 30-foot length of flowing muscular contractions, an amazingly efficient food processing system that keeps the body nourished, energized, and clean.

Of course, eating involves much more than the simple digestive process for a fully functioning and integrated human being. So, now that we

Fasting Wisdom

What we think and what we eat make what we are, physically and mentally.

—Edgar Cayce, American psychic and healer (1877–1945)

know the nuts and bolts, lets look at what's going on elsewhere in your body as you eat and digest, eat and digest.

The Anatomy of the Body-Mind

It's an old cliché: You are what you eat. Yet, this statement is more true than some people realize. Everything you take into your body becomes part of your whole self. As your body absorbs and accepts the nutrients from the food you eat, and as those nutrients travel all over your body to the cells that need them, you are transformed. You become the result of the nutrients you ingest.

But there's more. Eating is a powerful cultural and personal act. What we choose to eat and why we choose to eat it can be the result of a deeply personal decision, a political act, a protest, a support, a commitment to well-being, or a relinquishment of responsibility. Eating in the twenty-first century is much more than the simple fulfillment of hunger, but perhaps it always was much more.

Eating binds us to the earth. We can eat only what we are able to grow or raise on its surface. Eating acknowledges a human frailty: We must eat to survive. Eating represents a certain privilege when we have the food we want, or a prohibition when we can't have the food we want, or won't allow ourselves to eat the food we want.

That implies, of course, that we *want* food, and that desire for food, so often divided from our physical need for nourishment, is another source of joy or conflict, of great health or great pain. Fully savoring something we want and need can be one of the most profound joys of human existence. Eating a wonderful meal in a good spirit with full, live-in-the-moment appreciation is a truly spiritual as well as mental and physical experience.

Yet, desiring food beyond need, always wanting more, struggling with unfulfillment and excess are feelings that afflict millions of people trying to balance a surfeit of pleasure with good health and self-control.

Finer Fasting

Mindful eating means eating with your entire focus concentrated on the act of eating. Mindful eating can be a form of meditation, as the attention and all the senses focus intensely on the experience of how the food looks, smells, tastes, feels. It is also an exceptionally satisfying way to enjoy a good meal.

So, when you eat that steaming, savory bowl of vegetable soup, remember how lucky you are, pay attention to how good it tastes, appreciate how your body uses the nutrients you feed it, and eat your food in good company. And maybe tomorrow, fast. Nutritious food eaten with joy will feed your whole self, body, mind, and spirit in the same way that going without food for a little while can help all those different parts that make up you—your mouth, your stomach, your hands, your eyes, your heart, your mind, your spirit—come together into a vibrant, living human being far greater than any of its parts.

What Happens in the Fasting Body

You've seen what happens inside your digestive system when you eat, but what happens when you fast? What does your body do when it doesn't have food to process, or an external energy source? Even if you haven't ever purposefully fasted before, your body knows what it is like to fast because you do it every night when you sleep. Longer fasts are a magnification of what happens during the long stretch of night when you don't eat. Let's look at what the various parts of your digestive system are doing during a fast, whether just a few hours or just a few weeks:

- **Day one:** The first thing that happens when you stop eating is that your body recognizes it isn't receiving energy from an external source, so it turns inward to find energy. This turning inward stage is marked first by a breakdown of glycogen stores in the liver to make glucose, which the body and brain require to operate. These glycogen stores are typically depleted within about one day.

- **Day two:** When the liver's glycogen stores are used up, the body turns to its own protein and fat reserves and begins to break them down for energy. However, while the muscles and some organs can operate on this kind of fuel, some parts of the body, including the brain, cannot. In order to fuel the brain and red blood cells, the body manufactures the necessary glucose by converting glycerol from fat tissue and by breaking down amino acids from muscle tissue in order to make glucose.

- **Day three:** By now all the body's glucose stores have been depleted and the liver begins to manufacture ketones, a process called *ketosis,* which the brain, muscles, and heart can use as fuel when glucose levels are low. This *protein-sparing phase* is marked by a decrease in muscle wasting. This process is a survival mechanism that helps to spare muscle and organ tissue. Ketosis usually begins after about 48 hours of fasting for women and about 72 hours for men. Also during day three, toxin removal really picks up as the body breaks down fat and flushes fat-soluble impurities from the system.

- **And onward:** After day three, ketosis continues in the body, and while the body still uses muscle tissue to supply small amounts of glucose, muscle loss is minimal as long as adequate fat stores remain. However, in very long fasts, even someone who is overweight and has plenty of fat stores can eventually deplete too much muscle, causing serious health problems. For this reason, we recommend that anyone contemplating a fast gets a thorough medical checkup first to determine if body stores of protein and iron are sufficient to withstand a fast. Prolonged fasts (longer than a few days) should never be carried out without a physician's supervision.

Fast Talk

Ketosis is the state of the body during which the liver produces ketones for energy when glucose is unavailable. This phase of a fast is called the **protein-sparing phase**.

◆ **After the fast:** During a fast, your body stops producing digestive enzymes because they aren't necessary. For this reason, a sudden heavy meal can make you very sick if you've fasted more than a day. You probably won't want a very heavy meal, anyway, and you probably won't be able to eat one. It is always best to break a fast with small amounts of fresh fruit every few hours, so your body has a chance to reactivate its digestive enzymes.

Knowing what is going on inside your body as you fast can help you to understand how fasting feels, and also keep you inspired to stick to your fast. But how do you feel during a fast? What does ketosis feel like? What happens when your body flushes out toxins? Will you lose weight?

> **Fast Facts**
>
> According to Joel Furhman, M.D., in his book *Fasting and Eating for Health,* one in 20 people develop nausea and/or vomiting while fasting, but this is usually brief and rarely occurs more than twice during the fast. Furhman attributes the condition to dehydration, emphasizing that anyone on a fast must drink a minimum of one quart of water daily, whether thirsty or not. (See Appendix B, "Fasting Resources," for details on this book and others.)

Physical Changes During Fasting

During a fast, depending on how much fat and muscle you carry and how much excess fluid your body is holding, you will lose weight. Usually during the first day, as your body flushes out excess fluid and salt, you can lose up to two pounds or even more, depending on how much water you are drinking.

Much of this weight will return once you start eating again, so don't get too excited. Because your body has been trained to expect less food, your metabolism will slow considerably and your body will want to store more fat. Fasting and very low-calorie diets have been shown to increase levels of lipoprotein lipase, an enzyme produced by fat cells to help the body store fat. You will need to make very careful food selections to make sure the weight that comes back is muscle, not fat. After a week of fasting, the loss of muscle tissue may account for as much a one third of the total weight lost. This muscle tissue will be needed to help you burn fat through regular physical exercise when you begin eating again. Permanent weight loss can occur, however, as long as you don't return to your old habits as soon as your fast is over.

During your fast, your skin might break out. You might have bad breath. You might feel irritable from ketosis and inadequate dietary carbohydrate, or you might feel energized, even euphoric. When exercising, you may notice that your sweat has a strong smell. Your bowel movements may seem watery or mucus-y or look otherwise different from usual.

Your tongue may become heavily coated as toxins are eliminated. You might even stain your sheets or your clothes slightly brown as your skin releases what your body purges. If you fast for a week or two, toward the end you will become very hungry. Your tongue will lose its coating, your eyes will get brighter, and suddenly you'll feel ready to eat again. But let's see how a fast will work for our friend John.

John Does a One-Day Fast

John (not a real person, but perhaps he is a little like you?) is a 35-year-old computer programmer who spends a lot of time sitting at his desk and eating food out of a vending machine. He drinks lots of soda and very little water. Lately, he's been feeling very low on energy, even though he plays racquetball every week and goes to the gym two or three times a week to run on the treadmill.

John has decided to fast every Monday, to help boost his energy throughout the week. On Sunday night, he eats a light dinner (a salad and a salmon filet) and goes to bed, looking forward to his fast. In the morning, he isn't usually hungry, so he has a glass of water and goes to work. He tries not to look at the soda machine as he heads to his desk and gets to work.

> **Finer Fasting**
>
> Soda, including diet soda, is not juice and should not be a part of a healthy fast. Soda contains sugar and chemical preservatives, the kind of stuff your body is working so hard to eliminate. If you really must have that carbonation, try mixing a little club soda into fresh apple juice, or sip the club soda plain.

About 10:00 A.M., his typical hunger pangs set in, so John has a big mug of spicy herbal tea and another glass of water. This helps, and he goes back to work. At lunch, a group from his office goes out to a local restaurant. Not sure what to do, John agrees to come along. He doesn't want to miss anything, but he knows it will be tempting. Sitting next to co-workers ordering half-pound burgers with fries and club sandwiches is excruciating. The food smells so good, but John drinks as much water as he can stomach and tries to stay focused on the conversation, not on what kind of food is sitting on everyone's plate.

After lunch, driving back to the office, John feels buoyant and proud of himself for resisting lunch. He stops to buy a bottle of good mineral water and savors it on his way back to the office. Hunger pangs recur around 4 o'clock, but this time, they are duller and easy to resist. John has more tea and another big glass of water. Sure, he's heading to the bathroom a lot, but it feels good, like his body is already starting to cleanse itself. John goes home that evening after work and doesn't even feel like eating dinner. He has enough energy to go to the gym and do his usual workout on the treadmill, drinking more water to replace fluids lost while exercising and

> **Fast Facts**
>
> Citrus fruit juices, especially lemons, or vegetable juices made from kale, spinach, cabbage, and parsley are rich sources of vitamin C during a juice fast.

avoiding dehydration. Then he goes home, relaxes and reads for a while, and goes to bed feeling great.

In the morning, John isn't very hungry, but he eats some fruit for breakfast. For the rest of the week, John feels in control of his eating, his work, his exercise routine, even his own thoughts. He loses two pounds and has more energy than he has had for months. He vows to do it again next Monday.

Variations on a Fast

John practices one of the most common types of fasts, but people fast for many other reasons and in many other ways. While we will explain these different types of fasts in more detail later in this book, here is a brief description of some of the other options John (or you) might decide to try.

The Healing Fast

While many people fast for health maintenance, fasting is also incredibly effective for healing, if you are already suffering from a health problem. Doctors in fasting clinics report healing that seems miraculous, but the real miracle is the healing power of the body. Fasting just helps you get out of the way.

There are two types of healing fasts: the kind you do yourself to help heal your minor medical complaints, and the kind you do under medical supervision when you have a serious medical condition. Fasting should not be undertaken without a doctor's supervision for chronic conditions, such as heart disease, hypertension, liver and kidney disease, or diabetes. Here's the rule: If your health condition requires medical supervision, so should your fast. If you are under a doctor's care, then seek a doctor's care for your fast. Don't fast on your own if you have heart disease, but consider fasting under medical supervision.

If, however, you have arthritis and the doctor has told you that all you can do is exercise and take pain relievers, or if you get headaches a lot and your doctor has ruled out a serious condition, or if you are simply achy and stiff and feeling old, then you can do short healing fasts on your own.

Healing fasts for medical conditions are typically at least two weeks long, but if your complaints are minor—a sore knee that is taking a long time to heal, chronic colds due to a depressed immune system, tennis elbow, lower back pain—they may easily resolve with something as simple as a weekly 36-hour fast (which we'll discuss in Chapter 20).

The Fasting "Diet"

Some people fast just to lose weight, but fasting isn't effective if weight loss is your only goal. Used in concert with a plan to regain health (rather than just lose weight) fasting is much more effective. Periodic fasting (such as weekly or monthly) combined with a healthy, natural, plant-based diet can be effective for weight loss.

However, if you are clinically obese (and if you have any health problems related to being very overweight, such as hypertension or diabetes), you must be extremely careful with fasting, and should fast only with the supervision and approval of your primary care physician. This approval may be difficult to get. In rare cases, people who fasted for long periods to lose large amounts of weight suffered grave health consequences because they wasted away too much muscle. They fasted for too long, unsupervised or improperly supervised, and while they still had a lot of fat, they lost a critical amount of muscle protein, and they suffered serious heart problems related to severe muscle wasting. During a fast, the body will burn fat but also small amounts of muscle. The heart is a muscle we cannot afford to lose. For someone who is very overweight, this muscle wasting isn't evident, but it may be occurring, even under layers of body fat. Fasting for a very overweight person also does not address the basic issue of establishing new and healthier daily patterns of eating that improve the amount and quality of nutrient intake *and* result in permanent weight loss, which should be the primary objective for anyone whose body fits the clinical definition of obesity.

The Seasonal Fast

To get in tune with the earth, many people enjoy seasonal fasting of a few days to a week at the turn of each season. These seasonal fasts need not be total water fasts. They can be juice fasts or fruit fasts according to the season and what the earth in your region is producing at that time. Some examples of seasonal fasts might be …

- **A spring three-day apple diet.** Spring is the time for renewal and rebirth. Try a three-day diet in which you eat only organic apples and drink only apple juice and water.

- **A summer fruit-and-vegetable juice fast.** Summer is a great time to own a juicer. Try a one- to two-day fast on freshly juiced produce—apples, melons, peaches, berries, carrots, celery, greens, cucumbers, yams, beets, ginger—and lots of purified water. The experimentation and possible combinations are endless and half the fun!

- **An autumn grape fast.** Autumn is harvest time, and many wonderful foods are available. Grapes are one of the most ancient, and fasting on grapes and lots of purified water for three days is incredibly restorative, cleansing, and prepares the body for winter.

> **Fasting Wisdom**
>
> Even eating a very healthy diet can result in food obsession. An old Zen story tells of a man who visited a Zen monk and asked if the monk was a vegetarian, eager to explain that he was a strict vegetarian and therefore a highly spiritual person. The monk quickly reminded him that attachment to any idea like vegetarianism is a source of ego, not truth.

♦ **A winter soup fast.** The chill of winter is perfect for eating nothing but warm soup made from vegetable broth and finely chopped fresh vegetables, simmered gently in the broth for no more than 20 minutes. Try it for three days and you'll feel very good, very warm, and very comforted.

The Fresh Fruit Fast

While some would say it isn't a fast, eating nothing but fresh seasonal fruit feels a lot like a fast. During a fresh fruit fast, you eat nothing but fresh, organic, seasonal fruit … as much as you want! You'll find that you won't be able to binge on it. You'll eat just as much as you need as your body adjusts and remembers what it really requires. Summer is the best time for a fresh fruit fast because so many wonderful fruits are available. A fresh fruit fast can last for one day, or for as long as a week. Eat no meat or dairy products the day before beginning your fresh fruit fast, and come out of it gradually, sticking to uncooked fruits and vegetables the day after, and holding off on meat for at least another couple of days after that.

Finer Fasting

While periodic fasting can prevent the development of an ulcer as well as many other gastrointestinal disorders, you should not fast if you already have an ulcer. Follow your physician's instructions for care.

The Oatmeal Fast

This colon-cleansing fast is gentle on the stomach, and involves eating only oatmeal porridge, made with lots of water so it is very thin, with juice and/or a little honey if desired, three times a day. Also drink lots of purified water. This is an excellent one-day fast to help relieve temporary stomach discomfort.

The Least You Need to Know

♦ Digestion is a complex process during which your body moves the food you eat slowly through your digestive tract, breaking it down, extracting the nutrients it needs, and processing the rest as waste.

♦ The body, mind, and spirit are all affected by what you eat and how you eat.

♦ During a fast, the body uses its internal reserves for energy, burning excess fat and producing ketones to supply the brain with energy in the absence of large amounts of glucose.

♦ People fast for many different reasons, such as to heal or lose weight, and in many different ways, including fasts that include only some food like fresh fruit or oatmeal.

Chapter 4

The Spirit Is Willing: Overcoming Obstacles

In This Chapter

- ◆ A quiz to gauge your fasting success
- ◆ The physical obstacles to fasting
- ◆ The psychological obstacles to fasting
- ◆ The spiritual obstacles to fasting
- ◆ All about willpower (and why you won't really need much)

When you bring up the subject of fasting, people react in unusual ways. You are likely to hear some version of, "Oh, I could *never* do that!" "Fasting, oh, that's not good!" or "I would get a terrible headache!" Some people will merely raise their eyebrows and think you are strange if you decide not to eat when you have plenty of food available. "You gotta eat!" some will say. "Don't forget to eat!" "Make sure to eat!" "Let's go eat!"

Why is it so hard to skip a few meals? Because it *is* hard, at first. Let's consider the obstacles ahead of you. They are there, but they can be overcome, and the more you know about them, the better prepared you'll be to sail over them like an Olympic hurdler.

It's Not Easy

Fasting isn't easy, but the reasons it is so difficult have nothing to do with a real need for food. The obstacles in the path of someone who has decided to fast include physical withdrawal symptoms from an excessive diet, psychological difficulties based on your own assumptions and addictions and pressure from the outside world, and spiritual difficulties as you shift your body's energies. Even a one-day fast can be difficult—and the first day of a longer fast is the most difficult. But these difficulties lessen with knowledge, preparation, and especially, fasting experience.

But none of these obstacles is insurmountable, especially if you are prepared. But first, let's see where you stand when it comes to contemplating the physical, psychological, and spiritual obstacles you'll be bound to encounter during a fast.

> **Finer Fasting**
>
> Some people experience very few uncomfortable physical effects when fasting. You may be one of the lucky ones! The healthier you are when you begin your fast, the more comfortable and natural fasting will feel to you.

Your Fasting Success Indicator: A Quiz

Can you stand a mild headache? How do you take criticism? Do you have willpower when it comes to delaying pleasure? Before we discuss all the things that can get in the way of a successful fast, let's see how well you fare when it comes to analyzing your potential for fasting success.

Choose the best answer to each of the following questions, then tally up your answers according to the key at the end of this quiz.

1. When you have a mild headache, you usually …

    a. Resign yourself to a rotten day.

    b. Have an extra cup of coffee and a couple of pain relievers to fight that headache head-on.

    c. Stop whatever you are doing and launch into a 30-minute meditation/deep breathing session so your body can take care of the headache.

2. When you wake up in a grumpy mood, you usually …

    a. Curse your bad luck, grumble through the morning, and tell your co-workers they'd better avoid you.

    b. Force a smile and make yourself act like you are in a good mood. You'll buy yourself a big doughnut on the way to work, just to cheer yourself up.

    c. Sit down and think hard about what is making you grumpy, so you can do something about it before the day gets underway.

3. You are considering trying a fast, so you tell your friends about it. They immediately criticize the idea as being strange or unwise. How do you respond?

    a. Shrug your shoulders and agree that they are probably right. After all, they must know more about it than you do.

    b. Get defensive and resolve to start fasting at that very moment, just to show them.

    c. Tell them you are proceeding wisely, and refer them to this book, so they can learn about the wonders of fasting for themselves.

4. Most of the time, you feel as if you are …

    a. A victim of fate.

    b. On the defensive.

    c. In control.

5. The thing that worries you most about fasting is …

    a. You won't be able to stick with it.

    b. You might get too obsessed with it.

    c. You aren't worried. You are excited to get started!

Finer Fasting

If you need to lose more than 5 percent of your body weight, please see a doctor before you begin fasting, and conduct your fast only under medical supervision.

Now, count how many a's, b's, and c's you answered.

If you chose mostly a's, your fasting challenge is to let the fasting experience help you gain control. You tend to feel caught in the tossing and turning sea of circumstance. You sometimes lose sight of the fact that your life is your own and you can make it what you want. The wonderful thing about fasting is that if you can do this one thing, which is really *not* doing something, you will find that you gain control over many other aspects of your life you thought you'd never be able to manage. You have great potential for fasting success because you will be so pleased with the self-control you gain from your very first fast.

If you chose mostly b's, your fasting challenge is to let the fasting experience help you let go. You tend to cling, to dwell, to accumulate. You sometimes feel like you have to hold on to everything and keep everyone in line. Although your life often feels out of control, you do everything you can to get through the day. The wonderful thing about fasting is that, while it takes the kind of control you are good at, it also helps you to put things into perspective so you remember what is really important, what you really can control, and what is much better let go (such as the opinions of people you barely know, your attachments to material possessions, your fear of discomfort). You have great potential for fasting success because you will gain the feeling of freedom from letting go of the unimportant things in your life.

If you chose mostly c's, well, you know who you are! You are good and ready to start fasting and you have the right attitude in place. Your fasting challenge is to plan, execute, and put into place a fasting program to help improve your life. You'll find that fasting will help you feel cleaner, more energized, and more able to fight off illness or heal from injury. You'll think better, feel better, and look better. You are an ideal candidate for fasting because you are already pretty healthy and probably won't suffer from too many unpleasant side effects. So what are you waiting for?

Fast Facts
Some doctors now believe that hypoglycemia (an abnormally low level of glucose in the blood, commonly called low blood sugar) is overdiagnosed, and that the symptoms of what people believe to be hypoglycemia—headache, dizziness, mental confusion—are actually symptoms of withdrawal or detoxification from overly rich or overly processed foods or other chemicals such as caffeine.

Now that you've discovered what kind of fasting challenges lie ahead for you, let's look at some of the other challenges fasting presents to everyone. Fasting is physically challenging, psychologically challenging, and spiritually challenging. Knowing how each type of challenge might manifest itself in your fasting experience can help prepare you to overcome. And you shall overcome!

Fasting's Physical Gamut

The first and most immediate challenge when you begin to fast is your body's reaction. When you skip a meal, your body protests because it is accustomed to being fed. Some of the typical symptoms of physical discomfort during the first day or two of a fast are …

- Hunger.
- Headache.
- Stomachache.
- Slight nausea.
- Diarrhea.
- Excessive energy/nervousness.
- Stomach gurgling and grumbling.
- Lightheadedness.
- Intermittent weakness/fatigue.

People who fast regularly, and particularly those who, when not fasting, eat a plain diet, don't usually feel uncomfortable during a fast. They feel energized and clean. But when the body is accustomed to rich, fatty, heavy foods, excessive calories, and loads of chemical preservatives and colorants, the sudden absence of these things can be a shock to the system, and the body wants to get back to its "normal" intake. Would you mistake the cravings of an alcoholic or a drug addict as signs that the person needs alcohol or drugs to be healthy? Of course not!

But dealing with the uncomfortable symptoms of physical withdrawal and of the purging of impurities from the system can be difficult for some people, so much so that many will give up on fasting before a single day has passed. What can you do to get through that initial discomfort, to the part of the fast where you feel great? Here are some helpful hints:

> **Finer Fasting**
>
> When counseling people about changing their diet, Linda (your co-author) often hears comments such as they wish eating were something one could just stop doing, like smoking or drinking alcohol. Fasting is a way of doing just that, but with the intention of changing food choices and exercise habits. Fasting just might work for some people in concert with making healthy lifestyle changes.

- Keep in mind that the more often you fast, the less troublesome and frequent your symptoms will become. They will often disappear altogether.

- Drinking at least a half-gallon of good, pure water each day drastically reduces discomfort, much of which is due to dehydration rather than hunger.

- If you get a headache, drink a glass of juice diluted with some purified water.

- Stomach growling and gurgling may signal hunger to you. It is your body's way of noticing that it isn't getting it's normal load of food dumped into your stomach. But these sounds don't hurt, so while you will certainly notice them, you don't have to do anything about them.

- If you feel nauseated, try a cup of ginger tea with a little honey.

- If you get irritable, take a time out and breath deeply. Feed your body with the energy of breath.

- If you feel weak, rest. Short fasts shouldn't make you feel weak, though.

Keep reminding yourself that any discomfort is temporary. By the second day of a fast, most unpleasant symptoms will disappear, and discomfort is extremely rare after the second day. We much prefer short periodic fasting, like one day per week or even one or two half-days per week, over single long fasts for anyone hoping to maintain or regain health.

The periodic faster enjoys far fewer symptoms. The body learns how to recognize a fasting period and soon adjusts almost immediately. So it may not be great fun the first time you try it, but you'll feel so good afterward that next week it will be easier, and the week after that, easier still.

Fasting's Psychological Gamut

The mind is an amazing thing, and a powerful force. For some, the mere thought of fasting induces immediate feelings of mock hunger and reactive eating. It seems absurd that someone who is perfectly well fed and not due for another meal for several hours will be compelled to eat at the very suggestion of a fast, but it happens all the time.

The psychological obstacles to a fast are significantly larger and more intimidating than the physical ones. Some come from within us. What are we thinking, going without food when it is uncomfortable? Why are we punishing ourselves? Or, on the other side of the psychological coin, how could we have let ourselves become so unhealthy, so fat, so poisoned with junk? Is it really worth it to fast, or should we just give up and accept our failing health?

Some of the typical psychological symptoms during a fast are ...

- Food cravings.
- Frustration.
- Irritability.
- A feeling of isolation from others.
- A disconcerting euphoria.
- Self-doubt, especially when others criticize.
- Fear.
- Self-criticism, as you realize how thoughtless you have been with your body and how hard it is working to regain its health.

Humans are prone to negative self-talk, but that kind of talk is debilitating to good holistic health. The trick to staying strong in your resolve on a fast is to do a lot of research before you start (such as reading this book—see, you are already on your way!) and having affirmations ready to motivate you when you try to talk yourself out of it.

Affirmations and ready information are also helpful when you are confronted by someone who challenges your fast. This will happen! People who don't know much about fasting often assume it is dangerous or strange. Some medical professionals who aren't experienced with fasting may raise their eyebrows or discourage you from trying a fast. Just remember that fasting is generally not something that is taught in Western medical schools. As long as you have found a good doctor with legitimate credentials who supports your program, you don't need to listen to anyone else. Of course, your doctor may have good reasons for discouraging a fast if you have a medical condition, in which case you should certainly follow his or her advice.

So, when you criticize or doubt yourself before or during a fast, or when someone else criticizes or doubts you, remember the following statements. Memorize them. Have them ready in your brain. Post them on your bathroom mirror and on your refrigerator. Live them!

- My intuition tells me this is the right thing to do for my health, and I trust my intuition.
- I've researched fasting and I know it is not harmful to me because I am fasting in the correct way, with my doctor's supervision.
- Fasting restores health.
- Fasting builds inner strength.
- Fasting purifies.
- Fasting helps me to regain my self-control.
- Fasting fills me with energy, joy, and life.
- I don't need to eat today.
- I am not afraid to eat. I *choose* not to eat during this time.
- My body already contains everything it needs during my fast.
- I am successful at fasting.
- I am successful at eating well.
- I finally understand how to take care of myself.

Finer Fasting

Thought you'd get support from your friends? Think again. People tend to be unsupportive of someone who is fasting, either because they don't understand it and have heard it can be harmful, don't think they could do it, or are uncomfortable confronting their own health issues. Look inward for support instead.

And what about all that unsolicited advice you keep getting? As long as you feel strong in your own resolve, other people's opinions shouldn't really matter. Of course, that's easier to say than to practice. So, just to give you an additional boost, here are a few things you can say to people who question the safety or wisdom of your fast:

- I've researched fasting carefully and decided it's the best course for me right now, but thanks for your concern.
- Fasting really isn't as difficult as you might think. It feels great.
- Maybe fasting isn't right for you right now, but it's working very well for me.
- Don't worry, I'm under a doctor's supervision.

And if you just don't want to get into it, when offered food, politely decline: "That looks really good, but I'm just not hungry right now. Maybe later. Thanks, anyway!"

If you think someone would truly be unsupportive of your fast, just don't mention it. You aren't obligated to tell anybody you are fasting.

Fasting's Spiritual Gamut

Your spiritual side may not seem particularly relevant as a source of obstacles to fasting, but when you fast, your body's energies begin to shift and balance. Your spiritual side will float closer to the surface. And that can cause some problems, too.

Many of us claim to be spiritual people, but spend very little time seriously involved in spiritual pursuits. Who has the time? While many people attend church services once or twice a week and many more pray and/or meditate on a regular basis, few of us have integrated our spiritual sides into our personalities as thoroughly as we have integrated the mental, physical, and emotional parts of ourselves.

But during a fast, the physical self is put temporarily to rest, switched into self-cleaning mode, calmer and quieter. The mind, too, gets quieter and more peaceful during a fast, and once the psychological obstacles to fasting are conquered, the emotions tend to turn pleasant and joyful.

That leaves the spiritual side a lot more room to flex and expand. For this reason, many cultures rely on fasting to help induce visions, altered states of consciousness, and spiritual awakening. While you may not be interested in becoming a yogi on a mountaintop, you, too, can take full advantage of the spiritual space fasting grants your body.

But spiritual awareness can be a frightening prospect, too. To suddenly feel more spiritual, more aware, more in tune with your god or the universal consciousness or the energy of life or whatever you want to call it, can be daunting. You might wonder where these feelings are coming from. You might be afraid you are losing touch with reality. On the contrary, you are getting closer to your own inner reality.

> **Fasting Wisdom**
>
> A mind consciously unclean cannot be cleansed by fasting.
>
> —Mohandas K. ("Mahatma") Gandhi, Hindu religious leader and social reformer (1869–1948)

If you embrace your emerging spirituality during a fast by spending more time in meditation, prayer, and contemplation (in accordance with whatever your beliefs may be), you'll find that fasting holds another rich and wonderful reward. The spiritual space opened by fasting is the primary motivator for many people who fast. Let yourself explore it, rather than shy away from it, and you'll have overcome the final obstacle to successful mind-body-spirit integration through fasting.

All About Willpower

Willpower is tough, and while a few people have it, most of us willingly admit that we don't have as much willpower as we could. The dictionary defines willpower as "the ability to carry out one's wishes, decisions, or plans." Sounds simple enough. If you want to do something, if you wish to do something, if you decide to do something, or plan something, why wouldn't you just do it?

But humans are funny that way. We want to lose weight, we know what is required, but we just can't seem to pass up that giant cinnamon roll or that double pepperoni pizza. We want to get organized, but we just can't seem to make ourselves put things away after we are finished with them, or stay caught up on paperwork. We want to be kind, generous, loving people, but somehow, we do or say things that we know are not kind or generous or loving.

What's wrong with us? We're human. We have complicated wishes and desires constantly at odds with each other. So is there any hope for us? Is there any way we can really get through a fast, even if we want to, decide to, plan to?

Why You Need Only a Little

The great thing about fasting is that it doesn't actually take very much willpower. It's true! It just takes a little. The hardest part is skipping the very first meal, but all you need to do is *not* eat. Drink a big glass of water, a couple of cups of herbal tea, even some diluted juice. Fill up on fluids and go about your day. Keep yourself distracted. Every time you feel hungry, do it again. And before you know it, you'll feel great, you'll be energized, and fasting will seem effortless.

The Body's Built-In Technical Support Desk

During a fast of longer than one day, your body kicks in to help you feel good and keep you from feeling hungry by producing ketones (see Chapter 3, "The Anatomy of a Fast"). Your body also helps you keep fasting by giving you energy, a clear head, heightened senses, and an overall feeling of well-being. If you ever doubted fasting was good for you, you won't doubt it anymore when you see how good it feels. It is as if your body is saying, "Yes! Finally! Thank you! I'm going to reward you by making you feel great so you'll do this every now and then!"

How Focused Meditation Can Help

Sometimes, when psychological pressures overwhelm you and you want to break your fast (even a short fast like a half-day or one-day fast), meditation can help. When you begin to feel like you can't possibly avoid food, take five minutes, go to a quiet, secluded place where you won't be bothered, sit comfortably, take a deep breath, close your eyes, and concentrate on a positive image. Focus with all your energy on that one thing as you continue to breathe deeply. Let your body relax and take in positive energy from the air around you. Let yourself feel your body and let your body talk to you.

After five minutes, you probably will feel strong enough to withstand temptation. However, if you truly feel hungry and really do need to eat, go ahead and have some fresh raw fruit. But nothing other than fruit! This will put the least amount of strain on a fasting digestive system.

Your Willpower Checklist

No matter how much or how little willpower you think you have, keep this list handy. It is your checklist of willpower resources, and you can check on it whenever you need a boost:

❏ Do you feel good today? You deserve to feel good.

❏ Do you feel strong today? You have the right to feel strong.

❏ Do you feel in control of yourself today? You are allowed to direct your own behavior.

❏ Do you feel energetic today? You are designed to operate on energy.

❏ Are you being good to yourself today? Only you can truly take care of yourself, physically, mentally, emotionally, and spiritually.

Doing these things will help you to fast, but even more important, fasting will help you to accomplish these things.

The Least You Need to Know

- Fasting is hard to do, especially the first time, but it gets easier.
- The physical challenges of fasting consist primarily of symptoms such as headaches, nausea, and stomach cramps due to withdrawal from an overabundant and overly rich diet.
- The psychological challenges of fasting consist primarily of negative self-talk and the influence of people who don't know much about fasting or who discourage your efforts.
- The spiritual challenges of fasting consist primarily of accepting a willingness to open yourself to your spiritual side.
- Fasting takes only a little willpower. Your body takes care of the rest, making it easy after the first day.

Part 2

Fasting for Greater Spiritual Awareness

In this part we'll go into more detail about the spiritual aspects of fasting, including the best way to combine fasting with a meditation practice, how to use yoga, massage, and breathwork to boost the health-enhancing effects of short fasts, and a primer on the life-force energy often called chi, the energy centers in the body called chakras, and that radiant energy that surrounds each of us, our auras. Next are some profiles of famous spiritual leaders and teachers who used fasting as an integral part of their lives and missions. This part ends with a discussion of fasting centers and spiritual retreats, including a section on how to create your own fasting retreat at home.

Chapter 5

Fasting and Meditation

In This Chapter

◆ The link between fasting and meditation
◆ Everything you always wanted to know about meditation
◆ How to bring meditation into your fasting practice
◆ Guided meditations to try

Meditation is probably as ancient a practice as fasting. For thousands of years, humans have practiced mental focus as a means to better understand the nature of the world or as a spiritual practice. Meditation is a highly beneficial technique for sharpening the thought process and balancing and integrating the body-mind. In many ways, meditation and fasting are similar. They both take the focus away from the external world and direct it inside the body so that healing and balancing can take place.

So let's examine how meditation and fasting can be used together, each boosting the power of the other for a more concentrated physical, mental, and spiritual practice. If you thought fasting worked well, just wait till you try it with meditation!

Zen and the Art of Fasting

Zen is a nice buzzword Americans like to use to describe anything that is remotely spiritual or Eastern in flavor in our culture, but Zen is actually a Japanese form of Buddhism that has been embraced and adapted by Westerners, often as a philosophy without the Buddhist underpinnings.

Zen means meditation, and practicing Zen or having a Zen attitude or approach to life means simplifying, living in the present without attachment to the past or future, mindfulness in everyday life, paying attention, fully living each moment, staying awake (metaphorically), not striving or fighting but moving with the current of your life, looking inward, and seeking your own oneness with the universe. Zen is a deep and abiding satisfaction and joy in who and where you are right now.

Fast Talk

Zen is the Japanese word for meditation. The Chinese word is **Ch'an** and the Sanskrit word is **dhyana**. The Japanese word for sitting meditation is **zazen**.

Finer Fasting

Interested in meditation and Zen? Check out *The Complete Idiot's Guide to Meditation* by Joan Budilovsky and Eve Adamson, and *The Complete Idiot's Guide to Zen Living* by Gary McClain, Ph.D., and Eve Adamson. (See Appendix B, "Fasting Resources," for details.)

A Zen attitude can be helpful for someone battling with compulsive eating or the habit of overeating. If we are too attached to consumption, to excess, to the pleasure of eating rich foods in large amounts, we can't truly appreciate who we are in the present moment. We can't focus on what we are doing because we are too driven by our desire for food. Zen is about freeing ourselves from desire in favor of pure existence, unattached to desires that control us.

But Zen doesn't mean you stop enjoying yourself or your food. The best way to eat is with a deep and mindful appreciation. In fact, eating can be an incredibly Zenlike experience. But if we become too attached to eating, if we can't bear the thought of going without it, we have lost our Zen connection. In Zen, each present moment is a full and glorious experience, which we then let go in favor of the next present moment.

While fasting, a Zen attitude can help us to let go of our attachment to food and accept, appreciate, revel in the fasting process. It makes fasting a more profound and satisfying experience. And meditation is the key to getting there.

How Fasting Facilitates Meditation

The Zen form of sitting meditation, called *zazen*, involves sitting for a set period of time each day (five minutes is a good place to start) and simply focusing within, on the breath, how the body feels, what is happening in the present moment. Other traditions such as the yoga tradition also consider meditation a vital part of life. In Sanskrit, the word for meditation (one of the paths of yoga) is *dhyana*.

No matter the tradition, during meditation, the point is to train the mind to focus so intently on a single object that the object disappears and the unity of all things becomes apparent. Easier said than done, however! For the beginning meditator, distractions are inevitable. But, when thoughts about the past, the future, or anything beyond the present moment occur, the trick is to acknowledge the thoughts, notice them, then gently push them away.

Yes, sitting in meditation can be extremely difficult, especially for those who have never tried it. While it might seem a simple matter to sit and concentrate on the present moment, what really happens is distraction. You start to feel restless. You get an itch on a spot on your back you can't reach. Your mind races. What should you be getting done right now? What did you do this morning? Yesterday? What do you have to worry about that's happening later today, or tomorrow, or next week? What's on your grocery list? Your to-do list? Why can't you just get up and get something done?!

Luckily, fasting makes meditation easier. Fasting is an excellent way to help strip away the layers of illusion and attachment that keep us from successfully mastering a Zen attitude toward life, let alone five minutes of sitting meditation. When we fast, we stop focusing on the sensual pleasure of food and our focus, as well as our body's search for energy, turns inward.

The fasting person has a calmer, more tranquil demeanor. When you fast, your mind will have an easier time staying still. You won't obsess as easily over all the things you have to do. You'll feel quieter inside, and the concentration and focus required for meditation will come to you.

How Meditation Makes Fasting Easier

On the other side of the equation, meditation also does its share of the work to make fasting easier. During meditation, you consciously focus inward, rather than on outside, sensory stimuli. This focus is good practice for the brain, which is used to focusing most of its conscious attention on sensory input. What you see, what you hear, what you smell, what you taste, what you touch … your body takes it in, your brain processes it. You enjoy it, or don't enjoy it. But it's all about the senses.

Fasting Wisdom

Do not try to drive away pain by pretending that it is not real. Pain, if you seek serenity in Oneness, will vanish of its own accord.

—Seng T'san, 3rd Zen patriarch (died 606 C.E.)

Until you sit down to meditate. While you can notice the senses, they are not your focus. Your focus goes inward, to your breathing, to what's happening in your mind, divorced from its connection to the sensory input around you. If you choose to meditate while focusing on an external point, such as a candle flame or a picture or a star, while you are using your senses, they are so minutely focused on one thing that eventually, sensory input seems to dissolve and you and the point of your focus merge as one. Your focus becomes you.

When your brain gets used to thinking in this way, it is much easier to think—to *know*—that you can skip a few meals.

Is Meditation for You?

While we would argue that anyone can benefit from meditation, some people find meditation a lot easier than others. Consider whether any of the following apply to your life:

- Do you have trouble concentrating?
- Do you often feel frazzled or disorganized?
- Do you often lose things (car keys, cell phone, glasses)?
- Does your mind tend to race?
- Do you have trouble getting to sleep at night?
- Are you so forgetful that you fear you're becoming senile?
- Do you feel separated from your own spirituality, or wonder if you are spiritual at all?

Fasting Wisdom

I believe that it is essential to appreciate our potential as human beings and recognize the importance of inner transformation. This should be achieved through what could be called a process of mental development. Sometimes, I call this having a spiritual dimension in our life.

—His Holiness the Dalai Lama

These symptoms are all signs of mental stress, which meditation directly combats by teaching or exercising the mind to focus on one thing, training it to push away distractions. Meditators are often better able to focus on what they need to do, prioritize, and react more quickly.

Meditation can also be a highly charged spiritual practice. Different from prayer, which is usually some form of verbal or mental communication, meditation is simply sitting, concentrating, focusing. For those who meditate for spiritual reasons, meditation provides an ideal state in which to focus on, think about, and merge with a higher or inner power.

Setting the Groundwork

Meditation is an excellent way to help prepare your mind for a coming fast—even a fast of half a day. If you think you'd like to try meditation, you will be most successful if you know what to expect and feel ready.

Preparing for a Meditation Practice

You can meditate almost anywhere, and you don't need any special equipment, but mental preparation is essential if you are to be successful in your efforts at meditation. Knowing that meditation is difficult, especially for the unpracticed Western mind not raised in the tradition, can help you deal with the inevitable frustration at being unable to concentrate.

We are used to lots of sensory stimulation, television images that shift every few seconds, noise and color, conversation and challenge. Just sitting is exceptionally boring compared to all that. Yet, this very boredom is what helps to tone your mental process. Lifting weights is boring, too, but it makes you strong.

Remember these keys and think about them before you begin your meditation practice:

◆ Practice makes perfect. Really! Meditation is all about practice.

◆ Your mind will wander, but that's okay. It's what minds do. Just steer your attention gently back to your focus.

◆ You'll probably feel restless, but that's okay. It's what bodies do! Try to think past it. The more you meditate, the more comfortable it gets.

◆ One minute can feel like an eternity when you are just sitting there. But the more you meditate, the faster the time flies.

◆ Persistence and the determination and commitment to meditate every day, even if for only a few minutes at first, will pay off quickly.

Setting Up a Schedule

Whether you plan to meditate only during a fast or every day, you'll be most likely to keep it up if you work it into your schedule. Some people like to meditate first thing every morning. Others are better able to meditate in the evening, or even in the middle of the day.

During a fast, you may want to increase your meditation time. Here is a sample week you can use or adapt for your own purposes. Make sure you give yourself a comments section to record your experience. If you design your own schedule and meditate at the same time each day, you'll be making meditation a priority and a habit.

The following meditation schedule is designed for someone who will start fasting on Sunday:

	Time	Duration	Comments
Monday:	7:00 A.M.	5 minutes	Really hard!
Tuesday:	7:00 A.M.	5 minutes	Still hard—mind wandering
Wednesday:	7:00 A.M.	6 minutes	A little easier today
Thursday:	7:00 A.M.	6 minutes	Maintained good focus
Friday:	7:00 A.M.	7 minutes	Seemed long today
Saturday:	7:00 A.M.	7 minutes	Felt energized afterwards
Sunday/ Fast Day:	7:00 A.M.	10 minutes	Helped to focus on goals
	7:00 P.M.	10 minutes	I feel great about today!

Meditation FAQs

People who have never meditated have a lot of questions about it. Here are some of the most common frequently asked questions about meditation and the connection between meditation and fasting.

Can You Meditate Without Fasting?

Of course. Many people all around the world meditate without fasting. However, fasting can intensify and focus the meditation experience, and many people throughout history, both famous religious figures and "ordinary" people, have combined the two practices.

Can You Fast Without Meditating?

Sure. Plenty of people fast without meditating, but meditation does make fasting easier because it focuses your mind on your goal and helps to allay the temptation to eat compulsively or impulsively. Meditation encourages mindfulness.

What Physical Effects Does Meditation Have?

Meditation usually has a profoundly relaxing effect on the body, lowering blood pressure and pulse rate, and reducing or halting the production of stress hormones.

How Do You Meditate?

Sit comfortably on the floor (using pillows) in a cross-legged or kneeling position, or in a chair. Straighten and lift your spine. Don't slouch back. Close your mouth. Gently rest your tongue on the roof of your mouth. You can keep your eyes open, closed, or half open and unfocused. Begin by concentrating on something—an object, like a candle flame; a sound or *mantra* such as "peace"; or the feel of your own breathing. Some people begin by counting each breath, up to ten, then starting back at one. Once your mind is trained to stay focused, you won't need a point of focus anymore. You will simply sit in quiet and mindful observation. Begin meditating for two to five minutes, then gradually work up to 15 to 30 minutes once or twice a day.

Fast Talk

A **mantra** is a sound, word, or phrase repeated during meditation for focus. Some people believe that the vibration in the body generated by a mantra actually effects physical changes in the body.

Is Meditation Different from Concentration?

Yes. Meditation begins with concentration on a point of focus, but that is really a tool to help train your mind. Once focus is mastered, meditation is a period of rest for the mind, a state of alert awareness during which you don't follow or engage any thought, but simply and passively observe.

When Is Best to Meditate?

Everyone is an individual, and anyone can meditate at any time. However, first thing in the morning is a popular time for meditation, and some people believe it is the time when the mind is most prepared to meditate successfully, before the distractions of the day set in. Also, meditation is easier before a meal or during a fast than after a meal, when the body is busy focusing on digestion.

What Is the Goal of Meditation?

For some, the ultimate goal is to achieve the realization that the self and the universe are the same, and to perceive that oneness in a meaningful way. For others, meditation is an opportunity for religious reflection. However, many people have purely physical goals: mental clarity, stress reduction, or relaxation.

Do I Have to Be Religious to Meditate?

Certainly not. Meditation is not a religion, and while it can be a religious practice that fits easily into any major religious tradition (and plenty of minor ones), many people meditate for the mental and physical benefits alone.

Is Meditation Against My Religion?

No. Meditation is not a religion and is not exclusively associated with any religion. Instead, it can be a part of any religion, helping the religious practitioner to focus, worship, seek guidance, pray, or simply enjoy a more direct communion with God.

What Is a Zen Koan?

A Zen koan is a word puzzle, riddle, or story that doesn't seem to make logical sense. Practitioners of certain types of Zen meditate using the koan as their point of focus. When logic breaks open and the mind sees beyond it, the answer to the koan will be clear. In certain settings, the meditators present their answers to a Zen master so he or she can determine whether they truly understood. Koans train and stretch the thinking as well as hone the focus.

Fasting Wisdom

Curious about koans? Try meditating on a few of these Zen koans, which are meant to be illogical. Only when your mind is able to break free from the bondage of logical thinking and distinctions between one thing and another can you truly find the answer to these koans:

- What is the sound of one hand clapping?
- How does a goose escape from a long-necked bottle?
- Question: What is Buddha? Answer: This flax weighs three pounds.
- How do you proceed from the top of a 100-foot flagpole?
- When you have a staff, I will give it to you. When you have no staff, I will take it away from you.

What Is Guided Meditation?

Guided meditation is a form of visualization, in which the meditator is led to visualize certain scenes, events, or places for a particular goal. Someone meditating for stress relief might be guided in a meditation in which he or she is asked to imagine relaxing on a beach or sitting in front of a crackling fire in a cozy log cabin. Someone meditating for spiritual contemplation might be guided through a journey into the self represented by a staircase or an elevator descending into a private garden. The possibilities are endless, and guided meditations can be found in many different books. Meditation classes sometimes focus on guided meditations, during which a teacher guides the students.

Guided Meditations to Try

Guided meditations are a great way to begin meditating. They are more interesting than just sitting because they engage the imagination, but they still promote concentration because the meditator focuses on the words and the images suggested by the person leading the meditation.

> **Fast Talk**
>
> **Guided meditation** is a meditative form of visualization in which someone gives verbal cues to the person meditating to direct their attention to certain suggestive scenes or ideas. Common guided meditations have as their themes relaxing places such as the beach, communion with the earth, or cues for spiritual reflection.

Following are some guided meditations you can try. Relax, close your eyes, and have someone slowly read these meditations. Or record them yourself on a tape that you can play back for yourself. Each of these guided meditations is designed to work in concert with a fast.

For each meditation, get very comfortable, sitting on the floor or in a chair. Take a few deep breaths, relax, sit up straight, and then turn on the tape or signal the person reading to begin. Remember to read these slowly and to pause often to let the words sink in.

An Evening Meditation

This meditation is great for half-day fasts, such as fasting after 3:00 P.M. Try it in the evening, when you start to feel hunger pangs.

> Tonight is just for you.
>
> Tonight you have decided to honor yourself.
>
> Tonight you will focus on the inner you.
>
> As you breathe in, imagine filling your body with positive energy.
>
> As you breathe out, imagine releasing negative energy from your body.
>
> Imagine a warm band of light encircling your feet. Feel your feet relax into the warmth.
>
> Imagine the band of light slowly moving up your body. As it moves, your body gradually relaxes and tension dissolves away.

Notice how your feet feel. Your legs. Your stomach. Your arms. Your neck. Your head.

Let the warm light drain away all your tension and negativity.

Draw in light with the breath. Let go of tension with the breath.

You have honored yourself by taking care of yourself,

By releasing your tension and filling yourself with light.

By giving your body and your mind the rest they need.

Replenishing your whole being with clear, pure, clean, vibrant life energy.

A Weekly Meditation

This meditation is helpful during a one-day-per-week fast, or at the beginning of a week-long fast.

Take seven long, slow, deep breaths. With each breath, visualize.

Breath one: See yourself glowing with health.

Breath two: See yourself beaming with joy.

Breath three: See yourself strong and confident.

Breath four: See yourself thinking quickly and clearly.

Breath five: See yourself energized and alive.

Breath six: See yourself doing what you love.

Breath seven: See yourself loving and being loved.

This week, you will keep your happiness in the front of your mind. You will keep your health at the top of your priorities. You will love yourself this week.

A New Moon Meditation

Some people like to fast during the day of the new moon. This meditation will support your efforts to eat and fast in harmony with the lunar cycle.

The moon moves around the earth as the earth moves around the sun. Picture the full moon. See it in a dark sky, round, golden, brilliant. Notice the crevices and cracks.

Now, imagine you are floating. Breathe deeply and feel your body floating, lifting off your feet and gently rising into the air, up, up, through the clouds, slowly rising, peacefully floating into space until you see the moon ahead of you. Imagine gently, softly landing with your feet on the moon.

Now, imagine you are exploring the surface of the moon. Walk around and feel the rock under your feet. Look at the craters and crevices and chips of stone. Touch the ground.

Practice walking in the low-gravity environment of the moon. Take little jumps and feel yourself floating slowly up, slowly down. Have fun. Experiment. Play. All the while, the sky is a deep blue around you and you can see earth, waiting for your return.

Now, sit down on the moon. Relax. Breathe deeply. Notice the sun as it slowly sinks beyond the moon's horizon. The surface of the moon grows dim, the only sliver of light remaining where you sit. Think about how it is time for the moon to rest in shadow, just as it is time for your body to rest. The air is cool, cold, clear. You breathe, taking in the quiet, calm energy of the moon.

Now you feel tranquil. At peace with yourself. Imagine standing up, raising your arms toward earth, and slowly floating, up, up, back through the cool dark space, back through the clouds, back down to the ground, back down into your body. When you are ready, open your eyes and return your focus to the room.

> **Fast Facts**
>
> For centuries, farmers have planted and harvested crops according to the moon's cycle. Different plants are best planted at different phases. An almanac can advise you when to plant according to the lunar cycle during any given month. Eating and fasting according to these cycles can help you feel like you are living in closer harmony to the planetary and lunar cycles.

Meditations for Every Occasion

We could go on with many other meditations—the possibilities are endless. Seasonal meditations to coincide with solstice and equinox fasting are incredibly renewing and fulfilling. A new-year meditation can help you to begin a new year with the right mindset and preparation.

Try writing about your seasonal meditations. Be creative! After you write them down, read them on a tape and play them back to yourself. Spring meditations can be about renewal, birth, and revitalization. Summer meditations can be about growth, beauty, and communion with the natural world. Autumn meditations can be about shedding what you no longer need, forgiveness, and moving to the next stage of life, letting go. Winter meditations can be about turning within, warmth, purity, and miracles.

Each person has his or her own individual needs, life events, changes, and feelings that can inspire or require meditation. Whether you want to guide yourself through a meditation, find a teacher to help you, or just sit and focus, meditation can become an important and beneficial part of your life. When combined with fasting, you'll have some serious life-enhancing tools at your disposal.

The Least You Need to Know

◆ Fasting helps to focus the body inward, facilitating better meditation; meditation helps to turn the body inward and shut off the external senses, making fasting easier.

◆ People have fasted and meditated for centuries, and this combination is an important spiritual practice for people all over the world.

◆ Start meditating for only a few minutes at a time. Gradually work up to longer periods of 15 to 30 minutes when you are ready.

◆ Guided meditations are spoken to the meditator, who visualizes according to the cues. Guided meditations can be used for stress relief, relaxation, or to awaken spirituality.

6

Fasting and Spiritual Growth

In This Chapter

- ◆ What is spirituality and why do you need it?
- ◆ How fasting helps you to find your spiritual self
- ◆ Fasting for life
- ◆ Body-mind tools for getting better acquainted with your spiritual self

Much of this book is about using fasting to integrate the whole self: mind, body, and spirit. We've already talked about how fasting affects the body and the mind, and we've briefly mentioned spirit, but because spirit is a part of the self so many people admit they neglect, we've decided to devote a chapter to spiritual growth and the ways fasting can enhance it.

The spirituality movement has characterized the first years of the twenty-first century in the same way that the health-and-fitness movement characterized the last decade or two of the twentieth century. In recent years, the general population is doing pretty well materially, and yet, many still feel a sense of something missing from their lives. The link between the spirit and the body is far from unfounded. More than 50 studies have shown positive effects of spirituality on health and longevity, and researchers have actually been able to document physiologic changes in people involved in spiritual pursuits.

As people discover that a lack of spirituality impacts their health and happiness, more are seeking spiritual fulfillment.

What Is Spirituality?

While every health and fitness magazine on the racks these days seems to have an article on spirituality, many are hard pressed to define the term. Does spirituality mean religion? Going to a place of worship? Praying? Or is it something else?

While there may be many definitions of spirituality, we would define spirituality as the search for meaning in life. That search could target a higher power, or helping others, or an examination of the inner self in relationship to the world or the universe. To some, it could involve the practice of a religion. To others, it could involve service to humankind, or the formation of a personal belief system or moral code. Spirituality can simply mean taking a few minutes every day to stop whatever you are doing and look inward.

Whatever spirituality means to you, committing to a more spiritual life focus can broaden and enrich your life, and fasting can help.

Fast Facts

According to Andrew Newberg, M.D., a neuroscientist and the co-author of *Why God Won't Go Away: Brain Science and the Biology of Belief* (Ballantine, 2001), an area in the back of the brain responsible for processing spatial and time-related information experiences a reduction in activity during meditation. This phenomenon seems to give spirituality and the perception of universal unity a biological basis. [As reported in November 2001 issue of *Shape* magazine.]

What Your Spirit Learns from Fasting

The simple act of not eating—for one meal, for several meals, for a day or two—is a powerful spiritual tool. Because most humans are largely motivated by food, food keeps us externally focused (as we've mentioned before). But during a fast, when this rewarding external focus is removed, when we know we won't be eating anything, our spirits have the opportunity to float to the top of consciousness like a buoy that has been held underwater.

Fasting makes you feel good, clear, clean, and energetic. It makes you feel optimistic and it helps your spirit to take firmer root in your conscious mind. During a fast day, you may find it easier to stop what you are doing and reflect on yourself, your life, the things with which you are blessed. Fasting coaxes your spirit to come out and spread its wings. In other words, you'll be getting a lot in exchange for those missed meals.

During a fast, you may find yourself more drawn to the natural world and you may enjoy a heightened sensory perception. A walk through the woods on a crisp fall day or a stroll through a meadow in early spring—experiences like these become spiritual experiences during a fast, almost without effort.

How to Make a Spiritual Connection

Some people find it difficult to uncover their spiritual sides at first. Many people today don't go to church, don't practice any particular religion, or simply don't feel they have time to invest much energy in the exploration of their spirits.

Yet, those whose spirits are largely unattended often feel they lack something in their lives. Often, they try to fill up that empty space with something—by stuffing it with food or mind-altering substances like alcohol or drugs, or by getting into relationships with the wrong people, or any number of other self-destructive behaviors.

But what is lacking isn't food or drugs or bad relationships. Spirit is lacking. Spirit is what we are searching for. Where is it? How do we find it? If it's really inside, how do we uncover it? It's one thing to *want* to be more spiritually connected, but how do you do it?

Fasting, of course, is an excellent way to tune in to your spiritual side. By eliminating a significant sensory stimulus, fasting promotes an easier path inward. Ironically, a short break from food can feed that empty space better than a junk-food binge.

There are other ways to make a spiritual connection besides fasting that can be used in conjunction with fasting, or as a sort of spiritual warm-up before a fast. Choosing one spirituality booster each week can make a gradual but important difference in how you feel about yourself and how you see your life.

> **Fasting Wisdom**
>
> Life is occupied in both perpetuating itself and in surpassing itself; if all it does is maintain itself, then living is only not dying.
>
> —Simone de Beauvoir, French feminist and author (1908–1986)

Here are some ideas for spiritual boosts you can incorporate into your life:

- **Become a nature lover.** Spend 15 minutes outside each day in quiet contemplation of the natural world … even if all you have to look at is a potted geranium or a sapling planted inside a sidewalk square.

- **Give unto others.** Volunteer your time for a cause you think is important.

- **Examine your priorities.** Decide what you think is important: Make a list of your life priorities and post it where you can see it every morning.

- **Use your sixth sense.** The next time you have to make a decision, tap into your intuition. What does it tell you? It may be different from what your intellectual side tells you, but try giving your intuition equal weight and see what happens.

♦ **Try praying.** Whether or not you are religiously affiliated, you can pray. To god, goddess, spirit, to a benevolent higher power, to the universe, or to your inner self. Praying is really like communicative meditation. Talk out loud or in your head. What do you want to say? Let yourself express yourself.

♦ **Write about it.** Write how you feel, what you are looking for, where you think your life is going, where you would like it to go. Write about your personal philosophy, your expectations, your disappointments. Write about how it feels and how it changes you when you fast. Search, through writing, for what you believe, not just what you know or what you think. Sometimes you don't realize what you believe until you see what you've written!

> ### Fasting Wisdom
>
> In an article by William Webber called "What Good Can Come of the Evil from the Terrorist Attacks," posted on the Beliefnet website (www.beliefnet.com) in response to the September 11, 2001, terrorist attacks on the Pentagon and the World Trade Center, Webber relates evidence that after the tragedy, Americans everywhere were becoming kinder, more willing to help others, and more spiritual. Children reported improved family relations. Good Samaritan acts were on the rise. Attendance at houses of worship increased dramatically. One theory is that when people witness acts of heroism, it elevates their own sense of duty and goodness, causing them to act in kind, reconsider their priorities, and remember the importance of loved ones.

Fasting as a Spiritual Tool

Of course, one of our favorite spiritual tools is fasting, and you can set up a fast specifically for spiritual purposes. Intention is the first step. Let's say you plan to fast this Sunday. Before Sunday, preferably on Saturday evening, take some time by yourself to sit quietly, undisturbed, and set your intention. Decide what your intention is, and speak it out loud to yourself, or whisper it, or think it several times, or write it down. Here are some ideas for how you might word your intention. Of course, only you will know what intention will work best for your own fast:

♦ Tomorrow I will fast while focusing on my spiritual progress up to this point in my life.

♦ Tomorrow I will fast so I can feel what it is like for people who don't have enough food, because I want to raise my awareness of and connection with all people in the world.

♦ Tomorrow I will fast so I can focus more directly on the love of God.

◆ Tomorrow I will fast so I can feel more in tune with the cycles and energies of the earth.

◆ Tomorrow I will fast so I can feel humbled in the face of something greater than myself.

◆ Tomorrow I will fast so I can focus on my priorities and my long-term whole-self life plan.

◆ Tomorrow I will fast so I can focus on all the good things in my life, and the good that governs the universe.

If any of these suggestions speak to you, use them. If not, craft your own, but be sure that you begin any fast conducted for spiritual purposes with a clearly defined intention. That intention will help to guide you and give you something to hang on to and focus on when you are tempted to just grab that doughnut or that cheeseburger and give up on the whole fast. Yes, fasting is difficult in the face of lots of tempting food (most of which isn't very good for us). Just remember that difficulty can help to train your body, discipline your mind, and strengthen your spirit.

Fasting as a Life Path

Some people fast once or twice, just to try it, but many have chosen fasting as an integral part of their own life plan. This is just the kind of fasting we most advocate: short, periodic fasts incorporated into your life as a form of health maintenance, as a way to conserve resources, as a way to stay in touch with spirit and the natural world, as a way to be humbled and reminded of those with less … in short, as a simple, practically effortless practice designed to keep you in closer touch with yourself and the world around you.

The key to fasting as a part of your life's plan is to make fasting a regular commitment—as regular as eating on the days you eat, or brushing your teeth, or paying your electric bill. If fasting is something you simply *do* every Sunday or Monday or Wednesday or Friday or whenever, simply a part of your regular life, not something you have to struggle with or decide about each time, then it will become easier and easier until it is truly effortless. Your body will respond quickly to periodic fasting. Aches and pains, both physical and spiritual, will gradually subside. You'll feel lighter. More in touch. More whole.

Finer Fasting

The kind of fast you decide will best work for you depends largely on your life, your schedule, and your inclinations. We like a one-day-per-week fast, but you might prefer a couple of half-day fasts per week, or a monthly two-day or modified three-day fast. Beginners may wish to start with half-day fasts and work their way up to fasts of a day or two.

Other Fasting Boosters

For thousands of years, humans have been designing systems to help increase spirituality. Many of these systems focus on the physical body because this highly distracting human container can make a spiritual life challenging.

Bodies get hungry. They get tired. They hurt. Sometimes they itch. They get in the way. They get too fat or too thin. They age. They trip us up or obsess us so that we become insecure or vain or go through life with blinders, seeing little beyond physical problems or physical strengths such as attractiveness.

We aren't the first society to feel the need to get the restless, ever-changing body under control. Let's look at some tools and techniques borrowed from other traditions that can help facilitate better fasting and a deeper spiritual connection.

Yoga Poses for Better Fasting

As we first mentioned in Chapter 2, "Body and Soul: A Fast Trip Around the World," yoga is an excellent technique for learning to master your body. It has many different branches, but the most popular form in the West is *hatha yoga*, which concentrates on the practice of certain poses or positions (called *asanas*) to help get the body under control to better facilitate meditation and spiritual enlightenment.

While all yoga poses are beneficial and we would recommend taking a yoga class from a qualified teacher because of the excellent stretching, strengthening, and stress relief yoga provides, certain yoga poses are particular beneficial for encouraging productive fasting by stimulating the organs of elimination and helping to speed up the cleansing and purification the body undergoes during its rest from food. In yoga, poses are often balanced—forward bends followed by back bends, for example—to expand and then contract the body and keep everything structurally and energetically aligned. The best poses for a fast are those that expand the torso, particularly the abdominal area, and then contract or press on this area.

Fast Talk

Hatha yoga is a branch of yoga that concentrates on the yoga poses or exercises, called **asanas** in Sanskrit.

Even if you don't normally do yoga, you can try these poses during a fast:

- ◆ **Fish pose.** Lie comfortably on your back with your legs crossed or extended, whichever is more comfortable. Arch your middle and upper back and let your head relax backwards so the crown of your head is resting on the floor and your chin is pointing upward. If your legs are crossed, you can try to grab onto your feet. If not, rest your palms under your hips. There should be a space like a bridge between the floor and your back. Breathe deeply, and go back only as far as is comfortable. This position lengthens and stretches the stomach and abdomen.

♦ **Child's pose.** This pose curls the body forward, making it a good pose to follow fish pose, in which the body is arched the other way. Slowly lower your back and return your head to normal. Roll on your side and sit up. Cross your legs comfortably, then let your body sink forward, bringing your forehead toward the floor in front of you. Let your arms rest on the floor at your sides, fingers pointing behind you. You can also do this pose sitting on your knees and feet instead of in a cross-legged position. This pose contracts your abdomen and your liver and kidneys, helping to stimulate their function.

In a more advanced child's pose, sit with your legs crossed and one or both feet placed on top of the opposite thigh (called the lotus or half-lotus position, depending on if you use both or only one foot). When you bend forward toward the floor, your heels will eventually (when you are flexible enough) press into your abdominal region, further stimulating the organs of elimination.

♦ **A simple forward bend.** This is excellent for stimulating the body to cleanse and purify during a fast. Stand comfortably with your feet together and firmly planted on the ground (called mountain pose). Slowly bend at the waist, letting your arms and head relax forward as far as you can go comfortably. Feel the stretch in the back of the legs. You'll also be compressing your organs of elimination. Hold and breathe for one minute. If you get dizzy, immediately bend your knees and squat down or sit.

♦ **Bow pose.** To balance the forward bend by arching the body (the opposite position as in forward bend, lie on your stomach with your knees bent, feet extended toward the ceiling. Reach back behind you with your arms, lifting your upper body, and grab your ankles. Pull on your ankles while simultaneously attempting to straighten your knees so you fill your body with tension as in a bow. Let your body rock just slightly. Your abdominal area will be the part of your body rocking against the floor. Again, this stimulates the organs of elimination to do what they need to do during a fast. Hold for as long as is comfortable.

Finer Fasting

For a more complete treatment of yoga and/or massage, check out some of Eve's other books: *The Complete Idiot's Guide to Yoga* and *The Complete Idiot's Guide to Massage* (both co-authored by Joan Budilovsky) and *The Complete Idiot's Guide to Power Yoga* (co-authored by Geo Takoma). See Appendix B, "Fasting Resources," for details.

Yoga is a lot of fun, very relaxing, and an excellent cross-training technique for any sport. It is perfect for people who have been sedentary because it moves at an individual pace. It is also challenging for people who are in great physical shape. We think it is the perfect exercise complement for fasting.

Fasting and Massage

Massage is another excellent way to speed up the body's cleansing process during a fast. Like yoga, massage stimulates the organs of elimination, but you don't have to do the work! Somebody else does it (preferably an experienced and licensed massage therapist).

Massage does more than stimulate the liver and kidneys. It stimulates the skin, the lymphatic system, and the vascular system, promoting better, more efficient circulation. Circulation is key to cleansing the body of impurities, and massage can be an important key to maximizing your body's circulation and elimination. It even helps promote elimination through the skin!

While there are many different types of massage, the kind that works best to aid the body's cleansing efforts during a fast is the kind most readily available: Swedish massage. This form of massage uses different types of strokes on the skin to increase circulation and stimulate muscle tissue, encouraging the body to release and purge impurities.

Not only that, massage feels great! A good massage is relaxing and rejuvenating at the same time. Scheduling a massage during a fast can make you feel really good about yourself, and the stress-relieving effects can help you to get through your fasting day with an enhanced sense of well-being.

> **Finer Fasting**
>
> A few of the most common kinds massage techniques besides Swedish massage are …
>
> - Sports massage, a specific form of Swedish massage for athletes.
> - Shiatsu and acupressure, in which pressure points in the body are stimulated to free energy.
> - Reflexology, in which the hands and feet are massaged and are thought to correspond to the entire body.
> - Rolfing, a deep tissue massage, which gradually restructures and realigns the body.
> - Energy therapy, such as Reiki or polarity therapy, in which the body's internal energies are manipulated by the massage therapist; touching is typically light or nonexistent.

Breath Work During a Fast

While some people claim that the practiced meditator can live on nothing but life-force energy or *prana*—the Sanskrit word for life-force energy inhaled with breath—for long periods of time, we think humans cannot live on breath alone. However, during a fast, concentrating on deep breathing with the proper technique can work wonders to slow down that frantic urge to gorge and can imbue the body with a deep sense of peace and tranquility. Prana is similar to what the Chinese call chi, the energy that runs through the body in channels and is tapped or released with acupressure or acupuncture.

Deep breathing expels old air from the lungs and fills the body with the oxygen your tissues require. Many people never breathe very deeply, but the body works a lot better when the breath is deep and slow. A deep breathing session can make you feel so satisfied that you'll have no urge to eat.

Fasting makes deep breathing even more efficient because a full stomach limits the body's capacity for taking in a really deep breath, but an empty stomach lets the lungs expand to their full capacity. Also, with all that energy freed up from the digestive process, the body can concentrate on utilizing all that oxygen for other things such as healing.

Fast Talk

Prana is the Sanskrit word for life-force energy. In yoga, prana is the substance that animates the universe, and drawing it in with the breath is one of the best ways to maintain good health, extend life, and promote healing. Breathing exercises to fill the body with prana are an essential part of many branches of yoga.

Breathing deeply is easy with some practice. The trick is not to hike up your shoulders and fill your upper chest with air, but to keep your shoulders still and imagine gradually filling your body with air starting in the lower abdomen. This is easiest to feel at first when you are lying down flat on the floor. Put your hands on your abdomen and take a long, slow, deep breath. Concentrate on keeping your shoulders and upper chest still. Let the air fill up your abdomen. Feel it expand like a balloon with your hand. Then, slowly, release the air and feel the balloon (your abdomen) sink back down and deflate. You can even contract your abdominal muscles to help push out every last bit of old, stale air.

When you get the hang of deep breathing, you can do it sitting, standing, or during light exercise. Deep breathing is a great way to reverse the stress response, to help redirect a case of nerves or panic, and to bring back clear thinking. And of course, it is an excellent way to get past that initial hunger on your day of fasting. Let deep breathing fill you up with energy as an alternative to stuffing your face with food.

A yoga breathing technique that is particularly calming is to gently alternate nostrils during breathing. Gently shut your right nostril with your finger or thumb and inhale deeply through the left nostril. While holding your breath, release the right nostril and hold the left, then fully exhale through the right nostril. Then, do it the other way, inhaling through the right nostril and exhaling through the left. This breathing exercise is also very good for when you feel out of control or are obsessive about something. It helps you feel more balanced and centered.

Plumbing Your Creativity

Another great way to make your fasting more rewarding and more spiritual is to be creative. Keep a journal during your fast to record your thoughts. Try your hand at drawing or painting. Write a poem. Sing. Dance. It doesn't matter if you think you are creative or not, talented or not. Letting your creativity flow during a fast is fulfilling. It doesn't matter if you are "good" in the eyes of the world. Let your creativity expand and become your focus during a fast, just for you. And who knows … you might just get really good at something you never knew you could do!

Mapping Your Spiritual Path

If successful fasting starts with a clearly stated intention, it proceeds with a plan. A spiritual path is the same way. To have a more satisfying existence, to feel more fulfilled in your daily life, to feel like a more well-rounded and integrated individual, to fill up that missing space in your life, to feel connected to your inner self, to best understand who you are, you need to nourish and nurture your spiritual side.

People plan their finances. They plan their careers. They plan their families, their relationships, their schedules. Why don't more people plan their spiritual paths? Make a commitment to map out a plan for your spiritual path. Your plan, we hope, will include periodic short fasts, to give your spirit the chance to grow. It may include meditation, or prayer, or the ritual of religious observance. It may include helping others, or seeking truth, or getting to know yourself.

But whatever your methods, make sure you have a plan. Write it down. Design it like a business prospectus or a grant proposal or a map—whatever form suits you. Once your plan is in place, you'll know where you are headed. And that's a valuable asset in this life.

The Least You Need to Know

- ◆ Spirituality is the search for meaning in life.
- ◆ Many people today feel as if their lives are missing a spiritual element.
- ◆ Fasting can rid the body of the distraction of food, allowing the spiritual self more room to grow.
- ◆ Incorporating short, periodic fasts into regular life will help to balance body, mind, and spirit.
- ◆ Other tools such as yoga, massage, and creativity can help to make fasting work better and increase your sense of spiritual self.

Chapter 7

The Essence Beyond "Not Eating"

In This Chapter

- ◆ Do you have soul?
- ◆ How to free your chi
- ◆ Fasting and your chakras
- ◆ Cleansing your aura
- ◆ Tapping into the collective unconscious
- ◆ Soul: reality or metaphor?

Where is the seat of the soul? For thousands of years, people have wrestled with the concept of soul. Religions define it, philosophies search for it, and theologies decide where they think it goes after our bodies are gone.

Whatever soul is, most people agree there is something beyond the sum of our physical parts that makes us who we are. Something that can't be measured or examined under a microscope. Something that gives us that spark of life.

Whether or not you believe you have a soul in the traditional sense, the study of what we have inside us that makes us sentient beings is certainly fascinating (at least, it is to us, and we hope it is to you, too!). In this chapter, we'll look at some of those less measurable qualities that many cultures believe are as real as flesh, blood, and bone, and how those parts of you—your life-force energy, your chakras, your aura—respond to the cleansing and healing practice of fasting.

Fast Track to the Soul

How do you define soul? The answer is different for everyone. Maybe you believe the soul is linked to the Holy Spirit, survives after death and goes to heaven, or survives after death and is reborn into a different body. Maybe you believe the soul is a chemical reaction in the brain.

Some people believe the soul is part of or one of the psychic layers of existence beyond or within the physical body and can be realized by various physical, mental, and spiritual practices, including meditation, prayer, and of course, fasting.

While no one knows how to measure the effect of fasting on the soul, fasting does affect the body's life-force energy, sometimes called chi or prana; the *chakras* or energy centers in the body; and the *aura*. This life-force energy is the immeasurable energy that animates the body and all other life on earth. It also flows in pathways over the earth, through inanimate objects, and throughout the universe. Because mind, body, and spirit are one great, interconnected operation, purification and cleansing in the body are mirrored in the spiritual body. Life-force energy flows more freely, releasing blockages. Chakras are energized and balanced. The aura becomes clearer and brighter.

> **Fast Talk**
>
> The **aura** is the electromagnetic energy given off by the body. Auras change colors according to the quality or state of the body's energy at any given time, and it can reveal through dark or light spots physical problems and strengths. **Chakras** are energy centers in the body associated with certain physical, emotional, and spiritual aspects of the self.

Even if you don't necessarily believe in chi, chakras, and auras, you will certainly feel the increased clarity of thought and energy during a fast. Many people who fast for medical reasons report unexpected spiritual experiences, and we maintain that the holistic connection of the whole self is certainly affected on many different levels by healthy practices like short fasts.

Getting Inside Yourself

How do you know you have chi running through your body? How do you know you have chakras, or an aura? While some people naturally feel or have a sense of these less physical parts of the human being, others become more sensitive to them after reading or hearing about them from others. And some people don't believe they exist, since they are not parts of the body according to Western anatomy.

During a fast, when your body turns inward and you become more aware of your whole self beyond its attachment to sensual pleasures, you can try some exercises to get more in tune with or to better commune with your inner self. We like to think of this as having a conversation with your soul.

Sometime during the middle or toward the end of your fast day, sit comfortably, take a few deep breaths, and focus on the sound of your breathing. Feel your breath moving in and out of you. Breathe naturally, and simply pay attention. When you notice sounds from the outside world, or thoughts related to anything outside your own body, gently push them away and refocus on your breath.

Fast Facts
The life-force energy meridians that run through the body and the chakra energy centers are thought to be different from, but correspond to the central nervous system and its complex system of nerve impulses.

In, out. In, out. Feel the breath coming in and out of your nose. Feel the breath expanding and contracting your lungs. Feel the breath moving through your body.

Now, see if you can feel your heartbeat. Listen very closely for the sound and the feel of your heart. Concentrate on your heart, and on the area on your chest in front of your heart (your fourth chakra, but we'll get into that in a few pages). Focus on the sound and feel of your heart.

Now, see if you can feel your pulse. Put your fingers on your wrist or on the side of your neck. Feel your body's pulse. Listen to the rhythm, and visualize how your heart and your pulse help to power your circulatory system.

Continue to sit quietly, focusing on your internal body. Then, imagine looking deeper, deeper inside you. Visualize that inner spark, that spirit or soul, that makes you into the unique individual you are. Give your soul a shape, or a face, or a color. Visualize where you think it lives. Imagine filling it with light and positive energy. Talk to it. What do you want to tell your own soul? Remember to keep your soul talk positive and focused. You might say something like "This is me," or "I am perfect," or "I am love," or you might want to say something more directional, such as, "I am just where I need to be," or "Soul, lead me where I need to go," or you might want to direct your focus toward a higher power, something like, "God, please speak to my soul and guide us along the right path."

Finer Fasting

Ever wonder what you really believe? The Belief-o-matic quiz on the Beliefnet website (www.beliefnet.com) asks you a series of 20 questions about your philosophies and religious beliefs, then tells you what religion your beliefs are most closely affiliated with. It's fun, and you may be surprised by your results!

Let yourself sit with this inner focus as long as you feel it is productive. Then, slowly open your eyes, bring your focus back into the room, and feel the peace and inner centering you've gained from this short spiritual journey to the inside of you.

You can certainly try this exercise on a day when you aren't fasting, but you'll probably find it is much easier to do on a fasting day.

Free Your Chi

Chi, or life-force energy, is the force that many cultures believe runs through the body in certain channels, pooling in energy centers around the body but traveling back and forth, in and out, according to what you are doing, feeling, and thinking, and what external agents are acting on you, from the food you eat to the air you breathe to the words people speak to you.

Many eastern cultures also believe that when these energy channels get blocked and an area of the body is devoid of or flooded with too much chi, illness, pain, or psychological discomfort is the result. Traditional Chinese medicine and other Eastern-based therapies seek to balance and free chi in the body using different methods, from herbal remedies to massage to movements such as those in tai chi or yoga, to the insertion of acupuncture needles. The concept of chi is now quite familiar in the West, and many Americans know exactly what you mean when you say you are practicing tai chi or getting an acupuncture treatment.

Because fasting redirects the body's focus inward and promotes cleansing and purification, the energy that runs through the body's internal channels becomes freer, moves faster, and responds in a similar way to the physical body, by working through blockages and balancing and equalizing itself in the body. Deep breathing can help to further encourage this process by flooding the body with chi to help release and cleanse the internal energy channels. Used in conjunction with shiatsu massage or an acupressure treatment, a fast can have a profound effect on freeing and cleansing the body's internal energy.

Release Your Chakras

Chakras are the energy centers through which energy flows, sort of like intersections on the energy freeway. While the body contains hundreds of chakras, there are some major ones that are linked with certain aspects of the self. Blockages in certain chakras can result in physical, emotional, or psychological problems in certain areas of life. Certain exercises, meditations, fasting, and color therapy can help to unblock chakras, allowing energy to flow freely through and radiate from each chakra, promoting ultimate whole-self health.

Let's look at the chakras, one at a time. (Note: Different people describe the various chakras in different ways according to their own experiences and/or what they have been taught, so this list is based on personal experience and study and may differ from descriptions you've seen elsewhere.) See if you can sense where each chakra sits in your own body, and which of your chakras might tend to become blocked. Meditations focused on individual chakras during a fast can be extremely powerful for releasing and freeing the chakras.

The First Chakra: Instinct

The first chakra is located at the base of the spine. This is the seat of instinct. Your rage, your joy, your sexual urges, your hungers come from this chakra. When this chakra is blocked, you may feel out of touch with your instincts and your body, or stuck in your mind or intellect. When this chakra is flowing freely, you have a healthy rapport with your instincts. You can use them when you need them but you can also control them when necessary. When this chakra is overactive, your instincts may control your behavior even when it isn't appropriate.

The initial hunger you experience during a fast will come from the third chakra, which is used to taking things in, but after the first half day or so, your first chakra will become more sensitive and you'll feel more in touch with your instinctual nature. Meditate by visualizing a red pulse at the base of your spine to further energize your first chakra.

> **Finer Fasting**
>
> Short fasts enhance the sensitivity of all the body's chakras. However, longer fasts, especially in those who are inexperienced at fasting, can severely deplete energy within the chakras and can cause spiritual as well as physical harm. Don't fast for more than two or at the most three days unless you are very experienced and knowledgeable about fasting and are under medical supervision.

The Second Chakra: Elimination

The second chakra is located behind and just below your navel. This is the seat of elimination and it is essential that this chakra, more than any other, is activated during a fast. This chakra is the body's furnace. It generates heat to burn energy and it is in this chakra that impurities are flushed from the body during a fast. Located behind the colon, this chakra energizes and activates elimination, fat burning, and the purging of what we don't need. This is the seat of what yoga practitioners call *agni*, or the gastric fire. Agni keeps the body stoked like a furnace. It also heats and energizes the body with a little encouragement in the absence of food.

> **Fast Talk**
>
> *Agni* is the Sanskrit word for gastric fire, the source of elimination energy that burns energy and fuels the body.

During a fast, you can encourage the activation of your second chakra by massaging your abdomen or pressing with your thumbs just under your navel. You can also do the yoga bow pose (see Chapter 6, "Fasting and Spiritual Growth") or meditate on the second chakra by focusing on the area below your naval and visualizing a bright orange, crackling fire sitting inside your abdomen, slowly and gently burning away everything your body doesn't need.

The Third Chakra: Gut

The third chakra is located on the solar plexus, just below the rib cage. While the second chakra burns up and eliminates, the third chakra takes in and holds. This is the seat of the gut, where we take in our life experiences and hold them for future reference, as if on a video recorder. When something makes you nervous or giddy or afraid, those reactions come from the third chakra and are based in your past experiences (whether you remember them or not). Some would even venture to say that past life experiences are waiting here to influence your reactions. Being in touch with and open to your third chakra can help you to proceed through life with greater wisdom and enhanced intuition, but a blocked third chakra can subject you to panic attacks, phobias, anxiety, and neuroses.

During a fast, the third chakra becomes more sensitive and this is an excellent time to meditate on the third chakra, gently opening up to what your body has learned during your life. Visualize a yellow sun in your solar plexus shining down on everything you've ever learned, experienced, or felt. In the absence of the digestive process, you may experience a unique clarity during these meditations, recognizing things you never realized your body knew.

Fasting Wisdom

Whatever you do, devote your whole mind, heart, and soul to it. I once met a great sannyasin [Hindu ascetic] who cleansed his brass cooking utensils, making them shine like gold, with as much care and attention as he bestowed on his worship and meditation.

—Swami Vivekananda (1863–1902)

The Fourth Chakra: Emotion

The fourth chakra is the middle of the seven primary chakras along the center of the body. It is located just behind the heart and is the center of emotion and love in the body. Emotional reactions and love radiate from this chakra, and when it is blocked, we feel flat, unable to feel emotions, unable to feel or express love. When this chakra is open and flowing freely, we are in touch with our emotions and best able to give and receive love.

During a fast, the fourth chakra becomes more sensitive and we may feel more emotional than usual. To calm and balance this chakra during a fast, meditate on the heart. Visualize a full, lush, green tree in your heart center, branching out to everything around you and deeply rooted in your emotional center. Imagine this tree is your emotional life, grounded but able to reach in many different directions at once. Focus on the green of the tree and the feeling of peace in your heart as the tree rustles and breathes and moves gently.

The Fifth Chakra: Communication

The fifth chakra is located in the throat. It is the center of communication, and when it is blocked, you may feel unable to communicate well with others or to express yourself in an adequate way. When this chakra is overactivated, you may find it difficult to stop talking (or writing or sending e-mails).

During a fast, this center also becomes more sensitive, which is why practicing quiet meditation is helpful for the fifth chakra. Or, if you feel you need to unblock this chakra, a fast is the time to schedule a meaningful conversation, make that phone call, or write in your journal. Meditate on the fifth chakra by visualizing a patch of bright blue sky over your throat. Feel words, thoughts, ideas flowing unimpeded through this blue sky and landing exactly where they need to go.

The Sixth Chakra: Intuition

The sixth chakra is located on the forehead, between and slightly above the eyebrows. This is the third eye, or center for intuition, psychic abilities, foresight, and imagination. This is where we "see" beyond what our physical eyes can see. When this chakra is blocked, intuition, foresight, and imagination are stalled. When this chakra is open and flowing, you will be open to your own intuition and your creativity will be easy to access.

During a fast, your perceptions, intuition, and imagination are intensified due to the heightened sensitivity of the sixth chakra. This effect can induce spiritual insights, visions, and flashes of creative brilliance. To heighten this effect during a fast, meditate by visualizing a deep, indigo-blue eye or indigo circle on your forehead over your sixth chakra. Let your imagination flow through this indigo center and play. What do you see?

> **Fasting Wisdom**
>
> Acknowledge qualities like kindness and patience as seeds of self-nourishment that are growing inside you. They are the antidotes to the feelings of emotional hunger that come from grasping and clinging.
>
> —Ronna Kabatznick, Ph.D., from *The Zen of Eating* (Perigee, 1998)

The Seventh Chakra: Spirit

The seventh chakra is located on the crown of the head. This chakra is the highest and most spiritual chakra, and the passageway linking you to universal consciousness. This is the chakra that becomes fully open and activated during times of intense spiritual communion, and it is also the center for enlightenment in Eastern traditions. When this chakra is blocked, we feel separate from our spiritual selves. When it is open, we feel like our spirits are an essential part of our whole selves.

During a fast, like all the other chakras, the seventh chakra is more open and accessible. Spiritual perceptions come easier and those who seek communication with or experience of God or divinity or universal consciousness often find they are more able to achieve this communication during a fast. To further enhance the body's spiritual connection to universal divinity during a fast, meditate on the seventh chakra by visualizing a thousand-petaled lotus flower floating on a deep purple lake just over the crown of your head. Imagine the flower opening as your chakra opens to connect with a force larger than you, a force that is also you, however you visualize it or whatever you believe it is.

Cleanse Your Aura

Bodies generate electromagnetic energy, and this field, radiating from the human body, is called an aura. For thousands of years, people have perceived, talked about, considered, painted, and written about auras. Paintings by the old masters depict halos around holy figures, and some people believe these halos represent the bright auras surrounding those whose spirituality was particularly developed.

While some information you can find about auras in books or on the Internet may seem a little bit off the beaten track, a certain type of photography developed in Russia called *Kirlian photography* can show the body's electromagnetic field. Many people believe the physical or psychological illness or injury will show up as dark spots on the aura, and that the aura changes colors according to a person's health, mood, happiness, or in response to environmental changes. Some people believe that anyone can see auras with a little training.

Fast Talk

Russian scientist Semyon Kirlian developed **Kirlian photography** in 1939. This photographic technique reveals a colored halo around photographed subjects (from people to leaves). While skeptics claim the process doesn't actually reveal auras, many believe the process is good evidence for the existence of electromagnetic fields around all living things.

During a fast, as the body purges physical impurities from the digestive tract and energy blockages from the chakras, some people believe the aura is similarly clarified. People who see or train people to see auras say that people with good health, good intentions, and strong spirituality have clear, bright auras, while people in ill health, people with bad intentions, people out of touch with their spirituality, people caught up in materialism or personal gain or jealousy or other spirit-sapping physical and/or emotional conditions have cloudy or dark auras.

You can practice looking at auras during a fast, when you may be more in tune to seeing them. Stand in front of a large mirror, preferably against a white background, or look at a friend standing against a white background. The light in the room should be sufficient but not too bright. You can see auras best with your peripheral vision, so focus on your own or your subject's sixth chakra or third eye area, just above the eyebrows. Relax, breathe deeply, and gaze into the third eye. After a minute or so, you should be able to discern, with your peripheral vision, a colored halo around the form of the individual. Don't look directly at it. Keep using your peripheral vision but try to notice the color, the clarity, the size of the aura, and if there are any irregular spots of light or darkness.

The more you try looking at auras, the easier it gets. Skeptical? That's fine. Nobody says you have to do it, or even believe in it. But if you think it sounds fun, and are interested in seeing how your own aura changes with your moods and feelings, by all means, give it a try. Once you get good at it, see if you can tell any difference in your aura when you are fasting versus when you aren't.

Finer Fasting

A depleted, darkening aura during a fast can be a sign you have fasted too long.

Soul as Metaphor

Concepts like chi, prana, chakras, and auras can be challenging for some Westerners, while others embrace the concepts wholeheartedly. If you aren't a religious person and want scientific proof for things like chakras and auras, that's fine because that is who you are. But it doesn't mean you can't have a spiritual existence. Consider the soul, life-force energy, chakras, auras, even the existence of a higher power as a metaphor, or symbols for what we don't yet understand. Even the most hardboiled scientist will admit that there is much we don't know in the universe, and much we don't know within our own bodies and brains.

Long ago, people made up theories, stories, and myths to explain what they could see but couldn't comprehend—comets, eclipses, stars, earthquakes, lightning, fire, snow, tornadoes, thunder, the sunrise, and the sunset. Gradually, these stories evolved as the human race learned more and more about its external and internal environment.

This process continues today. Perhaps a soul, or a universal higher power, or a sixth chakra isn't exactly what we or anyone else suggests it might be. Perhaps it is something entirely different. But as the human race continues to seek and find truth and meaning in life, continues to learn and grow and evolve, those with open minds and spirits will be the first to perceive the things the rest of us haven't yet noticed. If this could be you, then how much richer and fuller and more complete your life and your whole self might be!

All we ask is that when you fast, sensibly and in a healthy way, you also remain open to those deeper, inner, unexplored parts of yourself. You are full of uncharted territory ... and much of the joy in living comes from exploration.

The Least You Need to Know

- ◆ Explore your own inner world during a fast for greater soul consciousness.
- ◆ Chi is the Chinese word for life-force energy that runs through the body via particular pathways or meridians.
- ◆ Chakras are energy centers along the life-force meridians where energy collects. Each of the seven chakras corresponds to a different part of the self, from instinct to intuition.
- ◆ Auras are the electromagnetic energy fields surrounding all living and inanimate objects.
- ◆ Even if you are skeptical about the existence of the soul, you can appreciate the exploration of your inner unknown as a life-enriching practice.

Chapter 8

Profiles in Enlightenment

In This Chapter

- ◆ Buddha's journey
- ◆ The fasts of Jesus Christ
- ◆ Fasting and Mohammed
- ◆ Fasting like the saints
- ◆ Fasting for social reform: Mahatma Gandhi and Mother Teresa

Fasting has enjoyed a high profile throughout the ages. Many famous spiritual figures have practiced fasting. Jesus, Buddha, Mohammed, and more modern figures such as Gandhi and Mother Teresa are all known for their famous fasts.

In this chapter, we'll look at some of the lives of the people who have shaped the world's spiritual history, and how fasting figured in their life paths.

Buddha and the Fig Tree

The story of the life of the Buddha, born as Siddhartha Gautama to King Suddhodana in the sixth century in ancient northern India (today's Nepal), is laced with myth and parable, but it illustrates for Buddhists and many other spiritual people the path of a human being who figured out how to wake up or become enlightened or fully aware during his lifetime.

Prince Gautama was rich, pampered, and in line for the throne. Completely sheltered in his daily life, the prince never left the royal courtyard. He married, gave his wife a son, and had every material possession he could ever desire. However, prince Gautama remained unsettled, as if, he felt, something was missing from his life.

To try to cheer up his melancholy son, the king took the prince on several royal rides through the city. During these visits, Prince Gautama saw some things that deeply disturbed him: an old man, a sick man, and a corpse. The alarmed prince asked his servant what these things were, and the servant (we can only guess he answered reluctantly) explained that human beings get old, get sick, and eventually die. Gautama was shocked! He had never realized that despite the trappings of luxury and money, humans would all eventually die. Even him.

On his last visit to the city, Prince Gautama spotted a wandering ascetic who possessed an unusual tranquility. It was the first sign of true contentment he had witnessed. And so, he gave up everything—his family, his money, his future as king—to become a wandering ascetic, to seek out the true meaning of life.

Fast Facts

Buddhists often practice short fasts in the spirit of the Buddha's Middle Way or adherence to moderation, but when they do eat, many Buddhists are vegetarians. The Buddhist philosophy of nonviolence extends to the killing of animals for food.

Fasting Wisdom

It is said that the Buddha, on his deathbed, told his followers the following (as quoted in *Buddhism Plain and Simple* by Steve Hagen, Charles E. Tuttle Co., Inc., 1997): "Be a light unto yourselves; betake yourselves to no external refuge. Hold fast to the Truth. Look not for refuge to anyone besides yourselves."

Prince Gautama lived for six years as a seeker. He studied under many teachers and starved his body through extreme fasting until he was so weak he could scarcely move. At last, he recognized that such extreme behavior wasn't doing him any good. He wasn't becoming enlightened. He was just starving himself! He drank some milk and his followers, who so admired his austerity, left him, thinking he had abandoned the search.

He hadn't, though. Instead, Siddhartha Gautama had recognized that following anyone else's path wasn't going to help him. He realized that he needed to look inward. And so, he sat under a fig tree and began to meditate. He decided not to move until he had finally apprehended truth and the nature of the universe. It took him 12 hours, but he did it. While meditating, the Buddha fasted, but this short, 12-hour fast was exactly what he needed. By the break of morning, he was enlightened.

After that, the Buddha practiced and preached the Middle Way, or moderation in all things. Unlike the Indian ascetics, he no longer advocated prolonged fasts. Instead, he advocated not too much and not too little in all aspects of life. During prolonged meditation, the Buddha fasted. During work and regular life, he ate—but never more than he needed.

The Buddha understood that like any other life practice, fasting is not meant to throw the body into an extreme state. Instead, it is meant to gently encourage mental clarity and a spiritual focus in a healthy way. Fasting helps you to increase your awareness, to wake up to your life. Exactly the way we like to practice it!

Christ in the Desert

The fasts of Jesus Christ, whose teachings are the basis of the Christian religion, are well known, but the one most people think of first is Jesus' 40-day fast in the desert prior to the beginning of his three-year mission.

Christians know the teaching well. After Jesus was baptized by John the Baptist, God called Jesus to go out into the wilderness for 40 days and 40 nights. Jesus fasted for the entire time. At the end of the 40 days, he became very hungry and the story goes that Satan came and tempted him to turn the stones before him into bread. Other temptations followed, all of which Jesus resisted. Finally, Satan went away and the angels came and ministered to Jesus. He then went back among the people to begin to spread the word of God, having solidified his spiritual mission through this prolonged fast.

Jesus mentions fasting several times in his preaching. He tells people not to make a big deal of fasting or to show off that they are fasting, because such a practice is a private spiritual practice.

While Jesus was an advocate of fasting, he was also a highly experienced and advanced spiritual practitioner. Many Christians today attempt to emulate this 40-day fast, but we recommend this only for people who are similarly experienced in fasting. Not for beginners!

Jesus certainly didn't advocate fasting to the extreme for anyone else, including his disciples. In one notable passage, he is questioned because his disciplines eat while others are fasting, and he replies that while the Son of God is among them, they ought to be celebrating, not fasting, and that they will have plenty of time for fasting once he is gone. He said, "Can the wedding guests fast when the bridegroom is among them?" To Jesus, fasting was a solemn and even mournful practice, a great and serious sacrifice for God.

Fasting Wisdom

A famous fasting passage from the New Testament book of Matthew (chapter 6, verses 16–18) quotes Jesus as saying: "And when you fast, do not look dismal, like the hypocrites, for they disfigure their faces that their fasting may be seen by men. Truly, I say to you, they have received their reward. But when you fast, anoint your head and wash your face, that your fasting may not be seen by men but by your Father who is in secret; and your Father who sees in secret will reward you."

But Jesus also understood that fasting was an individual practice, not a law or a rule that must be followed in an exact way to ensure piety. He tells a parable of a Pharisee and a tax collector. The Pharisee goes to the temple and prays, thanking god that he is not a sinner because he fasts twice a week and gives money to the church. The tax collector, on the other hand, ashamed and repentant, simply asks for forgiveness. In the parable, Jesus claims that God is more benevolent toward the tax collector because those who are humble, God will exalt, and those, like the Pharisee, who exalt themselves, God will humble.

In other words, fasting alone doesn't ensure a spiritual connection. It must be done with the right attitude and in the right way, preferably in private and as a kind of promise or commitment to God. This is the Christian view, and a view we also understand. For those who fast for spiritual reasons, keep in mind that fasting is a spiritual tool. It isn't, in and of itself, a spiritual answer.

Mohammed and the Delivery of the Koran

Mohammed, the Islamic prophet and deliverer of the *Koran* to the Islamic people, was born in 570 C.E. in Mecca. At the age of 40, Mohammed began his mission, but throughout his life he was intensely devoted to the practice of his religion, including prayer and frequent fasting.

Mohammed was a religious reformer and a political activist in first-century Arabia. At the age of 40, Mohammed was called by the angel Gabriel to begin his mission to deliver Allah's message to the Islamic people. He died in his sixty-third year (633 C.E.) of a fever after leading 40,000 people in a final pilgrimage to Mecca.

While Mohammed's life is controversial and many biographical accounts are probably apocryphal, most scholars agree that Mohammed was a man intensely devoted to his religion. An adamant practitioner of fasting, Mohammed received the following revelation (as recorded in the Koran in chapter 2, verse 183), following a three-day fast on his way from Mecca to Medina: "O you who believe, fasting is decreed for you, as it was decreed for those before you, that you may attain salvation."

Fast Talk

The **Koran** (or Q'ran) is the sacred book of the Islamic people and according to the Islamic religion, contains the revelations Allah or God bestowed upon the prophet Mohammed. The Koran is also the final authority on Islamic beliefs.

Ramadan, the month the Koran was revealed to Mohammed and the ninth month of the Islamic calendar, is the month when Muslims have traditionally practiced prayer and fasting. During Ramadan, Muslims celebrate and observe many different historical events from Islamic history, including the revelation of the Koran itself, various Islamic victories, days of forgiveness, and, during the last 10 days of the month, an intense commitment to fervent prayer.

Today, Muslims all over the world continue to celebrate Ramadan by fasting and prayer, as they remember their prophet, Mohammed. When Muslims fast, it's considered controlled or partial fasting, lasting only from sunup to sundown. They abstain from food and drink, including water, and sexual relations during those hours, and resume normal lives after the sun goes down.

Two meals are eaten during Ramadan. The *Fatoor* is eaten at sunset and the *Sahoor* is eaten before the sun rises. Muslims in polar regions tend to follow the same clock as those in Mecca, so they don't have to fast for the 20 hours of daylight they sometimes have there. Because the Muslim calendar is a lunar calendar (only 354 days), Ramadan is earlier every year. If it falls in winter, the daily fast is relatively short, while summer fasts are much longer. If an individual cannot fast for some reason, such as medical necessity or travel, the fast must be made up before the next Ramadan. Fasting begins for Muslims about the age of puberty (ten to 14 years), and is thought to strengthen the bond between members of their society who remember the less fortunate during this time. Fasting is also thought to provide health benefits by giving the stomach a period of rest, at least during the day, for an entire month.

Fast Facts

How to nullify a fast during Ramadan:

◆ Mistakenly breaking the fast just before sunset under the assumption that the sun has already set

◆ Continuing to eat, drink, or have sex just after dawn, and not realizing the error

◆ Intravenous injections of nutrients for health reasons

◆ Intentional vomiting

Fasting and the Saints

Fasting and Catholicism go way back, and the link continues today. Theodore Cardinal McCarrick, the Catholic cardinal for the Archdiocese of Washington, D.C., called for Catholics to fast one day a week in an act of "mortification and penance" in response to the ongoing war against terrorism which began September 11, 2001, with the destruction of the World Trade Center in New York City and damage to the Pentagon in Washington, D.C.

Cardinal McCarrick called for the fast to continue until the war comes to an end, and said, "We will ask God's providence to make our world safe for innocent people … to bring justice and peace to all the world and through that, to renew the world so that men and women everywhere will never live in fear again." McCarrick's spokeswoman said the cardinal did not specify what type of fast Catholics should follow, but on days like Good Friday, they typically eat only one regular meal and two smaller meals that together do not equal a regular meal. The elderly and sick are not expected to fast.

Historically, the Catholic saints have been zealous fasters. What do the saints of ancient and modern times have to say about fasting? Let's take a look (compiled from various sources, including the home page of the St. John the Baptist Russian Orthodox Cathedral in Washington, D.C., www.stjohndc.org):

> If thou, O man, dost not forgive everyone who has sinned against thee, then do not trouble thyself with fasting. If thou dost not forgive the debt of thy brother, with whom thou art angry for some reason, then thou dost fast in vain God will not accept thee. Fasting will not help thee, until thou wilt become accomplished in love and in the hope of faith. Whoever fasts and becomes angry, and harbors enmity in his heart, such a one hates God and salvation is far from him.
> —Venerable Ephraim the Syrian, monk and hymnographer (d. 373 C.E.)

> It is necessary most of all for one who is fasting to curb anger, to accustom himself to meekness and condescension, to have a contrite heart, to repulse impure thoughts and desires, to examine his conscience, to put his mind to the test and to verify what good has been done by us in this or any other week, and which deficiency we have corrected in ourselves in the present week. This is true fasting.
> —Saint John Chrysostom, Doctor of the Church (347–407 C.E.)

> A excellent faster is he who restrains himself from every impurity, who imposes abstinence on his tongue and restrains it from idle talk, foul language, slander, condemnation, flattery, and all manner of evil speaking, who abstains from anger, rage, malice, and vengeance and withdraws from every evil.
> —Saint Tichon of Zadonsk, patriarch of Moscow and martyr (1865–1925)

> Seest thou what fasting does: It heals illnesses, drives out demons, removes wicked thoughts, makes the heart pure. If someone has even been seized by an impure spirit, let him know that this kind, according to the word of the Lord, "goeth not out but by prayer and fasting" (Matthew 17:21).
> —Saint Athanasius the Great, patriarch of Alexandra (c. 297–373 C.E.)

> By fasting it is possible both to be delivered from future evils and to enjoy the good things to come. We fell into disease through sin; let us receive healing through repentance, which is not fruitful without fasting.
> —Saint Basil the Great, patron of hospital administrators (330–379 C.E.)

> As bodily food fattens the body, so fasting strengthens the soul; imparting it an easy flight, it makes it able to ascend on high, to contemplate lofty things and to put the heavenly higher than the pleasant and pleasurable things of life.
> —Saint John Chrysostom, doctor of the church (347–407 C.E.)

This is the instructive fast, it teaches the athlete the ways of the contest.
Draw near to it, study, learn to struggle shrewdly.
Behold he instructed us to fast with our mouths and hearts,
Let us not fast from bread and think thoughts
In which the hidden poison of death is hidden.
Let us confess on the fast day the First Born
Who gave us the word of life to meditate on.
—from St. Ephrem's Hymns on Fasting, number 1.6

Gandhi's Famous Fasts

The fasts of Mahatma Gandhi may be among the most known in the modern world. Gandhi spoke often about fasting—how it should be used, how it shouldn't be used, when it works, and when it won't work.

Mohandas Karamchand Gandhi was born on October 2, 1869, in western India. Gandhi spent his adult life working toward nonviolence and nondiscrimination in India and South Africa. Gandhi's campaign for passive resistance, which he called "Satyagraha," was often waged by fasting.

To Gandhi, fasting was a nonviolent way to speak to the sympathetic to help effect change. Gandhi expressed his view as follows:

> … [W]hat should a nonviolent person do when he finds his friends, relations, or countrymen refuse to give up an immoral way of life, and all arguments prove futile to evoke any response? (He) must not use a semblance of force to convert the wrongdoer. He even eschews the use of any harsh language. The first step is gentle and affectionate persuasion. When it fails to produce any salutary effect, voluntarily he invites suffering in his own body to open the eyes of the person who is determined to see no light.

Gandhi didn't fast for health or even for spiritual gain. His fasts were political in nature. They were designed to change the world—and they did. Many of Gandhi's fasts were conducted to atone for the immoral behavior of his friends, colleagues, or people in the communities with which he was involved. Other fasts were carried out to foster unity among disparate groups such as Hindus and Muslims and to protest government actions Gandhi thought were violent, dangerous, and not in the best interest of the country.

Gandhi's first fast in 1913 was a weeklong fast held to atone for immoral behavior of friends. In 1918, he fasted to protest low wages of mill workers in Ahmedabad. In 1919, he fasted for one day and prayed for the strength and resolution to begin his nonviolent resistance or Satyagraha movement.

> **Fasting Wisdom**
>
> A modern practitioner of fasting for peace, Vietnamese Buddhist monk, teacher, and peace activist Thich Nhat Hanh, whose latest book, *Anger: Wisdom for Cooling the Flames,* was released just one day before the terrorist attacks on New York City and Washington, D.C., encouraged people all over the world to fast for world peace. In an interview with *Publisher's Weekly* in October 2001, he advocated a meeting of compassionate listening with Taliban leaders and other perceived enemies. Nhat Hahn, whose own personal for-peace fast lasted for 10 days, proclaimed, "Compassion is the only means for our protection."

Although Gandhi was an unassuming, bespectacled, startlingly thin man who lived an ultimately simple and unadorned life, he had many enemies. To Gandhi, religion was no different from social action and his efforts to promote equality in South Africa and freedom in India triggered often-violent reactions in others. In the last month of his life, on January 12, 1948, Gandhi initiated a fast for communal peace in Delhi. On January 17, doctors warned Gandhi he must end his fast. The next day, the Central Peace Committee signed and presented a Peace Pledge to Gandhi, who then broke his fast. But on January 30, Gandhi was assassinated on his way to evening prayers.

Many of Gandhi's fasts were for only a day, and many more were for three days, but when Gandhi was fasting to atone for or protest against something he considered particularly serious, he often fasted for a week or two, and sometimes even longer. These long fasts seriously weakened the already emaciated Gandhi, but they were often incredibly effective, politically. When people remember Gandhi, they often first think of his fasts, and while we wouldn't recommend frequent prolonged fasting, we respect and admire the incredible efforts and accomplishments toward peace that Mahatma Gandhi was able to achieve during his lifetime.

> **Fasting Wisdom**
>
> Let us think not of Big Things but of Good Things.
> —Mahatma Gandhi
> (1869–1948)

Mother Teresa's Leadership

Mother Teresa may be the most famous missionary our culture can name. Her life was devoted to helping the poor. Born in 1910 in what is now Yugoslavia, Mother Teresa trained to be a nun in Dublin and in 1928 was sent to a mission in Calcutta, where she took her vows to be a nun. In 1950, she began her own mission, called The Missionaries of Charity, and throughout her life, she established over 50 mission projects throughout India, from children's homes to leper colonies.

When Mother Teresa won the Nobel Peace Prize, she delivered an acceptance speech that covered many important issues for her. Several parts of the speech revealed the sacrifices she had seen among the poor people in Calcutta:

> Some time ago in Calcutta we had great difficulty in getting sugar, and I don't know how the word got around to the children, and a little boy of four years old, a Hindu boy, went home and told his parents: I will not eat sugar for three days, I will give my sugar to Mother Teresa for her children. After three days his father and mother brought him to our home. I had never met them before, and this little one could scarcely pronounce my name, but he knew exactly what he had come to do. He knew that he wanted to share his love.

In another case, a man "fasted" from smoking:

> The other day I received 15 dollars from a man who has been on his back for 20 years, and the only part that he can move is his right hand. And the only companion that he enjoys is smoking. And he said to me: I do not smoke for one week, and I send you this money. It must have been a terrible sacrifice for him, but see how beautiful, how he shared, and with that money I bought bread and I gave to those who are hungry with a joy on both sides, he was giving and the poor were receiving.

Throughout her life, Mother Teresa often fasted and often suggested or led fasts for her followers and interfaith fasts to support certain causes. To Mother Teresa, fasting was a way to do without in order to provide more for others, a way to cleanse the spirit to be in closer contact with God, and a way to petition for social change. While she remained a strict practicing Catholic nun throughout her life, Mother Teresa's work has aided and touched people of all religions across the globe. She died in 1997.

Finer Fasting

For a Mother-Teresa-inspired fast, consider fasting for one meal or one day and giving the food or the money for food that you would have spent to a food bank, soup kitchen, or shelter.

The Least You Need to Know

◆ Buddha fasted for one day to attain enlightenment after years of extreme fasts that he then rejected in favor of a Middle Way or moderation.

◆ Jesus Christ fasted for 40 days at the beginning of his three-year mission to spread God's word. During his fast, he was tempted by Satan to break his fast but resisted.

◆ Mohammed fasted for three days, after which he was granted a revelation by Allah that fasting was decreed for all Muslims.

◆ Many Catholic saints fasted to purify the body and commune more closely with God.

◆ Mahatma Gandhi and Mother Teresa are two well-known modern-day social reformers who often practiced fasting.

The Fasting Retreat

In This Chapter

◆ The physical, mental, emotional, and spiritual benefits of fasting on a retreat

◆ Where and how to find a fasting center or spa

◆ The do-it-yourself fasting retreat

◆ Sticking with your fast

Fasting is easy to incorporate into your life, but when you undertake a fast for health and/or spiritual reasons, a fasting retreat can put you in a unique position to reap the maximum benefit from your fast.

Visiting a fasting center or spa, especially for longer, supervised fasts, can be an incredible, even life-changing experience. But you don't need to leave home to enjoy a fasting retreat. This chapter will also show you how to create your personalized fasting retreat in the comfort of your own home.

Why a Retreat?

Books on fasting (including this one) often proclaim that you can and should go on with your normal life during a fast. So you're not eating today. That doesn't mean you should stay home from work and lie in bed staring at the television. Movement, activity, and mental engagement—in moderation—can all make a fast more effective and enjoyable.

However, if you tend to overdo it, if you really want to focus on improving your health, or if your purpose for fasting is primarily spiritual and you want to take full advantage of the mental and spiritual state fasting tends to invoke, then a fasting retreat may be just right for you.

A fasting retreat gives you the space you need to take a short break from your busy life to concentrate more fully on your own body, mind, and spirit. A fasting center can provide a structured fasting retreat, often for the purposes of healing and often medically super-vised. A spiritual retreat can include fasting as one of its options, and is just right for an intensive spiritual focus. And a fasting retreat at home is the perfect way to spend some time with yourself and your own body, apart from your schedule, obligations, and all that food you tend to keep stuffing.

> **Fast Facts**
>
> In his book *Prayer Is Good Medicine* (Harper; SanFrancisco, 1996), researcher Larry Dossey demonstrates through studies that people who were prayed for, even when they didn't know it, healed or recovered faster than those who were not prayed for. Praying for others while fasting can be part of a spiritual practice.

A fasting retreat doesn't have to be long. One day is plenty, and plenty rejuvenating, too, for an at-home retreat. Fasting centers often have a variety of program lengths depending on need. But a fasting retreat does have to include privacy, quiet time, rest time, contem-plation time, and plenty of fluids. In the fasting center setting, a fast should also include plenty of supervision and professional guidance, both physical and emotional.

But before we jump into the nuts and bolts of a fasting retreat, let's review some of the benefits you'll get from taking time out of your normal life to concentrate on your fasting and on the effects it has on your body.

Enhancing Concentration

Life is busy, and for most of us, true concentration is a rare state of mind. Because of the nature of our complicated, multimedia, extra-social lives full of different priorities, we learn to split our concentration in many different directions at once.

But for the mind, that's a little like doing just a couple of repetitions of lots of different exercises without ever really working any of your muscles. Taking a break from the daily grind and the daily onslaught of demands on our attention—including meals and snacks and coffee and trips to the vending machine—can help you to focus more intensively on your mind. This kind of focus teaches your mind how to concentrate better.

Even one day of concentrated focus, whether through meditation or simply engaging yourself in a single task—writing in your journal, drawing, reading a book, listening to music—for longer than you normally would, can make a big difference in your own perception. You'll remember what it feels like to concentrate, and your brain will thank you.

> **Finer Fasting**
>
> Try this meditation exercise to enhance concentration. Choose an object that has meaning to you. Spend 15 minutes looking deeply at this object in quiet meditation. Contemplate every possible aspect of the object: its shape, color, texture, feel, smell, and the memories associated with it. Keep directing your mind back to the object if it wanders. Meditation teachers say that continuous concentration on an object will eventually dissolve all boundaries until you perceive yourself and the object as one. This is perfect concentration.

Nurturing the Spirit

As much as many of us would like to spend time nurturing our spirit, the harsh reality of life is that spiritual pursuits are often pushed to the bottom of our lists. We think we don't have time. Other matters seem more pressing, more immediate, more fraught with deadlines. But a fasting retreat makes space for nurturing the spirit in the same way it makes space for nurturing concentration and focus.

If you choose to engage in a fasting retreat for spiritual reasons, you can set aside blocks of time for meditation, prayer, or spiritual contemplation. You can write in your journal about your spiritual thoughts, accomplishments, and goals. You can chart your spiritual course for the next year, or five years, or decade, or longer.

At an organized spiritual retreat, you might receive valuable instruction, learn techniques for meditating or praying more effectively, and have the opportunity to expand your thinking about your spiritual path.

Simply making spirit a priority of your retreat can, in itself, make a difference in how you get through the day and how you feel about your life after your retreat is over. You don't even have to plan any scheduled activity if you are practicing your retreat on your own. A gentle, quiet day in which you simply consider your spirit and act kindly toward yourself can rejuvenate you for weeks.

Communion with Others

A fasting center or spiritual retreat offers an added benefit beyond making a space in your life for spiritual or self-contemplation. It also brings you into contact with others who are trying to do the same thing. If most of your time is spent with work colleagues or people who don't necessarily share your spiritual focus, fasting and other types of self-improvement can seem pretty lonely. At a fasting retreat, however, you'll be surrounded by people who want to do just what you are doing. You just might make some lifelong friends.

Even if you are retreating at home, you might consider allotting some of your day to time with someone else who shares your spiritual goals, or who is at least willing to listen to them with an open mind. We are social creatures and social interaction fulfills human beings. Let yourself be fulfilled in a positive way, rather than substituting too much food for a lack of social interaction.

Visiting a Fasting Center or Spiritual Retreat

If you think you need some guidance, want the experience of an organized retreat, or simply want to really get away from it all for awhile and get seriously healthy, consider visiting a spa or fasting center.

Many fasting centers around the world (from California to Thailand) offer medically supervised fasting, thorough health analysis, ongoing monitoring of the fast, and plenty of enjoyable health- and/or spirit-related activities. Talk to your doctor or local reputable health care professionals about where to find a good fasting center, or talk to local religious connections about where to find a good spiritual retreat. If you can find someone who has already visited a place, you'll get a good idea of what that place is like.

Fast Facts

In a study conducted at a fasting center and published in the *Journal of Manipulative and Physiological Therapeutics* in June 2001, researchers demonstrated that medically supervised water-only fasting for ten days with a two- to three-day pre-fast period and a seven-day postfast period of supervised eating significantly lowered blood pressure in hypertensive patients.

The experiences at fasting centers and spiritual retreats vary so widely that we feel we can't accurately describe them for you. Your experience might be completely different. Recommendations and research are your best weapons against a bad experience. Be sure to do that research before you send off a big deposit. Many of these centers and retreats can be very expensive, and while some people believe they are more than worth the price, others may not, especially if the experience isn't right for them.

In other words, do the work to make sure the fasting center or retreat that interests you is a good one, is in line with your personal beliefs, and is headed up by people who are professional and qualified.

Your Personal, At-Home Fasting Retreat

Maybe you aren't quite ready to fast for more than a day or two. Maybe you aren't too excited about plopping down 3,000-some dollars to visit a fasting center. Maybe you just want a break from your daily stress. If that sounds like you, then an at-home fasting retreat may be just what you need.

Fasting at home under certain structured conditions can be incredibly rewarding. Let's look at how you can take only one day off work (or do it on the weekend) and reap the benefits of a two-week vacation for your mind and body.

How to Set Up Your Retreat

The first step in setting up your at-home fasting retreat is to choose a day when you know you won't be interrupted. You'll need time at home alone, with no phone calls from work, visitors (unless you schedule them in), needy children, or other distractions. Phone friends, family, and work colleagues and explain that you won't be available on your chosen retreat day. You don't have to tell them why. If you have children, make arrangements for them to be elsewhere. Then …

1. The day before your retreat, get your house ready. First, clean. If cleaning the whole house is too much of a job for now, at least completely clean and declutter one room, such as your living room, bedroom, or kitchen. The room should feel clean and tranquil, not stuffed full of reminders about all the distractions of your life. Vacuum, dust, wipe down surfaces, and put everything away.

2. Next, change the sheets on your bed. When you rest, you'll want your bed to feel fresh and comfortable.

3. Set aside a comfortable sitting place for meditation, prayer, or contemplation. You might stack some pillows on the floor, prepare a comfortable chair, or dig out that meditation bench or meditation cushions

Fasting Wisdom

Silence suits me so well and I have such great grace and peace from it that I practice it in Lent and throughout the year and am greatly annoyed with others when I have to speak.

—Margaret Ebner, nun and mystic (c. 1291–1351)

Finer Fasting

You can meditate lying down, but chances are, you'll fall asleep. Meditation generally works better if you are seated with a straight back so your lungs have plenty of room to expand. Place your tongue on the roof of your mouth, close your mouth, breathe through your nose, and relax your eyes so your gaze is unfocused.

you haven't used in awhile. Candles, incense, pictures, relaxing music and a player, or other items that will enhance your meditation make great additions to this meditation/prayer area.

4. Make a plan for walking. During your retreat, you will benefit immensely from several leisurely walks in the fresh air. If you can't walk around your neighborhood, decide where you will drive to take a walk: a park, a nearby wood, a lake, or wherever you know the scenery will be beautiful and you'll feel relaxed. Truly nowhere to walk? Don't let that ruin your retreat. You can always just step outside your front door for a minute and let the sun shine on you.

5. Decide what to wear. You'll want to wear something loose fitting, comfortable, and soft, appropriate for the temperature and weather. Choose something that makes you feel really good.

6. Go to the store. Here is your list:

   - If you have a juicer, buy lots of fresh fruits (not citrus, as citrus juice is generally too acidic during a fast) and vegetables (same goes for tomatoes). Apples, pears, strawberries, blueberries, grapes, carrots, and celery are good choices. Locally-grown, in-season produce is best.

   - If you don't have a juicer, buy at least 32 ounces of fresh, organic fruit and/or vegetable juices. (And consider investing in a juicer. Fresh, homemade juice is much better for you than processed, store-bought juice. It contains the live essences of the plants, the least degraded vitamins and phytochemicals, and according to some, is more likely to retain the fruit's original vibrations and life energy.)

   - Herbal teas such as chamomile, ginger, peppermint, or cinnamon; or fruit teas such as orange, apple, or lemon.

   - One onion, garlic bulb, and bunch of celery for vegetable broth.

   - 64 ounces of pure, filtered water.

   - One fresh lemon.

And now you're ready!

Your Schedule, Your Rules

The great thing about an at-home fasting retreat is that you make the rules. You design your schedule and you decide your priorities.

Here is a sample schedule for how you might set up your day. Feel free to pick and choose, revise or adapt as it suits you. Make a commitment to yourself before your retreat begins that you will stick to your schedule and follow your own rules. This kind of inner commitment will help to make your at-home fasting retreat a success.

SAMPLE SCHEDULE:

The day before your retreat, eat light. Don't stuff yourself at any meal, and minimize your intake of animal protein. For dinner, have only fresh, uncooked vegetables and fruit. For example, you might have a vegetable salad and an apple. If you are hungry, drink juice. Or, you can opt to have an all-fruit meal. Just before bed, drink a glass of juice with a mix-in fiber powder (such as Metamucil) to get your colon started in its cleansing process.

7:00 A.M.: When you wake up in the morning on the day of your retreat, drink an 8-ounce glass of water with a quarter of a fresh lemon squeezed into it.

7:15 A.M.: Take a long shower and wash your hair. While showering, scrub your skin gently all over with a loofah sponge, skin brush, or washcloth to help exfoliate the dead skin cells and encourage the elimination of impurities through the skin. Relax and enjoy the warm water. You don't have to be anywhere today, so take your time.

7:45 A.M.: After your shower, dry off and if it's part of your normal routine, put lotion on your skin. Get dressed in clean, comfortable clothes.

8:00 A.M.: Sit down at the table and slowly sip 8 ounces of fresh juice. Savor each sip. Really pay attention to the flavor. Take your time.

8:15 A.M.: Spend an hour in your sitting area. Relax, breathe, meditate, pray, contemplate, or just think about your goals for the day. Listen to relaxing music. Light incense. Whatever focus you want to use for this time is fine. Just don't turn on the television!

9:15 A.M.: Make yourself a cup of herbal tea and take it back to your sitting spot. Relax, drink it, and pay attention to the aroma and the flavor. If you really need it, you can add a little honey to your tea.

9:30 A.M.: Take a walk. Spend about an hour walking at a moderate pace outside, taking deep breaths of fresh air. Or, if you don't have a place to walk, sit outside for awhile in the sun. (If you stay out for longer than a few minutes and the sun is out, put on sunscreen.)

10:30 A.M.: After your walk, drink 16 ounces of water with or without another quarter of a lemon squeezed into it. You might need to go to the bathroom about now, and if so, take your time.

11:00 A.M.: Phone a friend, check your e-mail, listen to the news, read a book, or do something else that involves contact with someone or something else. If a friend can come over, that's great, too. Just be sure you plan this contact to be with someone who won't try to get you to break your fast. This should be a relaxing and friendly

Finer Fasting

People are suggestible, and two of the biggest temptations during a fast are seeing visual representations of food and smelling food. Turn off the television and don't go where anyone is cooking food during your fasting retreat.

way to communicate with the outside world, not a temptation. Be careful if you watch the news on television because you'll probably be bombarded with commercials showing food, and you may be feeling hungry at this time.

12:00 noon: Time for lunch! Drink another 8-ounce glass of juice and make vegetable broth: Chop one onion in quarters and peel off the skin. Peel one or two cloves of garlic and cut them in half. Wash two stalks of celery and chop into 3-inch pieces. Boil the onion, garlic, and celery in 16 ounces of water for approximately 30 minutes, then strain the broth and discard the vegetables, or save them for soup on another day. Sit down and sip the juice and drink half the broth. Slowly! Relax and enjoy it, but don't give in to the temptation to eat solid food. Remember how good it is for your body to have this rest. Think about how good you'll feel tomorrow. It's worth holding off on food for now. And it's not like you'll never eat again! Save the other half of the broth for dinner.

> **Fast Facts**
>
> Even though you aren't very active on your fast day, you may find you are extra tired as your body works hard to purge impurities. Or, you may feel so energized that you have difficulty sleeping. Different people respond to fasting in different ways.

1:00 P.M.: Drink another 16 ounces of water, with or without lemon.

1:15 P.M.: Take another long walk in the fresh air. Breathe deeply. As you walk, test your senses. Do things look, sound, smell, feel sharper and clearer?

2:15 P.M.: Time for a nap. After your walk, go to your room and snuggle into bed. Even if you don't sleep, just rest. Let your body heal. Let your spirit surface.

3:15 P.M.: Drink 8 ounces of juice slowly, and if you still feel like you need something else, have another cup of herbal tea.

3:30 P.M.: Spend another hour in your meditation area, thinking, praying, meditating, contemplating, writing, drawing, listening to music, or doing whatever you feel like doing (except eating, of course).

4:30 P.M.: Call, e-mail, or visit a friend, or otherwise initiate social contact if you feel like it. Or, do whatever else strikes your fancy. Remember, it's your day!

5:30 P.M.: Drink another 16 ounces of water with or without lemon. If you can't finish it all, just keep it with you for the rest of the evening. This is the last glass of water you need to have (although you can always have more).

6:00 P.M.: Reheat and drink the rest of the broth, or make more if that isn't enough. Follow the broth with your last 8-ounce glass of juice.

6:30 P.M.: Take an evening walk or get some other form of moderate exercise. You might do an exercise video tape or even go to a yoga class or the gym. Just don't lift weights or do anything overly strenuous. Take it easy.

7:30 P.M.: Write in your journal about how your day has gone. What was easier than you thought it would be? What was more challenging? How do you feel now? How did you feel earlier? Did you feel more spiritual? Weaker? Stronger? More energetic? More optimistic? Or was it really difficult? Would you do this again? What are your future plans? Try to write for at least 30 minutes. Just let whatever you are thinking come out of your pen.

8:00 P.M.: Drink one last cup of herbal tea, finish your water, brush your teeth, and take a nice, relaxing bath. Scrub your skin all over again to encourage elimination through your pores. Relax in the bath and enjoy yourself.

Fasting Wisdom

There is a realm beyond the physical senses. It is a realm of mystery and spirit. It is an infinite and eternal dimension that transcends form and goes beyond time and space. The search for this domain has gripped the hearts of human beings throughout history. From the early biblical prophets who walked alone into the desert to fast and pray for divine revelation to Native Americans setting out into the wilderness to search for a vision, the pursuit of an inner world, beyond everyday physical reality, is one of mankind's oldest traditions.

—Denise Linn, from *Quest: A Guide to Creating Your Own Vision Quest* (Ballantine Books, 1997)

9:00 P.M.: Go to sleep! The body is best at repairing itself while you are sleeping. You may need to get up several times during the night to go the bathroom, but that's all part of the cleansing process. If you really can't get to sleep at 9:00 P.M., read a book, go out with a friend (but don't eat!), or practice some more meditation. You might try visualizing a vacation in an exotic place like a beach in the Bahamas or a trek through the Himalayas. See all the details in your mind. But, if at all possible, sleep. Most of us are sleep deprived, and a good, long sleep before you start your day again tomorrow will be a wonderful treat for your body.

The day after your fast: Stick to fruit and juice only for breakfast. You probably won't be too hungry. For lunch, have a salad with a small portion of whole grains. For dinner, eat soup or a salad, but keep all portions small. Avoid animal protein until the following day, during which you should include some yogurt. Make sure to keep plenty of fresh produce in your diet, at least for the next week.

Finer Fasting

If you are taking medications that should be taken with food, talk to your doctor before you fast. You may not want to fast while on that medication, or you may get medical approval to stop taking that medication for one day. Only your doctor can tell you the safest course.

How to Stick With It

You'll be tempted, especially in the first half of the day, to break your fast. The thought of food will be very tempting. If you have goals in mind before you begin, however, and stick to the schedule you have set, you should be fine. Just keep reminding yourself that it is for only one day. You can do anything for one day, especially when it is so good for your body, your mind, and your spirit.

Weakness, dizziness, and nausea are all possible side effects of fasting and do not mean you should eat. They mean you should *drink*—water, fruit juice, vegetable broth, or herbal tea! However, if you are very uncomfortable, have some fresh fruit, or gradually come out of your fast. A fruit-only or plant-food-only day is very healthy, too.

The Least You Need to Know

◆ Taking a fasting retreat helps you to de-stress, get healthy, enhance concentration, and nurture your spirit.

◆ Fasting retreats are available at fasting centers or other spiritual retreats, but you can also conduct your own fasting retreat at home.

◆ For an at-home fasting retreat, you'll need a day free of interruptions, a clean house (or at least a room) free from clutter, clean sheets on your bed, a comfortable place to sit, plenty of fresh fruit juices, and somewhere easily accessible where you can take a walk in the fresh air.

◆ You can stick with your fast if you stay motivated and keep your goals in mind.

Fasting to Live Better

This next part will show you how to integrate fasting into your life for a more holistic existence. We begin by looking more closely at the body-mind, which includes the emotions and spirit as well as the physical body and brain. We go on to talk about how a natural diet rich in plant foods and low in animal products plus healthy amounts of moderate exercise can further enhance life quality and whole-self health, followed by a chapter on whether you should use fasting for weight loss, or whether you should lose weight before instituting a fasting program. The section ends with practical advice on how to fit fasting into your personal schedule according to your own preferences, tendencies, habits, and personality, and a fasting planner you can fill out to plan your fasting as well as your eating and other holistic health goals for the next week, month, season, or year.

10

Fasting and Your Body-Mind

In This Chapter

◆ Your body-mind and how to make the most of it

◆ Integrating your body, mind, emotions, and spirit

◆ How to treat body-mind imbalances with holistic fasting

◆ Holistic fasting and the reinvention of you

Holistic this, holistic that. "Holistic" is a big buzzword these days, and most people have heard the word, but what does it mean? Some people think it means natural, or alternative, or New Age. Actually, though, holistic simply means anything that considers the big picture, the whole ball of wax, the soup to nuts (and those are all the clichés we can think of at the moment!). Holistic means looking at all the parts of a system, rather than looking at just one part in isolation, because the holistic philosophy is based on the idea that all things are connected and what happens in one part of a system affects all the other parts.

This theory isn't new or on the fringe. On the contrary, it is a well-understood scientific theory that elements in any system are related and are largely determined by their relationship to the other elements in the system. In fact, the word "holism" was coined a quarter of a century ago.

But what does that mean for you? It means that when you consider your whole self, you are more than just a body. You are more than just a mind. More than your emotions, more than your spirit. You are a complex, multifaceted, ever-changing collection of components. Whatever you do to one part of yourself—fasting, eating, praying, thinking, talking—will affect every part of yourself.

What's a Body-Mind?

So what's a body-mind? If we wanted to be entirely accurate, we would call it a body-mind-emotion-spirit. But that's a bit unwieldy. What we mean when we say body-mind is the self, the whole self, and nothing but the self. But we call it "body-mind" instead of "self" because we want to keep the idea in the front of your consciousness that we mean all of you, not just part of you.

We've already often mentioned the many ways in which fasting affects the body, the mind, and the spirit. Fasting, of course, isn't the only thing that impacts your body-mind. Everything you eat or don't eat, think or don't think, feel or don't feel impacts who you are and who you become with each passing moment.

So let's consider some of the implications of living in a body-mind. Recognizing how much everything you do affects you may help you to act, think, and move through life with an extra dose of consciousness and in a way that is most holistic, or healthy for and cognizant of your whole self.

You, Integrated

It's one thing to have a body-mind, but it's quite another to recognize and take full advantage of the knowledge that you are more than the sum of your parts. You are a unique and complicated whole being consisting of matter and energy created from an ongoing relationship between all your individual components.

Many of us tend to see ourselves as pieces of a puzzle. We have the structural piece: our bodies and how they work, or don't work. We have the emotional piece: how we feel, how we react to what happens around us, how we respond to how our body feels. We have the mental piece: what we think, how we talk, how we relate to the world around us, what we decide to do about our circumstances. We have the spiritual piece: our relationship with powers beyond ourselves, our communion with spirit, our prayer or meditative life, our contemplation of the meaning of life, our practice of religion.

> **Fast Facts**
>
> Some holistic health practitioners believe that physical disease can be caused by emotional or spiritual neglect.

Many of us see these pieces as fitting together to create a shape that is us. But what we don't always see or choose to recognize is the way these pieces integrate within us. The boundaries between the pieces quickly blur and disappear as we fit them together. The puzzle sits up and becomes three dimensional. The body, the emotions, the mind, the spirit blend and mix until they are no longer distinguishable. The energy created from the integration of all our parts animates us.

And so, when we eat, or pray, or feel angry, or think of a great idea, all the parts pulse with change, shifting and reorganizing, making us into something new. This is what makes living such an adventure, such an exploration and creative process. Everything you do helps to reshape your whole self. Consciousness of this process helps you to integrate even more fully. It helps you to maximize your potential.

How to Get There

Of course, it's easy to say, "integrate!" But it's harder to do it. How do you get to the place where you perceive yourself as a whole rather than as a sum of parts or, worse, a collection of compartments? Traditional religious philosophies from around the world have some hints for us. Many of them suggest that balance is the key. Too much emphasis on any one part of the self will throw the whole system out of whack. It dis-integrates your whole self, your body-mind, by pulling out one of the necessary elements and giving it too much weight.

In other words, if your focus is primarily on your body, the other parts of yourself won't get the time, attention, and nurturing they require. If you focus solely on what you eat and on pleasures of the body, or conversely, focus on depriving the body by not eating enough food and getting too much exercise, your physical self will throw the rest of you out of balance. Your mind, your emotions, and your spirit will suffer.

You can look at the body as being like a four-legged table, with each leg representing the structural, emotional, mental, and spiritual. If one leg is shorter than the others—in other words, if you give one part of your self less attention, or keep it from fully developing—then the table will be unbalanced.

Finer Fasting

Yoga is an excellent holistic or body-mind practice. It exercises the body in a way specifically designed to regain physical control, it nourishes the mind through relaxation techniques and meditation, it frees the emotions by activating the different chakras where many of these emotions are locked, and it feeds the spirit through breathing exercises thought to imbue the body with life-force energy.

Or, if you are always in your head, always thinking, overanalyzing, obsessively considering, to the detriment of your physical health or your spiritual or emotional well-being, these other elements of your whole self will be drained of energy. Your mind will rule your body-mind and you'll begin to feel less healthy, less energetic, less balanced. Things will start to go wrong because the system is out of balance, like a washing machine in the spin cycle with too many towels bunched up on one side.

The same thing happens if you let your emotions rule your every move and thought, or if you are so obsessed with your spiritual life that you neglect or mistreat your body or constantly chastise yourself for incorrect thoughts or feelings. Balance is the key to a healthy body-mind, and to find balance, you need to determine where you tend to put too much emphasis, and where you tend to neglect yourself. Only then can all the parts that make up your whole self begin to integrate.

Treating the Body-Mind

When you have a serious health problem, you should always visit a qualified health professional. Health professionals who practice *holistic health care* are increasingly popular because they use a more holistic approach, but whatever approach you choose, please see someone qualified to treat you if you are in pain or feel like your problem is serious, and always see a doctor for acute or emergency health problems.

Fast Facts
Holistic health care is just one of many names—alternative medicine and complementary medicine are others—for a form of health care that considers the whole person, including lifestyle, habits, attitudes, and personality, in the diagnosis of and treatment of disease. Instead of addressing only isolated symptoms or body parts as conventional medicine often does, holistic health care looks at the big picture and proceeds accordingly. Some holistic health care methods include chiropractic care, acupuncture, homeopathy, herbal medicine, energy therapy, and movement work.

But when your body-mind is suffering from imbalance—a condition that many people around the world believe is the precursor to any physical or mental disease—you can nip future problems by treating your own imbalance.

You know when your body-mind is not balanced if you suddenly begin to suffer lots of minor health complaints such as colds, headaches, achy joints; or minor emotional complaints such as the blues, irritability, or a short temper; or minor mental complaints such as an inability to concentrate or focus or keep track of things; or minor spiritual complaints such as an inability to feel sincere in prayer or a sudden aversion to meditation.

Even more revealing is a combination of minor symptoms: feelings of sadness you can't explain accompanied by a mild sore throat, low energy, and a flare-up in that dull pain you always used to get related to an old knee injury.

There are many ways to treat your body-mind when things get out of balance. First, look back on what you've been doing in the past week or two. Have you been eating a lot of junk food? Have you been getting less sleep than usual? Have you been skipping your meditation session? Have you neglected your daily walk because you've been too busy? Have you been more isolated than usual from your friends, or have you had less time alone than you like? Think about what part of yourself you may have been neglecting.

One of the most common ways we neglect ourselves is by overtaxing our bodies with too much or poor quality food, not enough or too much exercise (including physical labor), or by not getting enough sleep. Our culture likes to call the results of this kind of physical neglect "stress." Stress is a sign that the body-mind is out of balance.

If you find that physical neglect is exactly where you've been throwing yourself off balance, one of the fastest and easiest ways to set things right is to fast, even for a day, even for a half day.

> **Fasting Wisdom**
>
> Standing on the bare ground—my head bathed by the blithe air, and uplifted into infinite space—all mean egotism vanishes. I become a transparent eyeball; I am nothing, I see all, the currents of the Universal Being circulate through me; I am part or parcel of God.
>
> —Ralph Waldo Emerson, American essayist and poet (1803–1882)

Holistic Fasting

Holistic fasting, as opposed to medical fasting or spiritual fasting, is really all about attitude. If you feel generally out of balance, fasting for the purpose of balancing your whole self, your body-mind, is holistic fasting. Actually, all fasting is holistic because any fast affects your whole self, but some people fast just to correct a physical problem or just for spiritual renewal or solely for a social, political, or other reason. When you fast holistically, however, you fast with the conscious recognition that your whole self needs some work and you are going to allow it to repair itself by taking off the burden of digestion and the mental and/or emotional focus on food. Amazingly, this conscious intention has its own effects. When you fast for consciously holistic purposes, your body, emotions, mind, and spirit are better able to reintegrate. How you think has a direct influence on who you are and how well you can heal.

Fasting is a good way to restore mind-body balance. If you're having a bad day, feel like you're coming down with a cold, or are generally low on energy, the first thing you might be inclined to do is stuff your face. Don't do it! Overeating makes conditions like these worse because your body will be so overtaxed by digesting all that extra food that it won't be able to address the concerns it obviously needs to address: the basic repair of your physical, emotional, mental, or spiritual state (or a combination of any or all of these).

Instead, when you are feeling off balance, a one-day fast, or even a fast of half a day, will allow your body-mind to focus on rebalancing itself.

The body is an incredible self-healer of all its parts, if given the chance. Fasting gives it that chance, and holistic fasting takes you one step further.

Fasting's Body-Mind Power Tools

Fasting is a powerful body-mind tool when you set it to work on your whole self. As you fast, you'll notice changes rippling through your entire being, changes that affect you in many ways at once. Let's look at some of the ways a holistic fast can reset your body-mind to work better, feel better, and reinvent itself to be better.

Finer Fasting

If, during a fast, you feel as if your mental state is duller or you feel confused, you are probably dehydrated. Drink a big glass of juice and another glass of water. It's easy to forget to drink enough fluids when you are fasting. You should drink at least 64 ounces of water plus 32 ounces of juice on a fast day.

Finding Your Edge

If you've been feeling dull and slow to react, a holistic fast can quickly turn your mental doldrums around. You'll feel like your thinking is sharper, quicker, edgier. Your reaction time will improve, and you'll enjoy a mental energy you forgot you could possess.

Enhancing Your Mood

If you've been blue or irritable, a holistic fast can quickly improve your mood. During and just after the time when you are missing that first meal, you may feel nervous or irritable. Soon, however, as the fast begins to work its magic on your body-mind and your whole self begins to heal and rebalance, your mood will continually improve. By evening, you may feel practically euphoric.

Halting Your Compulsive Behavior

If you've been caught in a cycle of compulsive behavior—for instance, eating more food than normal and feeling out of control about it, or drinking more than usual and unable to slow down, or smoking more than usual and unable to control it, or doing anything else with a sense of compulsion rather than choice and self-control (spending money, having sex, working too much)—a holistic fast can quite suddenly cause a feeling of self-control to descend upon you. Things you thought you couldn't stop yourself from doing suddenly seem less desirable. In fact, fasting is one of the most effective methods for curbing compulsive behavior, from binge eating to drug use.

Fast Facts
According to the National Institute of Mental Health in Bethesda, Maryland, 2 to 5 percent of Americans experience binge-eating disorder. Many who suffer from this illness are overweight. Feelings of shame and disgust after a binge often lead to further binging, creating a vicious cycle. If you suspect you suffer from binge-eating disorder, seek medical help and/or counseling from a qualified professional before attempting to cure yourself with fasting. Without addressing the emotional component of binge-eating disorder, fasting can lead to more binging.

You, But Happier

If you've been feeling unhappy, especially if you aren't sure why, then a body-mind imbalance is probably to blame. Sometimes, unhappiness has a root cause in your life—a bad relationship, an unsatisfying job, family trouble—but these bad feelings help to imbalance your body-mind, making it difficult to see and clarify the problem.

A holistic fast can bring you a sense of deep peace and inner happiness. It can also help you to understand what things in your life are causing you to be less happy than you could be, and why. It can help you to discover solutions you might not have seen before because of the mental clarity and intuition a fast induces. If you feel like you need to reexamine your life and root out the areas of discontent, try a one- to two-day fast, during which you spend extra time in contemplation about your life. You may well find a way to make your life happier.

Fasting Wisdom

Diet-related diseases account for 68 percent of all deaths.

—C. Everett Koop, former Surgeon General

Body Meets Mind, Mind Meets Spirit

If you conduct regular holistic fasts—say one day each week or even one day each month—you will gradually begin to feel yourself integrating. As your body meets your mind and they begin to act, you'll be more able to see and put into practice behaviors and thoughts that benefit your physical and mental health. As your mind gradually becomes better acquainted with your spirit, you'll reap greater benefits from practices such as meditation and prayer that use the powers of the mind to unleash the powers of the spirit. As your body meets your spirit, you'll discover ways to eat, move, and act that will nourish all parts of yourself.

Regular, holistic fasting may be the easiest road to self-improvement because rather than you striving to change your own mental attitudes, relationships, or health habits, a fast virtually changes them for you by helping to heal you from within. When your changes start from within, outer changes eventually seem easy. If you no longer feel compelled to do things that are bad for you because of inner changes, then it will be easy not to do them! You won't be afflicted by unhealthy desires or tempted by the material world if you have learned to step back every so often and say, "No, thanks. I don't need this right now."

The greatest thing about periodic holistic fasting is that with each progressive step toward full integration, you'll find yourself feeling more human, more self-aware, less prone to your appetites, in better control of your own mind, and more spiritually mature. You'll be fulfilling the potential you always knew you had by reinventing yourself every day.

That's maximizing your human experience.

The Least You Need to Know

- A body-mind is your whole self, including your body, mind, emotions, and spirit—the you that comes from the complex interactions and influences of each of these parts on each other.
- A fully integrated body-mind recognizes the interactions of all its parts and is able to live with better awareness of how any act, thought, or feeling affects the whole self.
- Imbalances in the body-mind can affect any or all parts of the system.
- Short, periodic, holistic fasting—fasting with the intention of rebalancing the whole self—is one of the best and fastest ways to correct body-mind imbalances and integrate the whole self.

11

Fasting, a Natural Diet, and Movement

In This Chapter

- Making healthy food choices when you're not fasting
- How to naturalize your diet
- The best beverages
- Exercise for more effective fasting

Fasting may mean not eating, but eating is also an integral part of fasting. Obviously, you can't fast all the time. We need food for energy and to sustain us most of the time. Fasting is for only a little portion of life.

So what should you eat when you aren't fasting, to best sustain a healthy body-mind? A natural diet is incredibly important for getting the most out of a fast, particularly just before and after the fast. Let's look at your many choices and the best ways to eat for whole-self health.

What to Eat When You're Not Fasting

The food choices we are faced with today are truly mind-boggling. We can eat from the cuisine of almost any country in the world just by taking a trip to the supermarket. We can make instant food in a flash or a gourmet meal that takes hours of preparation. We can microwave frozen dinners and we can just add water for soup, chili, or chicken and dumplings.

With so many choices, it's easiest to choose foods according to what we like or what is convenient. However, it is easy to be seduced into thinking we like things that aren't really very good for us. You know what we mean: the snack cakes, the cheese balls, the toaster pastries, the frozen pizza rolls. All that stuff that our ancestors would scarcely recognize as food.

Our bodies get very attached to processed sugar, white flour, and foods fried or otherwise overloaded with fat. These "foods" may provide quick energy, but they also cause insulin surges (in the case of processed sugar and flour), which are known to be a powerful appetite stimulant. In other words, the more processed sugar and flour you eat, the more you want. It can be hard to stop, and in many people, these foods can trigger a binge.

High-fat foods taste good to us because, once upon a time, our ancestors required high-fat foods to live. Life was hard, the climate was harsh, people burned thousands of calories each day just trying to survive, and a high-fat meal could mean the difference between life and death. Today, however, life at a desk hardly justifies that bacon double cheeseburger and large order of fries, not to mention the fact that the fats in the foods we eat today are largely the hydrogenated kind that are treacherous to our blood cholesterol levels.

So what should we eat? The guidelines for healthy eating are simple: Control your portions and as often as possible, choose the most natural foods available.

Portion Control

One of the most important things you can do for your health and one of the best ways to maximize the effectiveness of a fast is to practice portion control.

America is not conducive to portion control. Compare the typical portion size Americans are used to with the portion sizes that are typical in other cuisines, and you'll see a big difference. We seem to have lost the connection to how much is rational, reasonable, and realistic to put into our stomachs at one time.

It's so easy to super-size, to order the "dinner portion," to sit at home alone and eat the whole pizza because you're bored. Eating huge amounts of food, no matter what the food, puts an immense strain on the digestive system. Indigestion, heartburn, gas, and bloating are all associated with overeating.

Fast Facts

At Roy Walford's laboratory at the University of California at Los Angeles, thousands of mice being fed 30 to 60 percent fewer calories are living far beyond their normal life spans. Theories abound regarding how caloric restriction works, but one postulates the existence of a single master gene responsible for aging that is turned on when excess calories are turned off. For more information, read *The Retardation of Aging and Disease by Dietary Restriction* by R. Weindruch and R.L. Walford (Charles C. Thomas, 1988).

The average stomach is designed to hold approximately 4 cups at one time, including liquids, and it can take six to ten hours to digest a meal. Imagine stuffing your whole dinner into a 4 cup measuring cup. If your measuring cup would overflow, you're probably eating too much. That Big Gulp from the convenience store alone will more than fill up your whole stomach, although it will move out of your stomach faster than solid food.

Of course, if all 4 cups of food are very high in fat, sugar, and processed flour—4 cups worth of chocolate chip cookies, or 4 cups worth of chili dogs and potato chips, for example—the situation goes from bad to worse. When eating foods like these, even portions smaller than 4 cups aren't good for your health, although eating a little bit of something that isn't good for you isn't as bad as eating a whole lot of something that isn't good from you. Remember, moderation is the key!

Whole Foods

Eating *whole foods* is another excellent way to maximize your health when you aren't fasting. Whole foods are foods that are still in their natural form. An apple is a whole food, but applesauce or an apple fruit snack is not. These processed forms are no longer whole, the way the apple was when it was picked off the tree.

A diet based on whole foods is far healthier than a diet based on processed foods like frozen microwavable dinners, processed luncheon meats, and other partially prepared dinners such as macaroni and cheese, canned spaghetti and meatballs, instant noodles, and other boxed "dinner kits." These processed foods are usually extremely high in sodium, which may be detrimental to blood pressure levels, and often contain huge amounts of preservatives, colorings, and artificial flavorings.

Fast Talk

Whole foods are foods that are in the same form as when they were originally harvested. Fresh, unprocessed fruits, vegetables, and whole grains are whole foods. Grain products with parts of the grain removed (such as degerminated grain, which is common) are not whole foods.

Finer Fasting

Whole foods generally contain much more fiber than processed foods. Most Americans don't get enough fiber, but fiber is essential for colon health because it keeps food moving quickly and effortlessly through your digestive tract, and may contribute to the prevention of certain cancers. Try to get about 30 grams of fiber into your diet every day with foods such as dry beans, whole grains, and fresh vegetables.

Foods like these can't hold a nutritional candle to whole foods, which generally contain a higher vitamin, mineral, fiber, and phytochemical content than processed foods, not to mention the absence of added artificial ingredients and sodium. Consider a salad full of fresh vegetables and a little vinegar and olive oil (although olive oil isn't a whole food, its high monounsaturated fat content is much better for your body than the hydrogenated fats often found in bottled dressings), a bowl of brown rice with steamed vegetables and legumes, such as lentils and beans, or a fresh, home-made soup.

Just remember, when choosing your next meal, to think whole food. The more processed, the further removed from its original form, the less it will nourish your body.

Organic and Local Foods

The organic food industry is still in its infancy. Largely unregulated, this industry isn't always reliable when it comes to exact standards for what is organic and what isn't.

However, organic food is still a safer bet than nonorganic because it is less likely to contain pesticide residues, wax, and artificial coloring, and it is less likely to be genetically engineered. Organic food often tastes better because it is fresher. It doesn't last as long on the shelf so that organic apple was probably picked more recently than that shiny, waxed apple on the other side of the store.

Foods produced in your area are also likely to be fresher and to require less preservation because it isn't traveling across the world to get to your table. Buying locally produced food supports the economy in your area, and can bolster the small family farm, if that is a cause you like to support. It's fun to shop produce stands for whole foods to add to your meals, and you'll also become more aware of what foods are in season so you can eat in closer harmony with nature.

The long-term effects of ingesting chemicals used in nonorganic farming aren't yet well understood and many people choose not to be guinea pigs, buying organic and locally produced foods instead of nonorganic foods produced in other countries or across the continent. While buying locally and organically may not always be possible, we think it is certainly the preferable option when you have a choice.

Fasting Wisdom

Is genetically engineered food or GM (genetically modified) food the root of all evil, or a perfectly safe way to keep food free from spoilage and contamination? Both sides have compelling arguments. The effects of consuming GM foods aren't yet fully known and gene experiments of food we eat certainly alters the food's natural form and, some say, life-force energy. However, genetic engineering can produce food with a better nutritional content that is less resistant to dangerous bacteria. Scientists and governments around the world continue to debate and explore the pros and cons of GM crops as they work to provide nutritious, healthy foods to the world's billions. What do *you* think?

Live Foods

Raw foods are an important part of the diet. Some people are so devoted to the concept of eating raw foods that they rarely eat anything else. Raw foods are foods that are unprocessed, unheated, and uncooked. Because cooking destroys many of the enzymes in plant foods, raw food enthusiasts believe food should never be cooked. Some associate the enzymes in plant foods with that plant's life-force energy, and claim that cooking destroys the life-force energy that humans can benefit from when eating the foods raw.

Raw foods include fresh fruits, vegetables, and nuts, probably the basis of the original human diet before we discovered cooking. While existing on such a diet would be incredibly difficult for most of us today, we can certainly easily include more raw foods. A salad and/or fresh fruit at each meal can make a huge difference in the quality of your diet. Plus, if raw foods do indeed imbue the human body with more life-force energy, this kind of eating before and after a fast can help to boost the healing action in the body that a fast is meant to initiate. In fact, most supervised long-term fasting programs require a raw-plant food diet for the days coming into and going out of a fast.

Considering Vegetarianism

Every year, more Americans decide to phase meat out of their diets and become *vegetarians*. Some even phase out all animal products, including eggs and dairy products, to become *vegans*, and some phase out even cooked foods, becoming *fruitarians*. Many studies have demonstrated that vegetarianism is good for your health, lowering your risk of heart disease, certain cancers, and many other minor illnesses. Vegetarians also seem to live longer.

Fast Talk

Vegetarians don't eat animal flesh, including poultry and fish. Some eat eggs and some eat dairy products such as milk, yogurt, and cheese. Some vegetarians stay away from cheese containing rennet, which is made from the stomach lining of cows. **Vegans** don't eat any animal products at all, including milk, yogurt, and cheese. Their diets are entirely plant based. **Fruitarians** go one step further, eliminating all cooked foods from their diets and focusing on a plant-based raw diet.

The reasons why vegetarians are healthy aren't precisely understood, but they probably have to do with a lower consumption of fat; a higher consumption of fiber, vitamins, minerals, and phytochemicals; and a generally lower-calorie diet than those who eat meat.

Vegetarians also tend to make better food choices in general, steering away from overly processed foods and foods with long lists of artificial ingredients. They may also have better health habits, exercising more and being more aware of staying at a healthy weight.

Fast Facts

An English study that compared the diets of 6,115 vegetarians and 5,015 meat eaters for 12 years found that the meatless diet yielded a 40 percent lower risk of cancer and a 20 percent lower risk of dying from any cause. According to William Castelli, M.D., director of the famed Framingham Heart Study, vegetarians outlive meat eaters by three to six years.

—#18 on Pamela Rice's "101 Reasons Why I'm a Vegetarian" list (www.vivavegie.org/vv101/101reas2001.htm)

Of course, there are many exceptions. Just because you don't eat meat doesn't mean you will eat in a healthy way and exercise. But, choosing to reduce or eliminate your consumption of meat can certainly be a healthy lifestyle choice. If it fits into your ethical thinking, all the better. Vegetarians often claim they feel more in harmony with the earth, and many people who practice yoga or Buddhism believe that being a vegetarian is an essential part of living a peaceful, nonviolent existence.

Even if you don't choose to become a vegetarian, try to eliminate meat consumption two to three days before and after a short fast, and at least a week before and after a long fast. Fasting reduces the digestive system's ability to digest meat because the enzymes required shut off temporarily during a fast. Eating meat right before a fast can slow the healing process because meat takes longer to digest than plant foods, and eating meat right after a fast can cause digestive distress and discomfort.

What to Drink

Eating is only part of the equation when it comes to what you put into your body for nourishment. Drinking fluids is an essential part of good nutrition, and no fluid is more essential to your body than water.

Water, Water, Everywhere ...

Your body is between 50 and 65 percent water (men have a higher percentage than women because they generally have more muscle mass and less fat, and muscle contains more water than fat). Water is essential for life and adults should drink at about 64 ounces of noncaffeinated fluids, mostly water, every day to maintain proper functioning of cells, organs, and the circulatory system.

But not all water is created equal. Tap water is usually safe to drink, but during a fast, filtered, purified bottled water is preferable. Keeping a supply of single-serving water bottles handy makes it easy to grab water instead of soda.

During a fast, be sure to drink 64 ounces of puri-fied water in addition to the juices and broths you may also be consuming. It's easy to get dehydrated during a fast. By the time you notice the symp-toms of dehydration, you are already very dehy-drated, so don't wait until you are thirsty to chug that H$_2$0!

Fast Facts
Bottled water is regulated by the U.S. Department of Agriculture as a food product, and must meet the same standards as tap water. Therefore, your bottled water may not be any different from your tap water. Check your bot-tled water to make sure it has been filtered using reverse osmo-sis for the best purity.

A Juice Rainbow

Nutrient-dense juices are great for fasting days as well as nonfasting days (except for orange, grapefruit, and tomato juices, which are too acidic and can be harsh on your stomach when you aren't also eating food). Making your own juice is fun, and freshly squeezed juice has the highest nutritional content. Drink freshly squeezed juice right away. And don't forget to add vegetables!

One of our favorite flavors of freshly squeezed juice is apple-carrot-celery juice, a great thirst quencher and very satisfying. Juice one apple, one carrot, and one stalk of celery for each serving. Of course, organic produce is best.

Even store-bought juice is a preferable alternative to soda or other sugary drinks. Choose juices that contain 100 percent juice (no added sugar in any form including high fructose corn syrup) and, if possible, organic and free of preservatives and artificial colors and flavors. Your local health food store is a great source for interesting juices if you don't want to make your own.

Herbal Teas, Please

Herbal teas are comforting alternatives to caffeinated teas and coffee. They give you all the warmth and ceremony of that morning cup without the caffeine.

During a fast, herbal teas can be an essential part of your day. Choose herbs that are safe and beneficial for you, individually. Here are some herbs to try for certain conditions you would like to address, either during fasting or nonfasting days. When consuming herbs or herbal teas for medicinal purposes, always consult your doctor or pharmacist; medicine is *medicine*, after all.

- White willow bark tea for arthritis. White willow bark relieves pain in a way similar to aspirin, without the stomach irritation.
- Peppermint, chamomile, or ginger tea to ease stomach distress and digestive problems.
- Rosemary tea for a headache.
- Valerian tea for insomnia and/or anxiety.
- Astralgus tea to prevent colds, and echinacea tea to end a cold faster.

Anytime Healing Broth

Whether you are fasting or not, vegetable broth can be a warming, fortifying comfort food. It can also be an excellent way to bolster your immune system if you make it with phytochemical-rich onions, garlic, shiitake mushrooms, and immune-supporting herbs like astralgus root (remove before eating), ginger, and thyme. Add some cayenne pepper, black pepper, and/or hot peppers to help clear your sinuses, chopped kale or collard greens for calcium, and any other fresh vegetables you enjoy, such as zucchini, celery, carrots, turnips, potatoes, and corn.

Finer Fasting

For a quick, easy vegetable broth, quarter one yellow onion, halve four cloves of garlic, roughly chop two stalks of celery, and slice a 1-inch piece of ginger root into four slices. Put in a saucepan and cover with 4 cups of purified water. Boil for 30 minutes, strain out the vegetables, and drink the broth.

Enjoy your healing vegetable broth whenever you have a cold, the flu, allergies, or any time. Eat it all winter long to stay strong against the onslaught of cold-weather viruses. A day of nothing but healing vegetable broth is almost like a fast, and will make you feel rejuvenated any time of the year.

Get Moving

Exercise is very important both during a fast and as a regular part of your life. Exercise keeps muscles strong, joints limber, and circulation working. Some studies have shown that regular exercise even makes you feel better, boosting mood and alleviating depression at a rate equal to antidepressant medication.

During a fast, exercise is a must, but not heavy, strenuous exercise. A couple of walks out in the fresh air on a fast day will help to keep impurities moving out of your system. You'll have the energy and the good mood to thoroughly enjoy a relaxing walk. You can even go to the gym and walk on the treadmill, but don't lift weights on a fast day. Weight lifting is one of the best exercises you can incorporate into your life, but your muscles need nutritional support when they are stressed, so lift weights only on the days when you plan to eat well.

If you are just beginning to exercise, consult your doctor before starting. Design an exercise plan that takes into account your fitness level and your general health.

Finer Fasting

It's easy during a fast to feel so energized and so inspired that you feel like exercising too much. Don't overdo it! Be sensible about exercise. Remember to practice moderation, and keep your vigorous exercise days for the days when you are eating. On those days, fuel up before a workout with complex carbohydrates, and have a little bit of protein after your workout to help muscle repair.

Your Best Exercise Picks for Fast Days

Fasting today? Try these exercises to make you feel great and help speed up your body's cleansing process:

- Moderate-paced walking, outdoors or on a treadmill
- Yoga
- Tai chi
- Low-intensity tennis, swimming, or cycling

Your Best Exercise Picks for Eating Days

Eating today? Try these exercises to make you feel great and keep your body, mind, and spirit fit and healthy:

- Brisk walking, outdoors or on a treadmill
- Weight lifting

- Jogging or running

- Any of the cardio machines at the gym (exercise bike, elliptical trainer, Stairmaster, ski machine)

- Aerobics classes such as step- and kickboxing

- High-intensity tennis, swimming, or cycling

But always remember: Don't push too hard. When exercising during a fast, or, for that matter, exercising at any time, be careful about overdoing it. If you become too tired or get out of breath, stop and rest. When in doubt about your exercise plan, talk to your doctor or a certified exercise physiologist about revising your fitness routine to maximize your individual health needs. Your goal is healthy exercise that makes you feel better and more energized, not exercising until you collapse, feeling drained and depleted! Remember, as the Buddha advised, everything in moderation.

The Least You Need to Know

- You can't fast all the time. When you do eat, make smart choices.

- Portion control is essential to good health. Aim for less than 4 cups of food and beverages in one sitting.

- For better health, choose whole foods over processed, organic foods over those produced using chemicals, raw foods over cooked, plant foods over animal foods.

- When choosing beverages, opt for purified water, fresh juice, herbal tea, and vegetable broth.

- Exercise is essential for good health. On fast days, stick to low-intensity exercise to help your body rid itself of impurities.

Chapter 12

Weighing In on Fasting

In This Chapter

◆ Assessing your weight loss needs

◆ When *not* to fast for weight loss

◆ When fasting for weight loss *can* work

◆ Finding yourself: the spiritual connection

◆ What you must know about fasting and eating disorders

◆ Other weight loss options—and why they may not be the best choice for you

Over half of Americans today are overweight, and almost a quarter of Americans are obese. Obesity in children has now been called an American epidemic, and the number of obese adults in the United States rose almost 50 percent from 1960 to 1994, according to the National Institute of Diabetes and Digestive and Kidney Diseases, a division of the National Institutes of Health.

Between 1991 and 1998, obesity numbers increased in every state in the country, in both genders, and in all races/ethnicities, age groups, educational levels, and smoking statuses. Clearly, weight is a national problem.

Not coincidentally, the huge number of overweight adults in the United States is linked to the huge amount of food available to us. Most cases of overweight and obesity are due to eating too many calories, plain and simple. Also high on the list of reasons why people gain too much weight is insufficient exercise.

So why don't people just eat less and exercise more? Alas, this simple formula is exceptionally difficult for many of us to follow. Compulsive eating, emotional eating, eating for comfort, and eating disorders are common in the United States, as is a sedentary lifestyle. Many of us try diet after diet, only to fail. Or, we lose weight, then gain it back.

Could fasting be the answer for the millions of overweight adults in the United States? For some, most definitely. For others, probably not.

The Difference Between Overweight and Obese

First, let's consider whether you really need to lose weight. If you are overweight, you might have more body fat than is healthy for you. Or, you might simply have a lot of muscle, which *is* good for you. People who lift weights are sometimes over the recommended weight according to standard charts, but are very fit and healthy. Obesity, on the other hand, means an excess amount of body fat, over certain recommended levels.

Fast Facts
BMI or **body mass index** is a number many health professionals use to determine whether someone is overweight or obese. BMI is calculated by dividing weight in kilograms by height in meters squared, or multiplying weight by 705 then dividing the answer by height in inches twice.

Today, the preferred method for determining a healthy weight is to measure *BMI*, or *body mass index*. BMI is a number based on a calculation of height versus weight. It doesn't take the body's fat content into consideration, but it tends to be pretty accurate. Your BMI can be calculated by dividing your weight in kilograms by your height in meters squared. To do this, multiply your weight in pounds by 705, then divide the answer by your height in inches. Divide by your height again. This number is your BMI.

For example, if you are 5 feet 6 inches tall and weigh 150 pounds, you would do the calculation like this:

$$150 \times 705 = 105,750$$

$$5 \text{ feet } 6 \text{ inches} = 66 \text{ inches}$$

$$105,750 \div 66 = 1602$$

$$1602 \div 66 = 24$$

Your BMI is 24.

If your BMI is between 18.5 and 25, you are probably at a healthy weight. A BMI between 25 and 29.9 is considered overweight, and a BMI of 30 or greater is considered obese. Most health organizations and health professionals agree on these ranges. So, the person in the previous example, who is 5 feet 6 inches tall and weighs 150 pounds with a BMI of 24, is at a healthy weight.

Of course, someone who often lifts weights might have a BMI of 26 and be healthy. Someone who doesn't eat enough and never exercises may fall into a so-called "healthy" weight range but not be healthy. The BMI system isn't infallible, but it is helpful to most people.

If your BMI is 25 or below, you are probably at a healthy weight. That doesn't mean you shouldn't fast. Fasting has many benefits that have nothing to do with weight loss. And, overweight or not, if you are sedentary, you should certainly consider adding exercise to your life. Regular exercise reduces your chances of dying from heart disease and lowers your risk of developing diabetes, high blood pressure, and colon cancer. It is excellent for relieving depression, and it will make you feel and look better.

Even if you are not overweight, you should also continue to consider improving your diet. Most of us can eat better and enjoy better health by improving our diets.

However, if your BMI is over 25 and you think you are probably at an unhealthy weight, or if your BMI is 30 or more, your health will certainly benefit if you lose weight. Obesity (or the often concurrent high-fat, low-plant-food diet) is a known risk factor for many serious health conditions, including …

> **Fasting Wisdom**
>
> … We associated less-than-optimal nutrition with poor growth and health, and common sense tells us that we do better if we are well nourished. In fact, most of us may be overnourished, and too much of a good thing may be doing us harm.
>
> —Andrew Weil, M.D., from *Spontaneous Healing* (Alfred A. Knopf, 1995)

- Diabetes.
- Osteoarthritis.
- Hypertension (high blood pressure).
- Stroke.
- Gallbladder disease.
- Uterine, breast, prostate, colorectal, kidney, and gallbladder cancer.
- Sleep apnea and other respiratory problems.

People who are obese are also more likely to have high blood cholesterol, excess body and facial hair, psychological disorders such as depression, complicated pregnancies and menstrual irregularities, and urinary incontinence.

According to the National Institute of Diabetes and Digestive and Kidney Diseases, most studies show that people with a BMI of 30 or higher have a 50 to 100 percent increased risk of death from all causes compared with people with a BMI between 20 and 25. Most of this risk has been attributed to cardiovascular-related causes.

> **Fast Facts**
>
> Only 22 percent of adults in the United States get at least 30 minutes of exercise five times each week (the amount many health professionals recommend), and 25 percent of Americans claim they don't pursue any physical activity at all during their leisure time.

So the question is, how do you go about losing weight and becoming healthier? Always talk to your doctor first to determine what weight-loss plan will be best for you. Seek counseling while working to lose weight, as many people have psychological and/or emotional issues associated with their weight problems. And then, consider whether short fasts might be right for you, as a way to boost your efforts. Start with the quiz in the next section.

A Quiz: Should You Fast to Lose Weight?

Fasting can be a highly beneficial health maintenance program for most people, but some people shouldn't use fasting for weight loss. Answer the following questions to help determine whether fasting for weight loss is a good idea for you.

1. What is your BMI?
    a. Under 25
    b. Under 30
    c. Over 30

2. How do you feel about your weight?
    a. I could stand to drop a few pounds.
    b. I eat too much, often out of boredom or just because I really enjoy eating.
    c. My weight and eating habits feel out of control and I'm often depressed or despairing about my inability to stop eating.

3. Have you ever been diagnosed with an eating disorder, such as anorexia nervosa, bulimia, or binge-eating disorder?
    a. No. I eat normally.
    b. No, although I do tend to eat too much.
    c. Yes.

4. How do you feel about your body?
    a. I like it.
    b. It could use some improvement.
    c. I hate it. I can't stand the way my body looks.

5. How is your health?

    a. Very good.

    b. Pretty good, although I tend to get lots of minor illnesses, especially in the winter.

    c. Poor. I am often ill or suffer from a chronic or serious health condition.

Tally your answers to see how many a's, b's, and c's you chose.

If you chose mostly a's, you are in good health and probably don't need to fast for weight loss, but you could easily benefit from short periodic fasts for health maintenance, high energy, mental clarity, and a more developed spiritual life.

If you chose mostly b's, you are probably a good candidate for fasting for weight loss. You need a health boost and you need to lose a few pounds but your eating isn't, for the most part, out of control, and you don't have an eating disorder. You just need to bring some order and healing to your diet.

If you chose even one c, be sure to talk to your doctor about fasting for weight loss and whether it would be right for you. If you chose more than two c's, fasting is probably not a healthy or safe way for you to try to lose weight. Eating disorders and other psychological symptoms related to food should be resolved before undertaking even a one-day fast. Also, fast only under direct medical supervision if you have any serious medical condition, whether you need to lose weight or not. Your doctor may have a weight-loss method he or she thinks is much better or safer for you.

Fast Facts

A study reported in the *Tufts University Health & Nutrition Letter* in April 1998 demonstrated that increased fiber intake can actually help the body to absorb fewer calories. In the study, an increase of fiber from 18 to 36 grams per day resulted in 130 fewer calories being absorbed each day for men, and 90 fewer calories for women who increased fiber from 12 to 24 grams per day. Because excessive calorie intake is the most common cause of obesity, increasing fiber content of the diet may be a good way to help take off excess weight.

When Fasting Is and Isn't Right for Weight Loss

The short version is just this: If you are in good health, are only a little overweight but not severely obese, and if your main problem with food is that you like it just a little bit too much, short periodic fasts, such as one day a week or several half-days a week, are probably an excellent weight loss method for you.

If, however, you are very overweight, suffer from a chronic or serious medical condition, have an eating disorder, or have serious psychological or emotional issues about food including a tendency to binge, then fasting is *not* a good weight loss method for you. Instead, talk to your doctor about alternatives.

Fasting Safeguards

If you decide to fast for weight loss, please proceed with caution and good sense. If you experience any of the following symptoms, remember that they are most likely due to dehydration. Drink a big glass of water. If uncomfortable symptoms persist, have some fresh fruit and ease out of your fast:

- Fainting
- Exhaustion
- Dramatic mood swings
- Binging
- Weakness
- Very low energy
- Depression
- Anxiety or panic
- Irrational thoughts

If you begin to feel pain or any other extreme physical condition during a weight-loss fast or any other fast, contact your health care provider. If your fast is in any way unpleasant, unbearable, painful, or disturbing, then for goodness sake, stop! Fasting is meant to be a pleasant and life-affirming experience. If it is anything but that for you, then perhaps fasting isn't right for you, at least not at this time.

Fasting for Self-Discovery

If you find that fasting for weight loss is right for you, then you have an exciting journey ahead of you. Finally being able to take off extra weight you've been carrying around for years is one of the most dramatic and obvious benefits of regular fasting. As the extra pounds come off, your energy increases, and so does your self-esteem. You'll uncover the you that was always there, hiding inside.

Losing excess weight through fasting feels great. It's exciting because it affects your whole self. Your physical health improves, your emotional state stabilizes, your mental health soars, and your spiritual self is finally unburdened by the correction of an imbalanced physical body.

Losing Pounds, Finding Yourself

So many of us who are overweight feel—*know*—that our physical potential is somewhere deep down inside of us. We know we could be fitter, stronger, leaner, more energetic. But, an attachment to food has been holding us back. We eat out of boredom, for amusement, because it's enjoyable, because we don't want to feel our emotions, because we don't want to face what our lives lack.

But an amazing thing happens when we stop this behavior, this eating in place of the other things we want and need in life. We find ourselves.

Who you are, as you surely know, is much more than your physical body. But, it can be difficult to know exactly who you are when you're feeling unbalanced, unwell, or unhappy. When you give your obsessions with the external world and the feeding of your senses an undue weight—when your daily focus is primarily on materialistic pleasures—the rest of you shrinks. You become unbalanced. And, consequently, you start to lose a sense of who you really are in the same way someone battling a chronic disease for a long period of time can sometimes forgets who he or she is apart from the disease.

Fasting Wisdom

There is only one real failure in life that is possible, and that is, not to be true to the best one knows.

—Frederic William Farrar, Dean of Canterbury (1831–1903)

But in either case, the essential you is still there. It is simply suffering from an imbalance, a temporary loss of self-awareness. When you are truly self-aware, you won't want to overindulge in food, just as when you are truly self-aware, your illness won't touch who you are inside.

Let Your Goal Be Balance

But here's the tricky part: How your body *looks* isn't indicative of your self-awareness. You can have a BMI over 40 and be supremely self-aware. However, if your BMI is over 40 *because* of an inner imbalance, an over-attachment to material pleasures, or, in simpler terms, *eating too much*, then you may well find self-awareness difficult. You are too externally distracted, and consequently, too mentally conflicted, emotionally confused, spiritually unfulfilled.

But putting your body and the fulfillment of your five senses in order, balancing them with the rest of you, will help you to find yourself again. And, the pleasant side effect of this kind of inner order is often the loss of excess weight. In other words, losing the weight won't help you find yourself and if this is your only goal, you may not enjoy success.

But, if learning who you are inside—the full, whole, complete you—is your goal, and you work on balancing your whole self in order to reach that goal, then things start to straighten themselves out. Weight comes off. Mental conflicts dissolve. Emotional confusion abates. Spirit rises and becomes fulfilled.

And ultimately, you'll know the joy of success—success as a whole person, not just the success of losing 10 or 15 or 20 pounds. That can be part of your success, sure. But unless you balance your whole self, that weight loss will be fleeting and you'll be back where you started in a few months.

> **Finer Fasting**
>
> When you learn to give equal attention to your physical, mental, emotional, and spiritual sides, you learn to listen to your whole self, not just your taste buds or your misguided self-talk telling you to fill your emotional hunger with a pint of Ben & Jerry's. This inner listening to the whole self makes self-control much easier. Only a little part of you wants to overeat. The rest of you would rather not.

How do you do it? There are many ways to balance the whole self, but as you already know from reading the first 11 chapters of this book, fasting can temporarily remove an excessive attachment to the physical from the equation, allowing the rest of you to catch up and reenergize. Short fasts help to deflate your physical obsessions, quiet your hungers, and balance the whole you. It's a great way to begin, and a great way to learn how to feel the healthy adjustments in your inner equilibrium.

The real key to lasting weight loss is, of course, to develop good eating habits. This is difficult to do for many people, and fasting can be a tool to help effect this change. Fasting combined with changes in diet to include more plant foods and nutrient-dense choices along with fewer processed foods and fewer choices that are high in fat and sugar will help you to establish good eating habits and maintain your weight loss.

Help for Eating Disorders

Eating disorders, however, are another matter. When you have an eating disorder, you have a psychological and/or emotional imbalance that must be addressed. In the case of an eating disorder, your physical imbalance is a result of your emotional or psychological imbalance, so simply correcting the physical won't help and can even be injurious to your health and mental well-being.

> **Fast Facts**
>
> Eating disorders are often accompanied by anxiety disorders, depression, and/or substance abuse disorders.

In the case of an eating disorder, you must seek professional help in order to get your mental and/or emotional state back in order. Once you've regained a healthy perspective, you can go to work on your physical self, but not before.

In the following sections, we describe some of the most common eating disorders and how to recognize them. If you suspect you might have one of these eating disorders, don't fast. Instead, call your doctor, counselor, or therapist. There will be plenty of time for fasting once you are sound and healthy again.

Anorexia Nervosa

Anorexia nervosa is an eating disorder in which people starve themselves in the mistaken belief that they are overweight. According to the National Institutes of Health, approximately .5 to 3.7 percent of females suffer from anorexia nervosa at some point during their lives. A much smaller percentage of men get the disorder.

Symptoms include an intense fear of gaining weight, resistance to maintaining a normal body weight and to the idea that low weight is dangerous to health, unrealistic body image, and unusual eating behaviors, such as eating only one or two kinds of foods in very small amounts. Women with anorexia often stop menstruating because of their low weight.

Anorexia is very dangerous to health and the death rate among women with anorexia is 12 times higher than the death rate for women ages 15 to 24 from all causes. Death from anorexia is usually precipitated by heart problems, severe dehydration, or suicide.

Bulimia Nervosa

Bulimia nervosa is an eating disorder in which people binge on huge amounts of food, then compensate for the excessive food intake by purging the food. Purging may take the form of vomiting, laxative use, enemas, excessive exercise, or even fasting. Fasting as a purgative measure is an unhealthy and even destructive practice when it follows a binge and is practiced out of guilt, shame, and a frantic attempt to "make up for" the excessive calories by refusing to eat.

According to the National Institutes of Health, approximately 1.1 to 4.2 percent of females suffer from bulimia nervosa at some point during their lives. As with anorexia, a much smaller percentage of men get the disorder.

Symptoms include a similar mental state to those suffering from anorexia nervosa: an intense fear of gaining weight and an unrealistic body image. People with bulimia nervosa associate self worth with body image to an extreme degree, and often feel intense guilt during a binge and great relief after purging. Binging and purging are usually done secretly.

People with bulimia nervosa are often at or around a normal weight, but may suffer from serious health problems due to frequent purging such as damage to the throat or teeth from repeated vomiting, laxative addiction, or problems related to unhealthy fasting practices such as dehydration or malnutrition.

Binge-Eating Disorder

Binge-eating disorder involves frequent binging on large amounts of food in a short time period, usually accompanied by a feeling of loss of control overeating, self-loathing or disgust, and guilt. Purging isn't associated with binge-eating disorder, but otherwise, it is quite similar to bulimia nervosa. According to the National Institutes of Health, approximately 2 to 5 percent of Americans suffer from binge-eating disorder in a six-month period.

Finer Fasting

Occasional overeating, especially as associated with special occasions such as holidays or infrequently for emotional reasons, does not constitute an eating disorder. However, if you are unsure about whether you have an eating disorder, see a doctor or a counselor to be sure.

Symptoms of binge-eating disorder include binge eating at least two days per week over a six-month period, distress, guilt, shame, secrecy about binging episodes, and often depression. Binge-eating disorder is a condition that has only recently been recognized, but many health professionals believe it is the most common eating disorder.

Compulsive Overeating

Compulsive overeating is a disorder characterized by frequent overeating against one's own will. The compulsive overeater doesn't want to overeat but can't help it, feeling compelled by psychological factors that have nothing to do with hunger. Compulsive overeating almost always results in being overweight or obese and requires psychological treatment. It differs from binge eating only slightly. A binge-eating disorder involves binging with normal eating in between. Compulsive overeaters overeat, although not necessarily to the extent of a binge, at almost every meal.

When You Must See Your Doctor

While there is absolutely no evidence that fasting causes an eating disorder, you may not realize you have an eating disorder until your fasting gets out of control. If you experience any of the following, please see your doctor immediately:

◆ You have been fasting and feel compelled to continue fasting past the point of good health.

◆ You have lost more than 10 percent of your body weight *after reaching a BMI of 25.*

♦ You binge uncontrollably before or after a fast.

♦ You sometimes cheat on your fast, then vomit or take laxatives to get rid of the food.

These are all signs of serious eating disorders. Don't ignore them. There is nothing wrong with seeking help for a health problem. Please do so immediately.

Other Weight Loss Options: First Do No Harm

The world is full of weight loss options, from pills to liquid diets to hypnotherapy to surgery. Many people who suffer from morbid obesity are willing to take drastic measures to achieve success with weight loss at any cost.

Most of the drastic measures people take for weight loss don't work very well, and if they do, they do so in a way that compromises health. The only drastic change we recommend for weight loss is a change of mind, one that leads to adopting healthy, balanced eating habits. Let's look at some of the other options first, and why they may not be the best choice for you.

Bariatric Surgery

Bariatric surgery, as this group of surgical procedures is known, involves shrinking the stomach and rerouting the intestine to limit the amount of food that can be digested and absorbed. After a bariatric surgery, the stomach, now reduced to a tiny pouch, can hold only very small amounts of food without severe consequences (sickness, vomiting, and pain).

While there are fewer complications today than when the procedure was first introduced in the 1970s and 1980s, it is still a traumatic assault on the body that leaves it less than whole. Furthermore, persons who undergo the procedure and have not addressed the emotional problems and lifestyle issues that led them to become obese in the first place can easily thwart the whole process by gradually restretching the "pouch" to its original size.

Fast Facts
Bariatric surgery is any surgery in which the stomach and intestines are altered to assist with weight loss. The so-called "stomach-stapling" procedure is an example of bariatric surgery.

Still, some overweight people believe bariatric surgery is the answer to all their problems. Here is a way they can defeat the digestive process, a process they view not as the miracle that turns food into energy, but as the enemy that causes food to turn into fat. With an impaired digestive system, they are physically prevented from consuming the quantities of food that can support a 300-pound body. Suddenly their portion sizes shrink to that of a two-year-old. No one asks them to eat more. No one accuses them of cheating on their diet. They are no longer hungry. And it will never go away. For the rest of their lives, eating more than a few ounces of food or drinking more than a half cup of liquid at one time can bring on sweats, chills, and nausea caused by food dumping directly into the intestine.

No, the diet of a person who has undergone this procedure is not like that of a person who is fasting. The difference is, the person who is fasting has chosen to do so, of his or her own free will. She has decided this is best for her body, and she can go back to eating whenever she wants—in a sensible way, and with a body that is whole and growing healthier by the minute. Fasting helps control the impulse to overeat and resets the brain to recognize real hunger and healthy food choices. There is no limitation to the faster's quest for personal wellness.

But a person who has only part of a stomach and a shortened intestine can only aspire to a single goal—that of weight loss. This person may have a thinner body, but it will never function the way it did before. It's almost impossible to get enough fiber or vitamins from food because the quantities are so small, and part of the intestine that absorbs important vitamins and minerals is no longer there. How much better it would be to find a way to get control of the impulse to eat, without such an invasive procedure!

Finer Fasting

After bariatric surgery, people are at a higher risk for nutrition-related diseases, such as osteoporosis and anemia, and dehydration is a constant threat. So much attention must be paid to their diet they have little time for anything else.

We don't recommend fasting for persons with a BMI greater than 30 without direct medical supervision, especially in the presence of an eating disorder. If, however, you have decided that bariatric surgery is the only route for you, we would ask you to first try several very short fasts under your doctor's and a nutritionist's care. These would enable you to experience for yourself the way fasting can turn off that desire to overeat by stopping the process of constant eating in its tracks. You may feel more in control, and less likely to want to change your body to change your eating habits. Isn't it worth a try before undergoing a procedure that could seriously compromise your health in other ways?

Liquid Diets and Diet Pills

If you believe that nutrition-in-a-can or a "miracle herb" or some new combination of "space age chemicals" is a weight loss panacea, think again. So-called diet solutions that promise results without effort or that don't address a mental and emotional adjustment toward food and eating are doomed to fail.

Sure, thousands of people have lost thousands of pounds (and spent thousands of dollars) on weight loss products, but in most cases, the weight comes right back on. Ever notice that in advertisements for those products profiling successful weight loss clients, the fine print always says "results not typical"? That's because typically, people don't lose weight with these products.

Real, permanent, lasting weight loss comes from a permanent change in eating habits, and that happens only with a change in mind. Doctors know it. Nutritionists know it. Even the people who sell weight loss products know it!

The Real Weight Loss Panacea

You know it, too, of course—only *you* can change you. We know it's so much easier to hope that a product will do the work for you. Unfortunately, that work has to happen from within. The good news is that once you do the work of altering your thinking, lifestyle, and food choices, the changes can be permanent and your health will only grow stronger as your waistline grows smaller.

Even making a few healthy changes in your diet without fasting can help stop the cycle of overeating. If your BMI suggests not just overweight, but obesity, then, ask your doctor for a referral to a registered dietitian, a behavioral psychologist, and an exercise physiologist. Weight loss is best addressed with a team approach, and together with these health professionals, you can come up with a plan to eat healthier, more nutrient-dense foods and incorporate physical exercise in your routine. You can also address some of those issues that are causing you to overeat in the first place. Then, when you've lost enough weight to simply be "overweight" and your doctor approves, you can try juice fasts or other limited fasts to help maintain that new healthier weight plateau.

We would never encourage an obese person to fast or make dietary changes without medical supervision, so please talk to your doctor about fasting and other weight loss options before proceeding. Obesity is a serious chronic health condition and must be treated as such. Arriving at the most appropriate strategy toward the management of obesity requires hard work on the part of the individual involved, as well as constant reevaluation and adjustment. It is a lifelong process that can employ several approaches toward eventual success.

Take one day at a time. Try your best to accept yourself and love yourself for who you are right now. Take care of yourself. Make food choices that nourish and sustain you. Exercise moderately every day, for the weight loss benefits, the overall health benefits, and the mood-boosting effect. Talk with your friends. Enjoy, really enjoy, your food. Taste every bite. And when your eating gets a little out of hand, take a break. Good health can be yours.

The Least You Need to Know

◆ Over half of Americans are overweight or obese, with a BMI or body mass index (weight in kilograms divided by height in meters squared) of higher than 25.

◆ Obesity is a known risk factor for diabetes, osteoarthritis, hypertension (high blood pressure), stroke, gallbladder disease, sleep apnea and other respiratory problems, and uterine, breast, colorectal, kidney, and gallbladder cancer.

◆ If you tend to eat too much but not for psychological reasons, fasting can be an excellent weight-loss tool—in addition to developing healthy eating habits when not fasting that allow you to maintain your goal weight.

◆ If you have an eating disorder, you should not fast and you should seek professional help to resolve your eating disorder before you suffer serious health problems.

◆ Consider lifestyle changes including medically supervised fasting before bariatric surgery and other drastic weight loss measures that can seriously compromise health.

◆ Lasting weight loss will only result from an inner change that can make external lifestyle changes permanent.

Fasting in Real Life

In This Chapter

- How to fit fasting into your schedule
- Discovering your food-related weak spots
- Your biggest barriers to successful fasting
- How to stop sabotaging yourself

By now, we hope fasting is beginning to sound like a great idea, but thinking about it is one thing. Actually fitting it into your life is another. It's easy to get excited about fasting, but when your fasting day finally arrives, you may find that first thing in the morning, you want nothing more than a big bowl of cereal, simply because you know you are supposed to be fasting.

In this chapter, we'll help you fit fasting into your real life, considering where your eating weaknesses lie, patching up your dietary problems prior to fasting, and looking at your schedule as a whole. How can you improve your basic daily diet, and when does it make sense for you to fast? We'll also give you some tools to help manage the inevitable barriers you will encounter if you make fasting part of your life.

Fasting and Your Daily Grind

Let's say it's Monday morning. The alarm goes off and you drag yourself out of bed. You get in the shower. You get out. You get dressed, you get your things together, and you leave for work. (If you work at home or at night, just adapt this scenario to your situation.) You're tired, you're cranky, and you really don't feel like spending the next 10 hours at your desk, but you know you don't have a choice. Only one thing fills your morning with a glimmer of satisfaction: On the way to work, you stop at the coffee shop and get a large double mocha latte and a bagel with cream cheese. Or, for you perhaps, it's a can of cola and a doughnut. Some of you probably make great choices, such as a piece of fruit and whole-grain cereal.

Whatever it is you feel you *must* have, you bring it to your desk and you savor each bite as you survey your to-do list. Suddenly, life seems a little bit better.

And now we're telling you to skip breakfast? Not at all! You may be withdrawing in protest at the very thought. You can't skip breakfast. You'd have a headache. You'd be even crankier. Worst of all, you'd have nothing to look forward to in the morning!

Let's make something very clear here: Fasting does *not* mean skipping meals. Not exactly, anyway. We want you to eat healthy meals and make good food choices. And then, on those selected fasting days, you may choose to fast during one or two meals, or for the entire day. But that's only for fasting days. Most of the time, *we want you to eat!*

The trick is to subvert your obsession with food, especially when the food choices you make are less than ideal and full of dependency-producing ingredients like processed sugar and caffeine. If this sounds like you, then you may have really good intentions and like the sound of fasting, but you may also dread how the actual practice of fasting will fit into your routine because you are terrified of giving up that double hazelnut latte with extra cream or that Cinnamonster pastry you so enjoy "rewarding" yourself with.

Even if you tend to skip breakfast, you may have a lot of emotional energy invested in that drive-through run at lunch hour, or that afternoon trip to the vending machine, or the bucket of fried chicken you plan to pick up on the way home.

Yes, we Americans love our food—especially our junk food. Food has become an important part of the daily grind, emotionally more than nutritionally. Food is our fuel, and good, healthy, energy-boosting food should be a priority. Unfortunately, that's not often our reality.

The truth is that junk food actually saps your energy, and occasional fasting can help your body to regain that energy it has been expending on the difficult job of digesting high-fat, high-protein, low-fiber foods. After the first few hours of a fasting day, you'll find you are probably in a great mood, once you get over the hump of emotional craving, and you'll feel lighter, quicker, clearer, and better than you do when you spend the whole day noshing on sugar and fat.

Finer Fasting

For some people, occasional fasting from solid food is much easier than giving up that cup of coffee or tea, but fasting is much easier if you first tackle your caffeine addiction. If you aren't willing to do so, drink some green tea in the mornings, just on fasting days. The small amount of caffeine, just enough to head off a caffeine headache, doesn't pack the jittery punch of full-strength black tea, coffee, or espresso. And remember, you can always go back to your cup of Joe tomorrow.

How's Your Day? A Quiz

But knowing that fasting is likely to feel good isn't the same as actually giving up that bagel with the brick-sized slab of cream cheese or that afternoon candy bar. The trick is to be mentally prepared for your daily weak spots—the times in your schedule when you are particularly emotionally dependent on a food- or drink-related habit. The following quiz can help you identify your trouble spots. Pick the best answer for each question.

1. What's your philosophy when it comes to breakfast?
    a. The bigger, the better—eggs, sausage, bacon, cheese, butter, waffles, syrup, great big pastries ... the works!
    b. Breakfast is for morning people, not me. I'm not usually hungry until later.
    c. Sometimes I grab something quick and easy and packaged on the way to work, and sometimes I don't.

2. By about 10 A.M., how do you feel?
    a. Ravenous. Time for something sweet!
    b. Just about ready for my third cup of coffee.
    c. Focused on work. I can hold out until lunch if I have to, or I might have some fruit or yogurt.

Fasting Wisdom

Many people with CFS (chronic fatigue syndrome) have experienced deep personal and spiritual renewal as a result of dealing with their illness. Alternative and complementary therapies which have been helpful are gaining wider acceptance.

—INR (Institute for Natural Resources) syllabus for "Immune Power and Fibromyalgia," *Arthritis and Autoimmune Diseases*, Second Edition, 2001

3. What do you usually eat for lunch?

    a. Whatever's being catered or whatever someone is bringing back from a nearby restaurant. I usually eat at my desk.

    b. I go out with the gang for a big, friendly, social lunch.

    c. I bring something light and healthy from home for maximum afternoon energy.

4. Around 3 or 4 P.M., how are you feeling?

    a. Ravenous again! Vending machines, here I come!

    b. Still stuffed from lunch. I don't like to eat between meals.

    c. Why hasn't anyone made another pot of coffee?

5. What do you usually do for dinner?

    a. I'm busy cooking something healthy.

    b. I'm ordering in, driving through, or going out.

    c. I'm not hungry. I don't like to eat in the evenings.

6. It's almost bedtime. What are you doing?

    a. Most days, I'm getting ready for bed. Nighttime isn't for eating.

    b. After eating light all day, I'm usually tearing frantically through the refrigerator for something, anything ….

    c. Eating cookies in bed.

Now let's look at your answers one by one.

Question #1

If you answered A: If you usually eat a big, hearty breakfast, morning will probably be the toughest time for you during a fasting day. Fasting will generally be easier for you if you get in the habit of making healthier and lighter choices for breakfast. Instead of that pile of bacon or stack of syrup-soaked pancakes, choose whole-grain cereal with low-fat milk, yogurt with fruit, or other light, high-fiber choices. Always have some fruit in the morning if you can. This habit will make your occasional fasting days much less effort because you won't be used to all that heavy, high-fat food. Simply changing your breakfast habit to include healthier food choices, even without fasting, will give you more morning energy. You can still make a big deal out of breakfast. Just choose healthier foods to make a big deal about!

On fasting days, be aware that you'll need to continue your breakfast ritual if breakfast is important to you. Sit down at the table or at your desk and, with some ceremony, prepare a nice cup of herbal or green tea, a glass of freshly squeezed fruit juice, and a glass of water. You'll be full after you drink all that liquid and you'll have given yourself the emotional fulfillment of breakfast without the solid food.

If you answered B or C: If you usually skip breakfast or can take it or leave it, mornings will probably be easy for you. Watch out for the psychological effect of suddenly feeling hungry even when you wouldn't normally be hungry just because you know you are fasting! As long as you stay in touch with your normal hunger process, you should be fine. However, you may have more trouble when midmorning or lunchtime arrives, so be ready.

Fast Facts

One large egg contains about 80 calories, 6 grams of fat, and 6 grams of protein. Not bad! But cook that egg in a tablespoon of butter and add three slices of bacon and three small pancakes with butter and syrup, and you'll be eating about 50 grams of fat and almost 600 calories. That's more than half the fat most people should eat in one day. Just imagine what a 3-egg omelette with 3 ounces of cheddar cheese would contribute (hint: about 60 grams of fat on its own!). And although the calorie count isn't bad, this meal has very little fiber, no fresh fruit or vegetables for vitamins and phytonutrients, and more protein than most of us require during a meal.

Question #2

If you answered A: For breakfast-skippers, midmorning is a dangerous time—unhealthy snacking is a real risk. After a few hours of working, hunger sets in and this group tends to grab something high in sugar, fat, or both. Nobody says you have to eat first thing in the morning, but doing so can head off midmorning binges. If you really can't face food early, however, learn to subvert unhealthy midmorning snacks by coming to work armed with healthy food. Bring a cup of yogurt, a piece of fruit, a whole-grain bagel, or a peanut butter sandwich on whole wheat bread for when hunger hits. You'll find it easier to pass up that box of doughnuts in the break room if you have something better at your desk. On fasting days, be sure to have a glass of fresh juice and/or some herbal tea during midmorning. You'll feel a surge of energy afterwards and you'll be ready to go.

If you answered B: If caffeine is your weakness, first cut down on the extra cream and sugary additives. If you love your latte, try one made with skim milk and no syrupy flavoring. Then, you might consider eventually cutting down to a single from a double. The next step might be to revert to regular coffee—you'll save a bundle of small change over time! And then, who knows. Decaf, anyone?

On fasting days, have some green tea and make an effort to take a break from what you are doing and relax. Practice some deep breathing and think about things that make you feel really good as you sip your tea. Or, some people find a quick, brisk walk in the fresh air is a great substitute for a caffeine fix.

If you answered C: So far, so good! Your snacks are generally healthy and your fasting efforts focused and strong. But weakness could hit you later in the afternoon, so don't become complacent. For now, enjoy how great you feel, both when you are eating well and when you are fasting well.

Question #3

If you answered A: You may be used to satisfying food, but if you eat at your desk while working on most days, you probably aren't paying attention to the eating process. That can mean eating more food than you need, eating food of lower quality than you really want, and generally missing out on the pleasurable and important process of eating. If you must work through lunch, do it on a fasting day. Sip your juice, water, or tea and make the most of your extra free time. If it isn't a fasting day, take 10 minutes to really focus on every bite of a light, healthy lunch. It's important to your body and to your mental health!

If you answered B: Lunchtime is tough when your co-workers usually go out. Office lunches are notoriously high in fat and calories and low in fiber. Even food choices that sound healthy, like a chicken Caesar salad, can be loaded with fat in the dressing and added cheese. But most restaurants do offer healthy choices, and just as with breakfast, if you are in the habit of eating light and making healthy, high-fiber food choices, those occasional fasting days will be easier come lunchtime. When your colleagues are ordering platters of burgers and nachos and jumbo chef salads, look the other way and choose a broth-based (rather than cream-based) soup with lots of veggies, a vegetable salad with dressing on the side, a light sandwich on whole-grain bread (nix the mayo in favor of flavorful mustard), or something off the "light" menu. Come midafternoon when everyone is slumped over their desks, you'll be high on energy and feeling great.

On fast days, you can still join your colleagues and never miss a beat, although you might find it easier to schedule your fasting day on a day when the group doesn't go out. If you do end up joining a lunch group on a fasting day, go along and order tea, water with lemon, and if they have it, vegetable broth. If it comes with vegetables in it, just sip the broth. If people give you trouble, you can always say your stomach needs a rest. You won't be lying. Or stay at your desk and get some extra work done. Impress your boss.

Finer Fasting

Office lunching can be tough for people who want to eat healthy foods. If you can convince everyone to go to the local organic-foods or natural-foods restaurant, you'll probably have more interesting choices in terms of juices, teas, and broths on fasting days. You might just get the rest of the gang hooked on healthy eating, too!

If you answered C: You may be used to eating healthy food, and that's excellent! But you may not be used to eating nothing at all. However, your healthy eating habits have given you an important advantage when it comes to fasting. You are probably less emotionally obsessed with food than people who get too attached to junk food. Healthy food has a way of normalizing hunger patterns. When hunger strikes, continue to drink juice, water, tea, and vegetable broth to keep your stomach full. You'll feel proud and energetic at the end of the day.

Question #4

If you answered A: Midafternoon may be the most notorious time of all for unhealthy snacking. However, that midafternoon slump—that time when you think that if you don't have a candy bar you'll fall asleep at your desk—is usually related to overeating at lunch. You can subvert this weak spot if you eat a light, healthy lunch with plenty of fiber and an adequate amount of protein—a turkey sandwich on whole-grain bread, a bowl of black bean soup, or a vegetable salad sprinkled with some shrimp or chicken, for example. There is nothing wrong with having a midafternoon snack, of course. If you are hungry, choose something with lots of vitamins, complex carbohydrates, and a little protein. An apple and a slice of cheese, whole-grain crackers with peanut butter, or yogurt with fresh berries are all great choices.

Once you are out of the habit of loading up on sugar for energy in the midafternoon, this time of day will also be easier when you are fasting. If you are fasting, chances are that you'll be high on energy and in a great mood by midafternoon. This is often the peak energy time on a fasting day. You probably won't be feeling very hungry by midafternoon, and you'll be plowing through your assignments while your co-workers eye you suspiciously, wondering why you look so happy. If you do find yourself struck with hunger during midafternoon during a fasting day, it's time for another glass of juice, a really big cup of water, or another steamy cup of herbal tea. That should do the trick.

If you answered B: If you don't eat between meals, you are a step ahead of the game when it comes to fasting. Yes, many sound sources of nutritional advice advocate lots of smaller, frequent meals, but even six small meals can be undertaken purposefully and without mindless snacking in between. If this is how you eat—with purpose and control during a meal, rarely snacking without paying attention between meals, no matter how many meals you eat—then you can undertake a fast with the same organized sense of self-control. Tomorrow, when you resume your healthy eating patterns, food will taste even better than usual, and you'll feel even lighter and more energetic than usual, too.

If you answered C: See the answer to 2B!

Question #5

If you answered A: If you usually derive satisfaction out of cooking at home—maybe you're even a gourmet cook who loves to choose only the finest ingredients or invent your own recipes—you probably have an appreciation for the cooking and eating process that many of us miss. That's great. Eating is an important, life-sustaining process that deserves your full attention for maximum physical and emotional benefit. During a fast, you can also get satisfaction out of creating your own freshly squeezed juices, designing different vegetable broths, even brewing your own herbal tea concoctions. If you can become just as committed to the process of creating health-sustaining juices, broths, and teas to drink during a fast as you are to cooking good food to nourish yourself and others, you may well have found the way to make fasting mentally and spiritually fulfilling in a way that suits your own individual inclinations.

If you answered B: If you are used to eating a big dinner from a restaurant or lots of processed food, you will be more susceptible to emotional hunger at dinnertime. Even though eating fat should shut down the hunger centers in your brain, many people who have practiced poor eating habits over a long period of time have lost this feedback mechanism and are no longer in touch with when they are really, physically hungry as opposed to when they are emotionally hungry. Also, if your big meal is low in fat and consists primarily of refined carbohydrates (an oversized bowl of pasta with tomato sauce, garlic bread, and a glass of wine, for example), you'll probably feel very hungry later on, as refined carbohydrates actually stimulate your appetite.

If you get in the habit of eating a healthy dinner that includes lots of vegetables, you can break the cycle of destructive evening eating. The wonderful thing about fruits and vegetables with a little fat and protein is that they actually curb hunger. They fulfill your body's nutritional requirements and the hunger—the real hunger—stops.

> **Fasting Wisdom**
>
> … [God says] … you must all be enlightened to know the transitory things of this world, that they all pass away like the wind. But you cannot know this well unless you first know your own weakness ….
>
> —Catherine of Siena, Italian ascetic and mystic (1347–1380)

By dinnertime on the day of a fast, you might be thinking about food again. If healthy food sounds great, you are probably ready to wind up your fast. Go ahead and have a healthy dinner. If you just want to gorge on junk, it's your emotions talking, not your stomach. In fact, this is a good test of hunger. If a big salad, a bowl of vegetable soup, or some fresh fruit sounds good, you are hungry. If it doesn't, you probably aren't really hungry. You are emotionally hungry. See if you can fulfill your emotional hunger in a better, more direct way. If you decide to continue your fast through dinnertime, let dinner be an event anyway. Have some hot, savory vegetable broth made from onions, garlic, celery, carrots, or whatever vegetables you have around. Even store-bought organic vegetable broth is good, and quick (look for the reduced sodium varieties). Sip it slowly with a spoon or from a big mug. Have more water and if you want it, more juice. Fill up on fluids and relax. Have a long conversation with your family or friends. Make it a ceremony to meet your emotional needs for an evening meal.

If you answered C: If you often skip dinner and are accustomed to not eating much at night, you are probably home free and feeling great by now. On the other hand, you may feel quite different after a day of fasting than you do after a day of eating. Take advantage of your natural eating habits and stay strong through the evening hours! You don't need to eat right now because it will soon be breakfast time again. However, if you are very hungry and healthy, nourishing food sounds good, go ahead and wind down your fast with a very light meal of plant foods, such as a vegetable soup or a light salad. You'll be nourishing your body without straining it after a gentle day of fasting.

Question #6

If you answered A: You are one of the lucky ones who has avoided the habit of nighttime noshing. Good for you! Eating right before bed is taxing to the body because it has to digest at the same time as it sleeps, and sleep is best reserved for other processes than digestion, such as healing, resting, and dreaming. If you've fasted all day, you may find yourself more hungry than usual at night, and that's okay. You're almost there, and you can probably hold out without eating. If you really feel like you need to eat something by the end of the day, keep it very light—a small bowl of soup, an apple, or a piece of dry toast. Take small bites and chew your food well, then go off to dreamland happy.

If you answered B: Some of us tend to eat light all day (when people are watching) and then binge at night when we are tired and feeling more vulnerable. *This is actually a sign of an eating disorder.* If you often binge at night and can't control it, feel guilty about it, don't want to eat but can't help it, then you should not be fasting. Address your eating disorder first; schedule an appointment with your doctor to discuss your eating habits.

If, on the other hand, you simply tend to be hungrier in the evenings (some people are, some people aren't), nighttime can be a time when you are more vulnerable to making unhealthy dietary choices. You may be tempted to wreck your whole day of healthy eating by going overboard. Studies show that eating large numbers of calories at night make you more susceptible to weight gain than eating those same calories during the day, probably because your body is less efficient at digestion while you are

Fasting Wisdom

According to Dr. Paavo Airola in his book *How to Keep Slim, Healthy, and Young with Juice Fasting* (Health Plus, 1971), freshly squeezed apple, carrot, orange, and celery juices are all good tonics for nervousness and insomnia.

sleeping. If you are usually hungry at night, get in the habit of eating something light and healthy that fulfills your hunger, such as whole-grain cereal with low-fat milk or low-fat soy milk, a soothing bowl of vegetable soup with whole-grain bread, or a peanut butter sandwich.

If you have made it through an entire fasting day, this is not the time to break down because chances are, you'll overeat and defeat all the work of your fast, as well as put an unusual strain on your body. Drink a big glass of juice or a soothing cup of tea. You can even add a little honey to your tea if it makes you feel better, but avoid solid food if at all possible. If you absolutely must eat something, make sure it's easy to digest and in a small quantity so you don't overtax your system, upset your digestion, and ruin a good night's sleep.

If you answered C: Complex carbohydrates in the evenings can help you sleep, as long as you don't overdo it, but simple sugars like cookies can become addictive and you may eat too many, taxing your digestive system. In general, though, a small snack at bedtime is probably fine—even if you eat it in bed, which can be a nice little sybaritic pleasure for some. If you are trying to eat less refined sugar, try a cup of warm milk with a little honey. It can be very soul-soothing.

On a day when you are fasting, evening is usually easy because you aren't hungry any-more. Your body has turned off the hunger switch. However, if you do feel tempted to eat, have some herbal or green tea with a little honey, then brush your teeth (which can help you to avoid eating because it makes your food taste funny and you may not want to brush them all over again) and go to bed. If you aren't tired, spend some time reading, organizing, or doing something else productive. No sense in wasting that good energy. Avoid exercising at night, however, which can make sleep difficult. Stick with relaxing, low-key projects, or take a nice long soak in the tub.

Finer Fasting

Some helpful hints for avoiding evening overeating:

- *Eat well during the day.* This is the most important thing you can do to sub-vert evening binges. Then you can remind yourself that you have had plenty of nutrition for the day and you don't need anymore.
- Stay out of the kitchen!
- Go to bed early.
- Avoid watching TV if you always eat while watching TV. Read a book, a magazine, or the newspaper.
- Stay distracted. Call a friend. Go on a walk or to the gym. Surf the Internet. Anything to get your mind off food.

The Barriers You Will Encounter

As much as we'd like to say that you won't encounter any barriers when you try to fast, we know all too well that … well … it just ain't so. You'll face many obstacles beyond matters of scheduling, especially when you first begin a fasting program. Your best defense is to be prepared, so watch out for the things you'll hear from your family, the attitudes you'll encounter from your friends, and the hidden hungers lurking inside your own body.

Your Family

Your family wants the best for you, of course, but they may not believe *you know* what's best for you. Parents raised in an era when fasting was virtually unheard of in mainstream culture may be utterly convinced you will destroy your health if you skip a single meal. Protective spouses may lecture, and even your own children may have a thing or two to say about it. They've learned about the food pyramid in school. They know good food is good for you. They know they aren't supposed to skip meals.

So how do you handle the naysayers in your family? Thank them for their concern, be happy that they care about you, and assure them (nicely) that you are following a special plan just for you that your doctor says is healthy, and not to worry. As long as you are in good health and your fasts are short (no longer than three days) and not too frequent (no more than one day per week, or three consecutive days per month, without medical supervision), your family has nothing to worry about.

> **Finer Fasting**
>
> Fasting isn't usually good for children and should never be practiced without close medical supervision. Explain to your kids that fasting is just for grownups, and when they are completely finished growing, they can begin to incorporate short fasts into their healthy lifestyle, too. In the meantime, continue to encourage your children to make healthy food choices.

Your Friends

Friends love to give advice, but unless they happen to know a lot about fasting, their advice on your fast may not necessarily be good advice, well-meant as it may be. Chances are, you'll hear about it from your friends if you decide to fast. Some of the comments we've heard:

◆ I would *never* do that.

◆ That sounds like a really bad idea.

◆ You'll slow down your metabolism and get fat.

◆ That doesn't sound healthy.

◆ What, are you crazy?

The simple fact is that only you and your doctor can decide if fasting is right for you. If you decide it is right for you, learn how to nod and smile and say "Thanks for your concern, but I'm confident I'm doing this in the best interest of my own health." If you can't take pressure from your friends, then don't tell them you are fasting.

> **Fasting Wisdom**
>
> Many otherwise enlightened people equate fasting with starvation—and starvation with certain death. They believe it would be unhealthy to miss a single meal. But they can rationalize overeating on the theory that it lets the body store up reserves for some hypothetical "rainy day" when there will be no food to eat. What they seem not to realize is that the body tolerates a fast far better than it does a feast.
>
> —Allan Cott, M.D., from *Fasting: The Ultimate Diet* (Hastings House, 1997)

Yourself

Your biggest obstacle is probably you. Your inner hunger, your psychological attachment to food, your emotional associations with meals, and all the things you've been taught to believe about the importance of eating every meal and cleaning your plate can all work against you. Search yourself for your beliefs and attitudes about food. Knowing what they are will help you to recognize them when you try to sabotage your own fast. Anyone can relearn and change unhealthy eating habits into healthy ones. You can do it, too. Just one fast and you'll see how great it feels. You'll be on your way to a younger, healthier, more energetic you.

The Least You Need to Know

- It can be difficult to work fasting into your schedule, but advance planning and a regular routine can boost your chances of success.
- Everyone has certain times of day when they are more susceptible to emotional hunger, as well as eating habits that are hard to break. Knowing your triggers, habits, and weak spots can help you to prepare for a fast with greater success.
- If you have a daily, weekly, monthly, and/or yearly eating and fasting plan, you'll know what to expect and you'll have goals towards which you can work for better health.
- Your family, friends, and even you may try to sabotage your fast. The more you know about fasting, the more confident you'll be about assuring people you are doing something healthy for yourself.

Your Fasting Planner

In This Chapter

- How to make an eating/fasting plan
- Daily, weekly, monthly, and yearly plans
- Special eating and fasting considerations for women
- Why men should consider occasional fasts
- Fasting for seniors: benefits and cautions

Now it's time to get organized. You know how you eat, you know what your weaknesses are, and you know, in general, when it makes sense for you to eat well and when it makes sense for you to fast. Let's do some planning.

Setting goals is an important step toward initiating a successful fast, and we don't just mean planning for tomorrow. Having a long-range plan that takes into account the unique qualities of your life, including your age and whether you are a man or a woman, can mean the difference between successfully integrating fasting into your life and giving up halfway through day one of your very first fast.

Setting Your Goals: Daily, Weekly, Monthly, Yearly

You'll find it much easier to fit fasting into your life if you set goals. Having daily, weekly, monthly, and yearly goals for your health give you a perspective in which to fit your fasting. When you have long-term goals, eating well makes more sense, and when you do fast, you'll be better able to put your physical and emotional hungers in perspective.

Keep your goals in a journal, on your calendar, posted on your refrigerator, or anywhere else where you will see them often so you can keep them in mind. Goals for health can include much more than fasting, but should also consider the fasting plans you want to follow. Remind yourself often of your goals to motivate yourself and keep yourself focused.

Goals should always be manageable. If you start with just a few things you know you can do, then you'll feel good when you accomplish them. The more you accomplish, the more goals you can set.

Your goals might look something like this, to start:

DAILY:

1. Eat five servings of vegetables.
2. Drink 64 ounces of water.
3. Avoid processed sugar.

WEEKLY:

1. Go on a one-day juice fast every Monday.
2. Lift weights each Tuesday and Thursday.
3. Take a 45-minute walk every Monday, Wednesday, and Friday.

MONTHLY:

1. Go on a three-day juice fast on the first weekend of every month (Saturday-Sunday-Monday).
2. Get a massage.
3. Try a new form of exercise this month.

YEARLY:

1. Go on a one-week raw-fruit-and-vegetable fast four times per year at the start of each season.
2. Visit the dentist each summer and winter.
3. Get a health checkup every January.

Maybe your goals will be simpler, or more numerous, or easier, or more difficult than these. This is just an example to get you started thinking about them. Whatever you decide your goals can and should be, write them down, look at them often, and incorporate them into your life.

> **Fast Facts**
>
> According to a national survey, at least 75 percent of the population in the United States experiences stress at least once every two weeks.

Perusing Your Schedule

One of the most obvious but often overlooked aspects of scheduling a fast is to plan fasting for days when you won't be put in situations where it would be very inconvenient or inappropriate not to eat. If your office goes out for lunch every Monday for a planning meeting, don't make Monday your fasting day. If you always cook a big Sunday dinner, don't fast on Sunday.

But, if you work late every Wednesday and then take a night class, Wednesday might be a good day for fasting because you'll be busy doing other things and won't be tempted. Plus, the energy you get from fasting will help you to get a lot accomplished.

Take a good hard look at your schedule and find the day during the week, or the weekend during the month, when you don't have food-related activities. Otherwise, you may be setting yourself up for goals you won't be able to fulfill.

Using a Fasting Planner

If you use a PDA, day timer, calendar, or any other kind of organizer, you'll probably find that a fasting planner is equally helpful. A fasting planner can be a part of your regular organization system, or it can be separate, in its own computer file or notebook or calendar page.

Your fasting planner maps out your fasting plans for the day, the week, the month, and the year. Use whatever system you like. You can copy the following templates for your own use, or adapt them to suit you.

Some people have only a weekly fasting plan, or a monthly, or a yearly. We suggest having several different plans so you can mix and match according to what is working for you at any given time in your life. We give you template suggestions for different fasting plans, and some suggestions for how you might fill them out. Have fun getting organized!

> **Fasting Wisdom**
>
> One of the biggest causes of a scattered schedule is not being sure what your goals and priorities are.
>
> —Julie Morgenstern, from *Organizing from the Inside Out* (Henry Holt and Company, 1998)

Your Daily Plan

Your daily eating plan should be designed to help you get the nutrients you need, and avoid the things that aren't good for you such as too much fat, sugar, and sodium, too many calories, and too many foods that are highly processed. You might plan to eat a certain number of fruits and vegetables each day, stick to whole grains, limit sugar, or forego fast food on most days of the week. Your plan might include how much water to drink each day, and even other health-promoting suggestions such as how much sleep, exercise, and relaxation you require.

Generally, we don't recommend a daily fasting plan. Some people fast every day before 10 A.M. or after 4 P.M., or on a schedule that works for them. We don't feel it is healthy to skip any meal on a daily basis. In fact, we prefer that you eat more frequent, smaller meals rather than a few large ones because large amounts of food at one time are very taxing to the body.

Finer Fasting

If you are healthy, experienced at fasting, do not have an eating disorder, are not overweight, and are in the habit of not eating for an extended period of time each day (never more than 12 hours, please, and never skipping more than one meal), and if you get enough calories and nutrients each day, short daily fasting might work for you, but again, we don't recommend it unless you do so with a doctor's approval.

The following template makes a good form for a daily fasting planner. You can also fill out one of these forms each day to keep track of your eating. Mark the time periods when you have decided to fast, and also, plan your meals. You'll be much more likely to make healthful choices and have the foods you really want on hand if you plan ahead. Last minute, unplanned meals tend to be the least healthful.

Time	Activity	Comments
6:00 A.M.		
7:00		
8:00		
9:00		
10:00		
11:00		
12:00 noon		
1:00 P.M.		

Time	Activity	Comments
2:00		
3:00		
4:00		
5:00		
6:00		
7:00		
8:00		
9:00		

Your Weekly Plan

A weekly plan could be arranged like the following template. Planning for each day of the week, both for fasting and for eating, will help you keep excessive eating under control, stick to your fasting plan, and make more healthful food choices. For example, you might decide to eat vegetarian on Sunday, juice fast on Monday, eat only raw plant foods on Tuesday. Wednesday might be a light-eating day of soup, salads, and whole cereal grains. On Friday, you may allow yourself a more extravagant meal, but make sure you still get adequate nutrition and don't eat too much at once. Again, these are only suggestions. Make a plan that works for you.

Finer Fasting

Don't get so sidetracked by obsessively organizing your schedule that you run out of energy to put it into practice. Let your scheduling system be flexible. As you gradually get more organized and have more energy, you may want to adapt your health plan accordingly.

Day	Eating/Fasting Plan	Comments
Monday		
Tuesday		
Wednesday		
Thursday		
Friday		
Saturday		
Sunday		

Your Monthly Plan

Your monthly plan won't be as detailed as a daily or weekly plan, but in it you can schedule monthly health maintenance activities such as a massage, a fitness event, trying a new healthy recipe, a monthly "vegetarian week," and any short fasts you want to try. That way you can look ahead at the beginning of each month and know what to expect. Having a scheduled routine each month makes it much easier to stay organized and on track.

Your monthly schedule could take the form of a calendar, as in the following template. Just fill in the numbers according to where the dates fall in the month you are planning. You might decide to schedule a two-to-three-day juice fast, fruit fast, or fruit-and-vegetable fast for the beginning or end of the month, or you might plan a short monthly fast around the full or new moon. Look on a calendar to find and mark down the lunar cycle on your monthly plan.

MONTH:

Sunday	Monday	Tuesday	Wednesday	Thursday	Friday	Saturday

Fasting Wisdom _____

… If we are suffering from a particular illness and through our knowledge we learn that a certain type of food is not good for us, even though we might have the desire to eat it, we restrain ourselves from eating it. So it is clear that the more sophisticated the level of our knowledge is, the more effective we will be in dealing with the natural world.

—the Dalai Lama from *The Art of Happiness* (Riverhead Books, 1998)

Your Yearly Plan

Even if you find it difficult to plan ahead more than 24 hours, having a yearly plan can give you a sense of security. When you have an annual plan, you are looking at the big picture, putting things into perspective, and preparing for the future. Your annual eating/fasting plan might include general health maintenance/disease-prevention goals such as medical checkups appropriate for your age, and could also include seasonal fasts or modified fasts, an annual New Year's fast, or it could incorporate elements from your daily, weekly, and monthly plans so that everything is in one convenient, at-a-glance spot.

For some ideas about how to plan for seasonal fasts, check out Chapter 22, "The Seasonal Three-Day Fast." Your yearly plan might look something like this:

YEAR: 20___

Winter Season Health Goals:

1.
2.
3.
4.
5.

Month	*Eating/Fasting Goals*	*Important Dates*	*Notes*
December			
January			
February			

continues

YEAR: 20___   (continued)

Spring Season Health Goals:

1.
2.
3.
4.
5.

Month	Eating/Fasting Goals	Important Dates	Notes
March			
April			
May			

Summer Season Health Goals:

1.
2.
3.
4.
5.

Month	Eating/Fasting Goals	Important Dates	Notes
June			
July			
August			

Autumn Season Health Goals:

1.
2.
3.
4.
5.

Month	Eating/Fasting Goals	Important Dates	Notes
September			
October			
November			

Fasting for Women

When planning for healthy eating and healthy fasting, women have some special considerations. Certain nutrients and other substances can help ease the discomfort of premenstrual syndrome, pregnancy, and the postpartum period.

Studies show that extra calcium in the week before menstruation can dramatically reduce the symptoms of premenstrual syndrome (PMS). Avoiding chocolate, alcohol, and high-fat foods may also help ease symptoms of PMS, even though you might find yourself craving these foods. Fasting can be a helpful way to stem cravings, but consider fasting on oatmeal and lowfat milk and taking a calcium supplement to avoid constipation and to get that calcium that is so helpful with PMS symptoms. Reducing processed food, sugar, and caffeine; drinking plenty of fluids; and getting adequate rest as well as emotional support can all ease the premenstrual period. Exercise is also key and will make fasting as well as PMS easier to handle.

During pregnancy, fasting is not a good idea. You may benefit from a fast, but your fetus won't. You should eat at least three small meals a day, and as the fetus grows and presses on your stomach, you'll soon see how important it is to make your meals small! (Can you say indigestion?)

Getting adequate nutrition is crucial for a healthy pregnancy, so make every bite count with nutrient-dense foods, plenty of fresh produce, and high-fiber foods like wholegrain cereals and beans. If you have cravings, drink a big glass of water first. You'll probably need to use the bathroom every 30 minutes anyway. Small amounts of most foods are fine, as long as nutrient-deficient foods are consumed only rarely. Most people now know to avoid alcohol and tobacco during pregnancy, which can compromise both the health of the fetus and your own health.

Most of us know that a low-fat, high-fiber diet may decrease a woman's risk of certain cancers such as breast cancer, and safe sexual practices can reduce the risk of certain cancers as well as venereal diseases. But how can fasting boost a woman's health? Primarily by keeping digestion working smoothly, which may be a factor in the prevention of cancers of the digestive system, including colon cancer; by helping to maintain normal weight; by regulating blood fat and cholesterol levels; and just as importantly, for its profoundly positive mental and spiritual effects.

The most important rules for fasting that women must remember are:

- On most days, eat a low-fat, high-fiber, moderate-calorie diet based on plant foods (fruits, vegetables, beans, and whole grains), and get 1,000 mg of dietary calcium every day (about 3 glasses of milk or 3 cups of yogurt).

- Never fast when you are pregnant.

- Never fast when you are breastfeeding.

- On days when you are experiencing premenstrual syndrome, try eating light and sticking to fresh, natural, whole foods with plenty of milk and yogurt for calcium. Or, try a one-day oatmeal-and-milk modified fast.

- During the postpartum period, adequate nutrition is crucial. Don't fast!

- Don't fast on a day when you plan to engage in strenuous exercise, especially exercise that taxes the muscles and joints such as running and weight lifting.

- Short fasts of one to two days can be excellent for combating chronic fatigue, a common condition in women possibly related to a high-fat, overly processed diet.

- Short fasts can help with weight loss, but you must not fast if you have an eating disorder.

Fasting for Men

Most fasting literature isn't gender specific, but fasting can be great for men who eat a well-balanced diet most of the time, get enough exercise, and are in good health. However, many men today don't get enough exercise and don't eat very well. Single and divorced men are more likely than men who live in a family situation to eat processed foods and fast food most of the time, and are much less likely to cook for themselves.

That translates into poor nutrition for many men. Whether men fail to make healthy food choices because they don't know how or because they don't feel it is important, those who eat a lot of processed food, too much fat, too many calories, and insufficient amounts of fiber and nutrients are more likely to suffer from serious health problems later in life.

Because of cultural pressures, men also tend to be less likely to admit to pain and discomfort, both physical and psychological. They are less likely to seek medical care, and the gap in life expectancy between men and women has remained wide: Men are dying sooner.

But, with a little effort, men can take a proactive stance when it comes to their own health by choosing to control those health-related factors they can control: diet, exercise, and stress reduction. Such steps benefit men and also the women who love them and the children who depend on them. Fasting, when practiced periodically in conjunction with healthy eating habits, can help to further enhance men's health by putting a stop to unhealthy eating behaviors, increasing energy, and helping men to become generally more aware of and in tune with the needs of their own physical, emotional, mental, and spiritual selves.

The most important things for men to remember when it comes to fasting are …

♦ Don't fast on a day when you plan to engage in strenuous exercise.

♦ Try to eat more fresh whole foods rather than packaged, processed foods, especially right before and after a fast.

♦ Get enough fiber. Aim for 20 to 35 grams of dietary fiber each day. Even when you are fasting, you can take fiber supplements.

♦ Many men suffer from undiagnosed eating disorders. If you tend to binge eat, purge after a binge, or starve yourself, please seek help and do not fast.

♦ Do fast on days when you are feeling low on energy, as if you are getting a minor illness, or if your thought processes seem sluggish.

♦ If you are at a healthy weight (or close to it) and in good health otherwise, regular short fasts, such as one day per week or two or three days per month, may help to prevent chronic diseases such as heart disease and certain cancers.

> **Fast Facts**
>
> National Men's Health Week, first celebrated in 1994 to raise awareness about men's health issues and disease prevention, is the week leading up to and including Father's Day.

Fasting for Seniors

Just because you hit the age of 65 or 70 doesn't mean you shouldn't fast. Short fasts can help seniors to stay healthy, redirect the body's focus away from food obsession, nurture the spirit, and even help to ease menopausal symptoms. Seniors with chronic disease conditions may benefit from medical fasting under the direct supervision of a physician, but please don't fast on your own if you have a serious medical condition.

Rheumatoid arthritis and other autoimmune diseases frequently respond well to short regular fasts or medically supervised longer fasts, but fasting is not an appropriate therapy for other conditions, especially if you have weakened the body. Just to be on the safe side, always check with your doctor before beginning any fast, even if you are healthy. If you stick to short fasts—the kind we recommend for almost everyone—fasting can make you feel more energetic than you have in years.

Fast Facts

According to an October 2001 Special Report from the Mayo Clinic Women's HealthSource, a recent study involving 400 people aged 70 or older in Australia, Sweden, and Greece revealed that those who ate lots of green leafy vegetables, beans, olive oil, nuts, and multigrain bread were less likely to have skin wrinkles, and those who ate more butter, red meat, and sugar were more likely to have skin wrinkles. Scientists believe that the antioxidant vitamins A, C, and E are probably the skin-saving elements, which tend to be more effective when consumed in food than when applied via skin lotions.

Please don't fast if you are underweight or weak. Fasting should be a healthy, vigorous practice, not an excuse to skip meals because you don't have an appetite and are losing strength. A physician should always address weakness and loss of appetite.

If, however, you are healthy, get moderate exercise, and feel good, then a one-day weekly fast can help to energize you and help your body to purge impurities more effectively.

The Least You Need to Know

- If you have a daily, weekly, monthly, and/or yearly eating and fasting plan, you'll know what to expect and you'll have goals toward which you can work for better health.

- Your eating and fasting plan should include plans for healthy living in daily life, not just plans for fasting days.

- Women can help to ease premenstrual symptoms, postpartum symptoms, and menopausal symptoms with targeted, modified fasts, but women who are pregnant or breastfeeding should never fast.

- Men can benefit from fasting to prevent chronic diseases and for more energy, stress reduction, and mental clarity, but shouldn't fast if they suspect they have an eating disorder.

- Seniors who stay active and continue to eat a healthy diet can also benefit from short, periodic fasting, but anyone suffering from health problems should not fast, or should do so only under the careful supervision of a doctor.

Part 4

Fasting to Heal the Body

This part examines more closely the link between fasting and physical health. We look at the plague of chronic disease in America and the ways in which healthy lifestyle changes combined with short, regular fasts can help to prevent and sometimes possibly even reverse chronic disease. We end this part with a look at the human immune system and how it works, as well as some of the more common immune-related diseases and digestive disorders that many believe can be largely resolved by the body's own healing power when aided by fasting.

Fasting for Physical Transformation

In This Chapter

- ◆ Americans and chronic disease
- ◆ Fasting for chronic disease prevention
- ◆ Fasting to build inner strength
- ◆ Fasting to heal the body

When people fast for good health, they usually do so with one of two objectives: either to prevent disease by maintaining good health and a strong immune system, or as a kind of treatment for chronic disease already affecting the body, allowing the body to heal itself by stepping out of the way.

Sure, many mainstream medical professionals aren't convinced fasting is a legitimate treatment for chronic disease. Studies on the subject are limited, even though fasting is one of the oldest known treatments for disease. In today's medical environment, studies addressing disease treatment are more likely to be designed around the effectiveness of medications rather than lifestyle changes.

However, many people—doctors, other health care professionals, and patients—claim, often based on anecdotal evidence or personal experience, that fasting can indeed effect a physical transformation in the chronically ill body.

Can fasting help to cure you of your chronic condition? Maybe. Let's look at what the evidence suggests.

America's Chronic Disease Plague

According to the Robert Wood Johnson Foundation's 1994 annual report, more than 90 million Americans live with chronic illnesses (an illness of long duration). Furthermore, the statistics make it clear that chronic disease is costing us in many ways:

- Chronic diseases account for 70 percent of all deaths in the United States.
- The medical care costs of people with chronic diseases account for more than 60 percent of the nation's medical care costs.
- Chronic diseases account for one third of the years of potential life lost before age 65.
- Over half of the people who die each year from cardiovascular disease are women.

According to the National Center for Chronic Disease Prevention and Health Promotion Chronic Disease Prevention website (www.cdc.gov/nccdphp/major.htm): "Arthritis and other rheumatic conditions currently affect nearly 43 million Americans, or about one of every six people. As the nation's population ages, arthritis is expected to affect 60 million people by 2020. The leading cause of disability in the United States, arthritis is estimated to cost almost $65 billion annually in medical care and lost productivity. Although prevailing myths have portrayed arthritis as an inevitable part of aging that can only be endured, effective interventions are available to prevent or reduce arthritis-related pain and disability."

Obviously, Americans are battling chronic disease and the numbers make it clear that chronic disease is a serious problem. The encouraging news is that many doctors believe lifestyle changes can significantly impact chronic disease rates. Number one on the list of lifestyle changes you can make to positively impact your health is (as you may have guessed) to quit smoking, but research points to dietary changes as a significant number two.

> **Fast Facts**
>
> One half of adult Americans have cholesterol levels above the desired 200 mg/dL.

Not Eating to Build a Better Body

But if dietary changes can significantly impact health, how is that relevant to fasting, which is, essentially, the absence of a diet? Actually, short periodic fasts can boost the power of positive dietary changes in several ways.

First, fasting for one day each week will help to stop the cycle of overindulgence in which so many Americans find themselves caught. Fasting helps to encourage moderation, portion control, and healthy food choices.

Second, when the body gets an occasional break from incessant digestion and can divert energy toward healing, the body is in the ultimate position to make the most of the nutrients and to digest most efficiently when healthy foods are reintroduced.

Fasting can, indeed, help you to build a better body if it is practiced in moderation, not by changing the body through any mystical process, but by freeing the body to be what it is designed to be: healthy, strong, and immune.

Rebuilding from the Inside Out

One of the theories behind *homeopathy*, a popular holistic health therapy involving remedies made with very small amounts of herbs and other substances, is that illness happens from the outside in, and that healing happens from the inside out. In other words, when an imbalance happens in the body, external symptoms will appear first.

Fast Talk

Homeopathy is a holistic health therapy developed by Samuel Hahnemann (1755–1843), a German physician who discovered that quinine induced the symptoms of malaria in a healthy person. Hahnemann developed the theory of homeopathy, based on the idea that "like cures like." Homeopathic remedies are highly diluted substances that treat the symptoms they would induce in someone without those symptoms. Homeopathy is considered a safe therapy because the remedies are so diluted.

For example, if you haven't been eating well or getting enough sleep or have been suffering from stress, the homeopathic theory is that you may first get an annoying skin rash or a breakout of acne. Next, if you fail to correct the cause of the imbalance, you might start to feel fatigued or have achy joints or develop a respiratory infection. And finally, if you don't address your condition over a long period, the imbalance could settle into a vital organ such as the lungs, the kidney, or the heart.

Healing, however, starts on the inside and as the body heals and repairs itself, symptoms recur in the reverse order from the way they first occurred. When you begin to eat less and better quality food, get more sleep, address your stress, get more exercise, take homeopathic remedies or herbal remedies designed for your condition, and otherwise treat your body in a way that allows it to start healing itself, you might have a recurrence of the symptoms of your respiratory infection as the body cleanses and purges the build-up of impurities. After this clears up, you may develop another skin rash or breakout. The healing is moving from the inside out. After skin problems and other external problems finally resolve, balance is often restored.

This process is slow but works with the body's natural healing rhythms. However, short periodic fasts can help to speed up the process, not so much that it becomes dangerous or any more uncomfortable than it already is, but just enough to help you see the changes and healing taking place in your own body.

A one- or two-day fast is appropriate at the first signs of a physical imbalance. A recurrence of a rash flare-up, a scratchy throat, an upset stomach, a dull headache, a particularly achy morning—these are all signals of the beginnings of an imbalance. A short fast may be all your body needs to get things back in order, subverting that spreading rash, that cold, that indigestion or diarrhea or constipation, that migraine, that joint pain flare-up.

Cleansing for Strength

As long as you maintain healthy habits, your body really is pretty good at keeping itself clean, but a short juice fast will give it an extra jump-start at cleansing, especially if your good habits have been slipping.

During a fast, your body steps up its natural self-cleaning process and the result can have immense benefits on your overall health and healing power. As the body searches for sources of energy in the absence of food, it first turns to sugar and fat from the bloodstream, normalizing blood sugar and blood fat levels. The toxins stored in fat cells are released, processed, and removed from the body as fat is burned for energy. The colon will become more efficient at sloughing off its lining, especially if you take a fiber supplement (preferably one containing psyllium husks) on the morning of your fast. Your body will also purge excess mucous, environmental toxins, and digestive waste.

Some of this cleansing process can be uncomfortable or unpleasant, as your sweat and breath may smell stronger, your skin may break out in acne, and you may experience headaches and irritability or other aches and pains. These unpleasant symptoms of cleansing are only temporary, however. Rest assured that afterwards, you'll feel great: cleaner, lighter, and more energetic.

> **Fasting Wisdom**
>
> I'm often asked about colonic irrigation as a means of "purification." This is totally unnecessary. The entire lining of the colon sloughs off and is regenerated every day. The best way to care for the colon is to let its own natural physiological actions keep it clean and in good working order. You can help by eating a high-fiber diet, drinking plenty of water, and exercising to help move your bowels regularly.
>
> —Andrew Weil, from his "Ask Dr. Weil" website (www.drweil.com), Q&A archives

When the digestive tract from stomach to colon is clean and empty, when the tongue is uncoated and the breath and even sweat smell sweet, when your skin is clear, you'll feel stronger and you'll be stronger, too, because a body unimpeded with excess food and excess waste is in optimal condition for self-healing, for physical activity, for quick thinking, for happiness, and for spiritual fulfillment.

Your Great Inner Healing Power

In our society, we tend to look outside ourselves for answers. We look for medicines or supplements or other magic bullets to "fix" our health. Yet, what many of us don't realize is that a great healing power exists inside each of us.

In traditional Eastern healing practices, this inner healing power is generated by the life-force energy (or chi or prana) that runs through certain channels and along certain pathways in the body. When life-force energy gets blocked or depleted, an imbalance occurs which, when left unchecked, eventually results in illness and pain.

In the West, the inner healing power of the human body is a function of the immune system, a complex process governed by a network of organs and tissues in the body (for more on the immune system, see Chapter 16, "Fasting to Improve Health").

But whether you consider your inner healing power a function of free-flowing chi or a crackerjack lymphatic system, knowing and nurturing your inner healing power is the key to great health and the prevention of, or quicker recovery from, chronic disease.

> **Finer Fasting**
>
> Many health care practitioners recommend taking vitamin and mineral supplements to ensure against deficiencies from a diet lacking in variety. However, too much of certain vitamins and minerals, such as vitamin A, selenium, zinc and iron, can actually weaken rather than strengthen your immune system. Ask your doctor about selecting the optimal vitamins and relevant combinations and dosages to maintain and boost your health.

You probably already know that there are many things you can do to promote your own inner healing power, such as eat a healthy diet and get a moderate amount of exercise. But you can do other things, too, to bolster your body's natural healing energy. Implementing one or two each week can soon make a real difference in your healing reserves:

- Eat more fresh, raw fruits and vegetables. Try to eat at least two servings of raw fruits and/or vegetables every day. The phytochemicals including antioxidants in raw fruits and vegetables are beneficial to the body in many ways, and the life-force energy in raw produce may help to intensify your own life-force energy.

- Eat more whole grains. The whole grain contains many nutrients and phytochemicals that processed grains such as white flour don't contain. These substances may help to fine-tune your body's healing power.

- Reduce your consumption of animal products (meat and dairy products). Animal products are harder to digest, putting more strain on the body. Some people also believe that consuming an animal that was killed imparts negative energy to the body.

- Eat more whole, natural, organic foods and fewer processed foods.

- Don't eat too much food at one time. The body becomes immensely strained by having to digest large amounts of food.

- Get 30 to 60 minutes of moderate-intensity exercise on most days, including some kind of strength training such as weight lifting, jump roping, or yoga. (Yoga exercises are specifically designed to release life-force energy so it flows freely and unimpeded through the body.)

- Vary your exercise routine. If you continue to surprise your body, you'll achieve physical fitness faster and you'll use more and different muscles more often.

- Get eight hours of sleep on most nights, even if you think six or seven hours are enough for you. Most Americans are sleep deprived, and many don't even know it.

- Don't drink too much alcohol. Excessive alcohol consumption has been linked to a host of health problems.

- Manage your stress. Evaluate whether you are under stress and do something about it. Meditation, deep breathing, relaxation techniques, and lifestyle changes such as shifting career directions or resolving unhealthy relationships can make a huge difference in how healthy your body feels.

- Be good to yourself. Positive self-talk, self-care, and a commitment to taking care of yourself all promote faster healing and better health.

- Cultivate personal integrity. Know what you believe is important in life, and act accordingly. People who act according to their personal beliefs tend to be happier and feel more confident and satisfied with their lives, no matter what those beliefs are.

♦ Consider holistic health care options. For minor complaints and chronic pain, consider visiting an herbalist or a doctor who practices homeopathy. Find someone who comes well recommended and has a good reputation as well as solid training.

♦ Don't neglect your mental health. If you are feeling overwhelmed or unhappy, figure out why and what you can do to change it. Nobody should spend his or her life unhappy. See a counselor if you want support in your quest to find personal happiness.

♦ Give your body an occasional restorative break by fasting on fresh organic juice and purified water for a day or two every week, every other week, or every month.

> **Finer Fasting**
>
> Two widely available herbs have been shown to boost immune system function. *Astragalus membranaceus* is especially helpful as a preventive medicine to keep the immune system strong, and *Echinacea purpurea* is a helpful herb for short-term use at the first signs of minor illness such as a cold.

The Healing Power of Fasting

Scientists have yet to be able to prove exactly why fasting appears to initiate such dramatic, almost miraculous healing processes in the body. Whether or not fasting directly impacts the immune system is still a matter of speculation, but some research suggests that fasting does just that. Because of the dearth of studies on fasting, there is much science still doesn't understand. However, fasting's long history stands as evidence for its great healing power, and contemporary anecdotal evidence is widely available.

Many doctors practicing today claim to have seen hundreds of patients with serious chronic diseases go into complete remission after an extended, medically supervised fast. While we would never recommend fasting for more than three days without medical supervision, we have read many seemingly reliable accounts of fasts of up to 60 days in fasting clinics with constant monitoring by qualified professionals that have resulted in the resolution of diseases such as advanced rheumatoid arthritis, asthma, and serious digestive disorders.

> **Fasting Wisdom**
>
> Prayer, art, and healing all come from the same source: the human soul. Research has shown us that a person in prayer, a person making art, and a person healing all have the same physiology, the same brain wave patterns, and the same states of consciousness.
>
> —Michael Samuels, M.D. and Mary Rockwood Lane, R.N., M.S.N., from *Creative Healing* (HarperSanFrancisco, 1998)

The Healer Is You

The bottom line when it comes to fasting and healing is this: You have an innate and powerful healing mechanism inside you. It doesn't matter what you call it or even exactly how it works. What matters is that it does work, and it works even better if you treat your body, mind, and spirit with care and respect.

Practicing a healthy lifestyle is the first step, and the most important. It is a powerful healing mechanism over which *you have control*. Respect your body as a whole and recognize that emotional pressures can negatively impact your inner healing power, perhaps even as much as unhealthful habits such as smoking, drinking too much alcohol, eating too much junk food, or sitting all day.

Let your body do what it needs to do without getting in its way. Every so often, let your body replenish itself. Stop the incessant cycle of digestion, just for a day, just once a week or less. Your healing power will soar.

The Least You Need to Know

- Over 90 million Americans live with chronic disease.
- The most powerful healing mechanism we have at our disposal is our own inner healing power.
- Short periodic fasts help to build inner strength by cleansing and redirecting energy to shore up the body's healing reserves.
- Nurture your inner healing power through physical and mental lifestyle changes including short fasts.

Chapter 16

Fasting to Improve Health

In This Chapter

- ◆ Your immune system and how it works
- ◆ Assess your own immune function
- ◆ What happens when the immune system breaks down
- ◆ Optimize your immune system with fasting, lifestyle changes, and spirituality

If you weren't interested in improving your health, you probably wouldn't be reading this book, and you certainly wouldn't have made it this far! But we imagine that you, like us, want to take your health into your own hands. You know that the things you do and the way you think and live affect your health.

The state of our health is largely due to the state of our immune system, which is our body's primary defense against disease. When we come into contact with germs, our immune system keeps them from making us sick … most of the time. We heal ourselves … most of the time. But without a strong immune system, our body starts to break down. Keeping our immune system working at peak efficiency is essential for good health. This chapter will show you what you can do to help your own body help itself.

Your Immune System: A Mini Primer

The human body has a weapon against disease: the *immune system*. The immune system is specifically designed to keep us healthy through a network of organs and tissues that are programmed to recognize foreign substances such as viruses, bacteria, and diseased cells, and eliminate them. In a healthy body with a healthy immune system, viruses should have a pretty hard time taking hold. Bacteria will be destroyed before they cause infection. Mutated or diseased cells will be dispatched before they can cause cancer or other problems.

But unless our immune system is healthy, it won't work as well as it could. We might get that cold, that flu, that infection, even cancer. Keeping the immune system healthy is the most important thing we can do to preserve our own health because the immune system is our primary biological ally in the war against disease—a war taking place every day inside of you.

> **Fast Talk**
>
> The **immune system** is a network of organs and tissues that destroy foreign or harmful substances in the body such as viruses, bacteria, and tumor cells.

> **Fast Facts**
>
> The primary organs of the immune system are the ones doctors used to remove often, thinking they didn't serve a function: the tonsils, adenoids, appendix, spleen, and the thymus gland. Now we know better, and although these organs sometimes must be removed due to severe infection, this practice is much less widespread.

Before we look at the ways in which we can help to strengthen our own immunity, let's look briefly at what, exactly, the immune system is, and what, exactly, the immune system does.

What Is an Immune System?

Your immune system isn't limited to a single organ. Instead, many different organs and tissues throughout your body contribute to the overall workings of the immune system. The immune system has substations all over your body to provide the proper kind of defensive weapons wherever germs or other biological invaders may enter the body.

The primary organs of the immune system are the tonsils, adenoids, appendix, spleen, and thymus gland. The bone marrow, white blood cells, and lymphoid tissue also comprise essential components of the immune system. Each of these components works together to provide an immune response in the body whenever necessary.

How Does It Work?

The immune system starts a highly efficient and effective set of complex chemical reactions whenever the body is invaded by something that doesn't belong inside it—whether a virus or a splinter, the immune system launches its search-and-destroy mission. In fact, certain immune cells called macrophages actually attack and destroy viruses and certain other foreign elements by "shooting" holes in them with certain chemicals.

The immune system can even learn! Through more complex processes of intercellular communication, the immune system can remember what viruses, for example, have attacked it and will remain on a sort of chemical "high alert" in case the same viruses return, so that response time is much quicker and more efficient if a virus makes a reappearance.

How Healthy Is Your Immune System?

You can tell your immune system isn't working up to par if you seem to get every minor illness that goes around. Lots of things can tap our immune system's energy reserves, sometimes without us even knowing it! But your body will offer you clues. Check off any of the following items that apply to you, or that have applied to you in the last year, then read on to estimate whether or not your immune system is functioning at peak capacity:

- ❏ You get more colds than other people you know.
- ❏ You've recently had an infection that lasted more than a few days or which you couldn't get rid of after a single course of antibiotics.
- ❏ You eat a lot of animal products including meat.
- ❏ You eat a lot of sugar.
- ❏ You eat a diet high in saturated fat.
- ❏ You eat less than three servings of fruits and vegetables every day.
- ❏ You get less than seven hours of sleep on most nights.
- ❏ You rarely drink water.
- ❏ You tend to eat very large meals.
- ❏ You rarely exercise and lead a sedentary life.
- ❏ You feel as if you are under stress much of the time.
- ❏ You are overweight.
- ❏ You smoke tobacco.
- ❏ You smoke marijuana.
- ❏ You drink more than four alcoholic drinks each week if you are a woman, more than seven if you are a man.

> **Finer Fasting**
>
> Smoking marijuana is against the law, but that isn't the only reason to pass up this habit. Marijuana use has been shown to suppress immune system function, and could make you more vulnerable to disease.

❏ You are a pessimist.

❏ You feel socially isolated.

❏ You have an underactive thyroid.

❏ You have food or respiratory allergies.

❏ You often get skin rashes or hives.

❏ You are often tired even when you have had enough sleep.

❏ You have been told you have chronic fatigue syndrome or a similar disorder.

❏ You have unexplained pain in any part of your body.

❏ You suffer from depression.

❏ Your joints often hurt.

❏ You have been diagnosed with cancer of any type.

❏ You have been diagnosed with rheumatoid arthritis, lupus, or another autoimmune disease.

❏ You have been diagnosed with heart disease.

❏ You have been diagnosed with diabetes.

❏ You have been diagnosed with multiple sclerosis.

❏ You have been diagnosed with fibromyalgia.

❏ You have any other chronic disease not listed above.

❏ You have recently suffered a physical or emotional trauma.

❏ You have recently suffered a severe injury.

Now count how many boxes you checked. Any one of the items on this list is either a sign of or a risk factor for a depressed immune system. If you checked several, chances are good that your immune system isn't working up to par.

Fast Facts
Many more women than men are diagnosed with autoimmune diseases each year. While some scientists attribute the difference to the fact that women tend to be more likely to seek medical help for their health care concerns, others believe there are other factors predisposing women—especially those who are employed and are in their child-bearing years—to autoimmune diseases. The cause of this phenomena remains under investigation.

When the Immune System Goes Awry

Many things we do, even the way we think, can adversely affect productive immune function, but sometimes our immune systems go awry due to reasons other than lifestyle. In the case of prolonged infection or disease, we can suffer from reduced immune function. Or, in the case of *autoimmune diseases*, our immune systems go haywire and become over-reactive, mistakenly attacking the body rather than foreign invaders to the body. If you suffer from an autoimmune disease, it is equally critical to practice lifestyle changes that encourage immune system balance.

Let's look at some common immune-related disorders.

Fast Talk

Autoimmune diseases are diseases that cause the immune system to attack the body, or self, rather than foreign substances such as viruses and bacteria. Autoimmune diseases are not contagious and may be heritable. Some common autoimmune diseases are multiple sclerosis, rheumatoid arthritis, systemic lupus, Type 1 diabetes, psoriasis, and inflammatory bowel disease.

Chronic Fatigue Syndrome

Chronic fatigue syndrome, or CFS, is an insidious condition that cannot be precisely diagnosed from any test and cannot be cured. CFS saps energy and saddles the sufferer with flulike symptoms, from aches and pains in the joints and muscles to fever to extreme fatigue. Unlike the flu or other similar conditions such as mononucleosis, CFS doesn't usually go away. Once called the "yuppie flu" because the first wave of people diagnosed with the disease were wealthy Caucasian women in their 30s and 40s, CFS has now been diagnosed in many different ages, genders, and races.

Fast Facts

The Centers for Disease Control estimates that chronic fatigue syndrome or something resembling it affects more than 500,000 Americans each year.

According to the National Institute of Allergy and Infectious Diseases, a division of the National Institutes of Health, many scientists believe the disease is probably due to some sort of faulty interaction between the immune system and the central nervous system.

While nonsteroidal anti-inflammatory drugs and antihistamines can sometimes help with some symptom relief, there is no definitive cure, just as there is no definitive diagnosis. Many medical professionals continue to doubt the existence of CFS, but an increasing number of doctors have begun to recognize CFS-like symptoms in all types of patients, not just the originally recognized "yuppie" group. However, women do seem to develop the disease more often than men.

According to anecdotal claims, fasting has been shown to relieve the symptoms of CFS and restore energy, especially when practiced in conjunction with a low-fat, plant-based diet.

Rheumatoid Arthritis

Rheumatoid arthritis is an autoimmune disease in which the immune system targets and attacks the linings around the joints, causing usually symmetrical pain, stiffness, redness, and swelling. In other words, you might experience symptoms in both knees, both hips, or both hands, whereas with osteoarthritis, you experience symptoms in joints that have endured a lot of wear and tear.

Besides joint pain, redness, and swelling, other symptoms of rheumatoid arthritis include fever, loss of appetite, low energy, anemia, and rheumatoid nodules or lumps of tissue over affected joints. Rheumatoid arthritis pain usually begins in the feet and hands, and can progressive over the course of many years, eventually invading bone and causing severe damage.

Early diagnosis can help to keep the disease under control, although there is no cure and the cause of rheumatoid arthritis is still unknown. Rheumatoid arthritis affects 2.1 million Americans and, as is the case of other autoimmune conditions, it affects mostly women: 1.5 million women in the United States have rheumatoid arthritis; only 600,000 men have the disease. Most people develop rheumatoid arthritis in middle age, but onset in the 20s or 30s is not uncommon, according to the Arthritis Foundation.

Rheumatoid arthritis is one of the chronic diseases that, according to research, seems most responsive to fasting and dietary changes. Research suggests that medically supervised fasting of about a week in conjunction with subsequent dietary changes (switching to a vegan or vegetarian diet) can have a profound affect on the occurrence of rheumatoid arthritis symptoms. Because of the similarities of their symptoms, rheumatoid arthritis and lupus (see the following section) are often mistaken for each other.

Fast Facts

A study done in Oslo, Norway, in 1999 showed significant benefits to patients with rheumatoid arthritis who fasted for seven to 10 days followed by a vegan (no animal products), gluten-free diet for 3.5 months, followed by a lactovegetarian diet (plant foods and milk) for nine months, as compared to a control group. Researchers concluded the beneficial effect might be explained by significant differences in fecal flora (colonic bacteria) between the study and control groups. *American Journal of Clinical Nutrition*, Sept. 1999.

Lupus

Systemic lupus erythematosus, also called lupus or SLE, is an autoimmune disease that can be mild to life threatening. According to the Lupus Foundation of America, more than 16,000 Americans develop lupus each year, and 500,000 to 1.5 million Americans have been diagnosed with lupus.

In lupus, the immune system attacks different systems in the body: the skin, joints, blood, or any major organ. Symptoms vary dramatically among people suffering from lupus. Some people experience only joint pain and/or skin lesions causing pain and stress. In others, the disease can become fatal when it attacks major organs such as the kidneys.

Lupus may be heritable but also seems to be triggered by certain events or environmental causes, such as ultraviolet light, antibiotics, or stress, in those susceptible to the disease. About 10 to 15 times more women contract lupus than men, and black and Hispanic women are more likely to contract lupus than Caucasian women, for unknown reasons.

As with other autoimmune diseases, lupus is often treated primarily for symptom relief and with drugs that suppress the body's over-reactive immune response, and with medically supervised fasting.

Multiple Sclerosis

In multiple sclerosis, or MS, the immune system attacks a few or many different parts of the body, resulting in a wide range of symptoms from person to person and even from day to day. This frustrating disorder is, like many other autoimmune disorders, difficult to diagnose and has no cure. And, again, it is more common in women, affecting two to three times more women than men.

Fasting Wisdom

Some people believe multiple sclerosis has an environmental cause early in life, due to the following well-established epidemiological facts about MS (according to the National Multiple Sclerosis Society):

- Worldwide, MS occurs with much greater frequency in higher latitudes away from the equator, than in lower latitudes, closer to the equator.
- In the United States, MS occurs more frequently in states above the 37th parallel (from Newport, Virginia, to Santa Cruz, California).
- Before adolescence, an individual born in a high-risk-MS area who moves to a low-risk area acquires the new risk level.
- MS is more common among Caucasians than other races.
- Certain outbreaks or clusters of MS have been identified.

According to the National Multiple Sclerosis Society, some of the many symptoms of multiple sclerosis, from mild to advanced, can include tingling, numbness, pain, blurred or double vision, muscle weakness, impaired balance, spasms, tremors, changes in bladder, bowel, and sexual function, cognitive changes such as forgetfulness or difficulty concentrating, speech and swallowing problems, and mood swings. Some people are only mildly or moderately affected by symptoms. Others are severely affected and may be unable to walk or talk. Some people experience only a few symptoms, and some experience a wide range of symptoms.

Fasting for Immune System Balance

We've emphasized how fasting helps you to get out of your body's way so it can heal more effectively. This is particularly true in the case of autoimmune disorders. Paradoxically, fasting boosts suppressed immune function but also suppresses overactive immune function in the case of autoimmune diseases.

This is one of the fascinating effects of fasting, and one of the reasons it may be such an effective treatment for autoimmune conditions. This suppression of overactive immune function is the other side of the equation. During a fast, the body seems to develop the ability to balance immunity, restoring it or recalibrating it to its natural, healthy state.

Freeing Your Body-Mind for Healing

Once again, we would like to remind you how intricately your entire self is connected. Many studies have demonstrated the link between mental state and physical health, between lifestyle (from diet and exercise practices to spiritual satisfaction) and disease rates. The core of this response seems to be that everything we do, think, eat, believe, and practice can impact the immune system.

If you are under mental stress, anxiety, or depression, energy is channeled away from healing. If you are injured or unhappy or lonely, energy is channeled away from healing to address these other needs.

Finer Fasting

Don't let an infection go untreated. Untreated infections sap the immune system of its reserves. On the other hand, don't take antibiotics if you don't need them. Antibiotics do nothing against viruses. They are for the treatment of only bacterial infections. Take antibiotics only when prescribed by a doctor, and only for the condition for which they were prescribed. Never take a few leftover, older antibiotics from something else, and always finish your prescription as directed. Antibiotic misuse helps bacteria to grow more resistant, making future infections harder to cure.

But, if you eat fresh, whole, healthful foods and keep your body moving, you create more energy for healing. If you practice stress management, maintain a positive outlook, and nurture all sides of yourself, you create more energy for healing.

And, if you don't overburden your body with too much of anything—too much food, too much stress, even too much exercise—you'll allow your body to redirect all that surplus positive energy to where your body most needs it. Don't neglect your spirit when planning your immune system self-care. Give yourself space to enjoy your life, plan and journey toward your goals, and stretch your mind beyond your daily routine. Let yourself consider and pursue spiritual as well as physical and material goals. Let yourself be happy.

And last but certainly not least, don't forget that regular, short fasts can make all these goals more accessible by freeing your body's energy and balancing all your many aspects, including your inner healing power.

These are the keys to balancing your own immune system and harnessing your internal energy for healing.

The Least You Need to Know

◆ Your immune system is a function of many different organs and tissues in your body that recognize foreign or non-self elements and destroy them to keep the body free from disease.

◆ Autoimmune diseases happen when the immune system mistakenly sees the body as "other" and attacks the body's own tissues and organs as if they were viruses or bacteria.

◆ Some common autoimmune diseases include rheumatoid arthritis, lupus, and multiple sclerosis. Autoimmune diseases are more common in women, for reasons scientists don't yet understand.

◆ Balancing your immune system through lifestyle changes and a spiritual focus as well as fasting can help your body to remain stronger against disease.

Fasting for Better Digestion

In This Chapter

◆ The digestive process
◆ Digestive disorders and why they happen
◆ How fasting helps to improve digestion
◆ An Eastern perspective on digestion

You eat, you digest. You eat, you digest. You eat some more, and you continue to digest. The digestive process in your body (which we explained in detail back in Chapter 3, "The Anatomy of a Fast") is an amazing and efficient way to get the energy and nutrients out of the foods you eat to help your body function. But your body isn't designed to digest 24 hours per day. It is designed to digest reasonable amounts of food several times per day.

Too much eating of too-large portions consisting of too-rich food puts your digestive process at risk for disease. Other factors can also cause digestive problems, including heredity, bacteria, and stress. In this chapter, we'll look at some of the problems you might experience with your digestive process, and how fasting can help.

Your Digestion at Work

Your digestion may be just fine. After you eat, you feel full for a while, and then eventually you get hungry again. If you eat healthy foods in moderate amounts, drink plenty of water, and get enough exercise, your digestive system is probably in good shape because these are the three elements that contribute to healthy digestion.

But even if you think your digestion is fine, if you tend to eat lots of high-fat and/or high-sugar foods, if you seldom drink water, if you lead a sedentary life, and if your diet is low in fiber, you may be headed for trouble. Just as that car you keep driving and driving and driving and letting stand idling for hours keeps on going, just as that furnace running 24/7 all winter long seems okay, your digestion may seem, for all practical purposes, to be just fine.

Until suddenly, something goes wrong. The engine seizes. The furnace suddenly quits working. You develop indigestion, constipation, a stomachache, diarrhea, gas, or heartburn. You feel horrible, and you wonder why your body has betrayed you.

> **Finer Fasting**
>
> Sometimes, drinking a large glass of water at the first sign of heartburn is all it takes to feel relief. Try drinking water before automatically popping a handful of antacids.

For others, the digestive process is hardly effortless and is the source of long-term chronic pain, as in the case of ulcers, colitis, inflammatory bowel disease, or other chronic diseases and conditions of the digestive system.

No matter what your digestive system status, you can make the most of your digestive health by changing your habits for the better. But first, let's look at some of the things that can go wrong with your digestive system, and why scientists think they happen.

When Your Digestion Stops Working

Sometimes, it seems, you can eat whatever you want and feel great. At other times, even a healthy meal can upset your stomach.

While the difference may be related to your stress level, mental state, or any number of other factors at the moment (remember, you are a whole, integrated person so what affects your mind may well affect your digestion), that doesn't mean your food choices aren't important, or that you won't experience digestive problems even when you are in a good mood. Always remember that you are a whole person and everything you do affects everything you are.

That being said, here's what sometimes goes wrong, for any number of reasons, including what we do, how we live, what we eat, how we think, how we feel, what we are exposed to, and what we inherit.

> **Fasting Wisdom** _____
>
> In certain Eastern cultures and according to many holistic health practitioners in the West, the attitude with which you eat any food can affect how well your body accepts and digests that food. A fresh salad loaded with organic vegetables won't sit well if you eat it while you are in a rotten mood. A candy bar eaten joyfully, mindfully, and with complete attention to the pleasurable experience will go down just fine.

Indigestion

Indigestion is a general term to describe digestion that isn't working quite like it should, or the discomfort associated with this condition. Many things can cause indigestion, from eating too fast or eating too much or eating something that is too high in fat or too spicy to a serious illness that compromises the body's ability to digest food properly. For example, some chronic diseases may inhibit digestion so that food takes much longer than usual to get digested.

Heartburn

A feeling of burning behind your breastbone, often accompanied by regurgitation of stomach acid and bile salts into your esophagus, characterize heartburn, a common digestive complaint caused when the sphincter that closes off your esophagus from your stomach opens or abnormally relaxes. Heartburn is sometimes mistaken for a heart attack because the chest pain it induces can be so severe.

According to the Mayo Clinic website (www.mayoclinic.com), some of the substances that can cause the esophagus to relax, resulting in heartburn, are …

- Fatty foods.
- Chocolate, caffeine, onions, spicy foods, mint, and some medications.
- Alcohol.
- Large meals.
- Lying down soon after eating.
- Tranquilizers, such as benzodiazepines including diazepam (Valium) and alprazolam (Xanax).
- Theophylline (Slo-Bid, Theo-Dur), an asthma medication.

> **Fast Facts**
>
> According to www.mayoclinic.com, every day as many as 10 percent of adults experience heartburn.

Chronic heartburn resulting in inflammation of the esophagus is called gastroesophageal reflux disease. In most cases, however, heartburn is easily controlled by limiting portion sizes, reducing consumption of the foods and drinks that cause it, and by losing weight.

Gas

Everyone's digestive tract generates gas because gas is a by-product of digestion, plain and simple. Everyone has to pass those gas bubbles, through burping or flatulence, numerous times throughout the day. However, sometimes our digestive system produces excessive gas. Larger or frequent gas bubbles can cause discomfort, even sharp pain. Gas may sound like a trivial complaint or something to inspire giggles, but gas pain can be a real problem for some people.

Most people produce about 1 to 3 pints of gas a day and pass gas through burping or through flatulence about 14 times per day. These amounts are normal. Most gas is odorless, but the odor associated with flatulence comes from small amounts of gas containing sulfur released by bacteria in the large intestine.

Eating or drinking too quickly, or drinking carbonated beverages, results in swallowing excess air, a common cause of excess gas. Swallowed air is usually released through burping. Foods high in carbohydrates are more likely to produce gas than foods high in fats and proteins. According to the National Digestive Diseases Information Clearing House (a division of the National Institutes of Health), the carbohydrates most often to blame are …

- **Raffinose.** The notoriously gas-producing bean is high in raffinose. Cabbage, Brussels sprouts, broccoli, asparagus, and whole grains contain smaller amounts.

- **Lactose.** Many people don't have a sufficient amount of the particular enzymes necessary to digest this sugar found in milk and milk-containing diary products. Even those who aren't lactose-intolerant in youth may develop problems digesting lactose as they age because enzyme production decreases with age.

- **Fructose.** This sugar occurs naturally in onions, pears, artichokes, and wheat, and is added to many processed soft drinks and fruit drinks.

- **Sorbitol.** This sugar occurs naturally in apples, peaches, pears, and prunes, and is the sweetener used in many dietetic foods and sugar-free candy and gum.

> **Fast Facts**
>
> According to Tamara Schryver, M.S., R.D., editor of *Dietitian's Edge*, the definition of fiber is changing. If proposed changes are adopted by the Institute of Medicine, fiber will be broken down into dietary fiber and added fiber. Total fiber will be the sum of these two categories. The terms "soluble" and "insoluble" are being phased out in favor of the terms "viscosity" and "fermentability."

◆ **Starches.** Starches such as fruit and beans may cause gas because they aren't completely broken down until they are in the large intestine, where they are fermented by colonic bacteria that releases hydrogen, carbon dioxide, and methane gas.

◆ **Fiber.** Fiber also causes gas, but not the insoluble type that passes right through your body undigested (such as in wheat bran and some vegetables). Instead, it is the soluble type of fiber, as found in apples and many other fruits, oat bran, beans, and peas that cause gas because soluble fiber, like starch, isn't completely digested until it reaches the large intestine.

Constipation and Diarrhea

Quite simply, constipation is an uncomfortable condition in which your body becomes unable to pass stools and/or stools become very hard and difficult to pass. Diarrhea is the opposite condition, in which stools become very loose and watery, and it becomes difficult *not* to pass them.

Constipation is often caused by three things: insufficient dietary fiber, insufficient exercise, and insufficient fluid intake. Correcting these insufficiencies is usually enough to correct the problem, although if the problem becomes chronic, you should certainly see your doctor, as it could signal a serious health problem.

Diarrhea is more often caused by a virus, bacteria, or parasite, but can also be caused by alcohol, caffeine, or foods that irritate the digestive tract such as chocolate or spicy foods. Antibiotics can also cause diarrhea. If diarrhea doesn't resolve in two or three days or if you become dehydrated, see a doctor immediately.

A high-fiber diet rich in plant foods may cause some initial digestive discomfort in the form of some initial excessive gas or even mild diarrhea, but don't let that be an excuse to revert to less healthy eating habits. Your body will quickly adjust to higher fiber and carbohydrate and your digestion, as well as your overall health, will benefit in many ways.

Ulcers

People used to believe that spicy foods and stress caused ulcers, but scientists now understand that most ulcers, or peptic ulcers, are related to a bacteria called *H. pylori*, and can be quickly cured with antibiotics. About 5 to 10 percent of Americans will at some time develop a peptic ulcer, called a gastric ulcer if in the stomach and a duodenal ulcer if in the duodenum, a section of the small intestine. It isn't clear whether the bacteria actually causes the ulcers or is simply present when there are ulcers, but researchers are studying ulcers to learn more. While diet doesn't cause ulcers, it can certainly ease the pain ulcers cause. Reducing stomach acid is the key to reducing ulcer pain. A mild, low-acid diet during treatment is best. Your doctor may also suggest you take antacids, quit smoking,

Finer Fasting

Let herbs be your ally as you seek digestive health. Peppermint tea settles indigestion and relieves gas. Chamomile tea is a mildly sedating anti-inflammatory that can also ease digestive complaints, and cinnamon tea can help to stop diarrhea. For general digestive balance, include steamed dandelion greens in your diet.

quit drinking alcohol, and take only acetaminophen instead of aspirin or nonsteroidal anti-inflammatory pain relievers such as ibuprofen.

Gastritis

This painful condition is marked by an inflammation of the stomach lining, causing pain in the upper abdomen and sometimes nausea and vomiting. Gastritis is caused by excessive stomach acid and is usually easily resolved by eating gentle foods and quitting smoking and drinking alcohol. As for ulcer sufferers, people with gastritis should take only acetaminophen for pain relief instead of aspirin or nonsteroidal anti-inflammatory pain relievers such as ibuprofen.

Irritable Bowel Syndrome

Irritable bowel syndrome (IBS) is an uncomfortable but very common problem affecting an estimated 35 million Americans and ranking second only to the common cold as a cause of lost work time in the United States. Most likely to affect young women, IBS causes abdominal pain, cramping, bloating, gas, diarrhea, or constipation. Due to uncoordinated and/or overactive muscles in the digestive tract, food is pushed through the intestines too quickly, causing symptoms associated with improper digestion.

Unlike other more serious bowel conditions like those associated with inflammatory bowel disease, IBS is more uncomfortable than life threatening. However, it can cause many problems for those who suffer from it, from pain to depression to an inability to participate in "normal" activities of life.

IBS is usually a chronic condition but symptoms can abate, then flare up again during times of stress or in response to certain foods or practices such as smoking or drinking too much alcohol. Lifestyle changes are key to managing IBS. Many health care providers recommend some or all of the following IBS care strategies:

◆ Gradually increase your intake of dietary fiber (too much too soon can worsen symptoms temporarily).

◆ Avoid foods that tend to irritate your condition. For some people, these foods include alcohol, caffeinated beverages, chocolate, spicy foods, fruit and fruit juices, raw vegetables, dairy products, high-fat foods, high-sugar foods, nuts, and red meat. Only you know which foods set off your own symptoms.

◆ Practice stress management techniques such as relaxation, yoga, meditation, and deep breathing. Stress can set off an attack of IBS, and stress management may help to keep symptoms under control.

◆ Eat small meals at regular times every day.

◆ Drink plenty of fluids, including at least a quart of water each day.

◆ Exercise regularly.

> **Fasting Wisdom**
>
> A crust eaten in peace is better than a banquet partaken in anxiety.
>
> —Aesop, Fables

Inflammatory Bowel Disease

Inflammatory bowel disease, or IBD, refers to any of several different conditions, the most common being ulcerative colitis and Crohn's disease. These two diseases are very similar and are often mistaken for each other. Symptoms of both conditions are chronic diarrhea, abdominal pain and cramping, blood in the stool, fatigue, reduced appetite, and in severe cases, weight loss and fever.

Crohn's disease consists of inflamed areas anywhere from the mouth to the rectum, although most commonly inflamed areas and large ulcers occur in the lower part of the small intestine or the colon, with healthy tissue in between inflamed areas. In ulcerative colitis, inflamed areas are usually limited to the colon and may include small bleeding ulcers.

IBD can be very serious, may be hereditary, and although the cause is unknown, it is probably an autoimmune condition in which the body attacks its own healthy tissue. Some scientists believe IBD may be a response to an as-yet unidentified bacterium or virus. And, because IBD is more common in industrial nations, many believe it may be the result of a high-fat, highly processed diet.

In addition, both Crohn's disease and ulcerative colitis increase your risk of developing colon cancer. Treatment usually includes anti-inflammatory and/or immune-suppressing medication and treatment that directly address symptoms, such as pain relievers and lifestyle changes, including eating smaller meals, increasing fiber and protein, decreasing fat intake and dairy products, drinking more liquids, and eliminating foods that cause flare-ups, such as foods likely to produce excess gas.

> **Fast Facts**
>
> People who develop IBD usually contract it between the ages of 15 and 35. It is equally common among men and women but is most common in Caucasians. If you are Caucasian, you are five times more likely to develop IBD than if you are Jewish and of European descent.

Fasting and Your Digestive System

In Chapter 3, we showed you what happens in your body when you fast. The rest and restoration that happens in your body during a fast can have a significant effect in healing and restoring the health of your digestive system. Short fasts are best, especially for those already suffering from digestive disorders.

When you fast regularly, you build an automatic rest into your digestive routine. Although the link between diet and the cause of digestive complaints is nebulous, the link between diet and symptom relief is well understood for many different digestive complaints. In addition, a healthy diet of moderate portion sizes with occasional fasts probably helps to keep a healthy digestive system working optimally.

Activate Your Second Chakra

Remember your chakras, which we described in Chapter 7, "The Essence Beyond '"Not Eating'"? Your second chakra, located just behind your naval, is the seat of digestion, of the gastric fire (*agni*) that burns food for energy and eliminates impurities from your body.

For a holistic approach to healthy digestion, in addition to a healthy diet and exercise, keep your second chakra activated. Here are some second-chakra strategies:

Finer Fasting

Crystal healers believe crystals contain certain energetic healing properties related to their color and structure that can help soothe your digestive system. If you suffer from constipation, sluggish digestion, gas, malabsorption of nutrients, poor circulation, or obesity, rest on your back with red or orange crystals or stones on your lower abdomen. If you suffer from heartburn, acid indigestion, acid reflux, diarrhea, or ulcers, use purple, blue, or green crystals or stones.

- Get or give yourself a massage on your lower abdomen.

- Try yoga poses that stimulate the abdominal area, such as the bow pose, in which you rock on your abdomen while holding your heels with your hands over your back, or any pose in which the body is folded over at the abdomen, such as standing or seated forward bends.

- Try abdominal acupressure. See if you can locate a sensitive area in your lower abdomen by pressing gently with your thumbs. (This is also great for relieving menstrual cramps.)

- Drink tea with ginger and/or other spices like pepper and cinnamon.

- Relax on your back and breathe deeply into your abdomen.

- ◆ Visualize a flame in your lower abdomen activating your entire digestive system.

- ◆ If you suffer from heartburn or feel a burning sensation in your digestive tract, visualize cooling blue and green and soothing water flowing through your abdomen.

The Least You Need to Know

- ◆ Even a seemingly healthy digestive system can eventually lose function if it is abused through constant overload.

- ◆ The digestive system is subject to many different disorders like indigestion, heartburn, gas, constipation, diarrhea, ulcers, gastritis, irritable bowel syndrome, and inflammatory bowel disease.

- ◆ In addition to healthy lifestyle changes like eating a high-fiber, plant-based diet and increasing fluid intake and exercise, fasting can help to ease the symptoms of digestive disorders and may help to prevent them from occurring.

- ◆ Keep your second chakra healthy for a holistic approach to good digestion.

Part 5

Four Fasts and How to Do Them Right, Plus Fast Variations

This part takes all the information in the book thus far and puts it into practice with chapters that map out individual fasts and exactly how to do them, including schedules, menus, shopping lists, calendars and timetables, journal templates, and inspiration. This part begins with a fasting primer filled with terminology and preparation information, and ends with some fasting variations, including fruit fasts, oatmeal fasts, raw-foods fasts, and even fasts from spending money, the media, and talking.

Chapter 18

Getting Into the Spirit: Your Fasting Primer

In This Chapter

- ◆ Get ready, get set: what to know before you fast
- ◆ Physical, mental, and spiritual pre-fast preparation
- ◆ What to expect during short and long fasts
- ◆ Why you should consider mind-body transitions

Perhaps up to this point you have simply been reading, mulling over the information, and considering whether or not you actually want to try fasting. In this section of the book, we jump right in! It's time to give fasting a try, and with the help of our step-by-step guides, you should have an easy time.

But before you find the fast you want to try, invest in that juicer, and give it a go, and read this chapter, which will get you physically, mentally, and spiritually prepared for your fast.

Before You Begin

What do you need to do to get ready for a fast besides stop eating? Plenty. Because most of us are so emotionally attached to food and because our routines are so ingrained, getting physically, mentally, and spiritually prepared is essential for success.

Even if you think you are ready to try a fast, give these tips and strategies a try. Fasting, especially the first time, is a lot harder than you think. It's all too easy to start out with great intentions in the morning and to give up before lunch. It's fine not to fast, but if you decide you really want to take advantage of the many benefits of short periodic fasts, then a commitment is in order, and so are some preparatory measures.

Physical Preparation

To physically prepare for a fast, you need to ready your digestive system for the temporary absence of food. This isn't such an unusual thing to do. Have you ever noticed that you don't sleep as well when you eat too much right before bed? You may toss and turn, wake up frequently, and face the morning feeling sluggish and even, ironically, famished. That's because you haven't eased into your nighttime "fast." Instead, you've overburdened your digestive system.

When you eat a light, healthy, low-fat dinner, however, you are more likely to sleep well and wake up refreshed. You'll be more able to control your eating at breakfast, and you'll feel better all day.

A full-day fast is just a little bit different than the fasting you do every night when you sleep. One obvious difference is that you are awake, which makes it more difficult not to wander towards the refrigerator and eat something less than healthy.

Finer Fasting

For a perfect pre-fast dinner to ease you into a one-day fast for the following day, make a big salad with lots of fresh organic vegetables and about a half cup of white or red beans, topped with about a tablespoon of olive oil and a splash of good vinegar. Have one or two pieces of fresh fruit for dessert.

To prepare yourself for a fast, eat nothing but plant foods on the day before and the day after a fast, and avoid refined carbohydrates such as white flour and white sugar products. Because animal products (meat, dairy products) are more difficult to digest than plant foods, plant foods help to ease your digestion toward its resting period. And, because refined carbohydrates are powerful appetite stimulants, avoiding them will help your appetite normalize.

Another way to prepare your body for a fast is to gradually reduce portion sizes the day before, and to gradually increase portion sizes the day after. Let dinner be your lightest meal the day before a fast, and forego the nighttime snacks. By the next morning, you probably won't even be hungry—at least not physically. The day after a fast, have a light breakfast consisting of one piece of fresh fruit, and gradually increase your portion sizes with each meal until dinner is back to your normal size.

This kind of physical preparation or digestive system "priming" is essential for success because it helps to control your hunger. Then, you can focus on your emotional eating issues, which are probably much more powerful an obstacle to a successful fast than mere physical hunger.

Finer Fasting

Don't chew gum while fasting. The chewing action starts the digestive process, which can be very uncomfortable if there is no food to digest.

Mental Preparation

Mental preparation is just as important as physical preparation if you want to make it through your fast successfully. Your mind is perhaps your most powerful appetite stimulant, and can tie you to food in an emotional way that is hard to resist. You are used to eating food at certain times, and habits can be very difficult to break.

For many of the same reasons diets often fail, attempts at fasting often fail. People don't like to change habits that are pleasurable, even if those habits are damaging to health. Smoking, drinking alcohol, drinking caffeinated beverages, taking drugs, and binge eating are all physically addicting but also extremely powerfully emotionally addicting. Removing a comfortable, pleasurable habit can be unpleasant. How do you prepare yourself?

One of the most powerful things you can do to redirect your mental state toward a path of positive change is to talk to yourself. Continually remind yourself of the things you know but tend to forget at the peak of a craving. Photocopy or cut out the following list of positive self-talk cues for use during your fast to keep your mind on track and your mental state positive and productive. If you say something enough, eventually it will become reality for you, so let positive self talk be your ally.

Fast Facts

During an extended fast of more than two or three days, sudden extreme weakness could be a sign of plummeting potassium levels. Your physician should test for this condition. Gradual loss of energy is normal.

The day before the fast, pick the following cues that seem most relevant for you. Memorize them, and repeat them to yourself every hour on the hour. By tomorrow, you'll be in a good mental state for fasting:

- ◆ "I am strong enough to fast for one day."
- ◆ "I enjoy food, but I can go without it for one day."
- ◆ "I am committed to developing my whole self."
- ◆ "My spirit is stronger than my cravings."
- ◆ "Inner balance will increase my health."
- ◆ "My fasting day will be a day of exercise for my mind and spirit."
- ◆ "I can achieve inner discipline."
- ◆ "I am worth taking care of."
- ◆ "I deserve to reach my full potential."
- ◆ "I will stop confusing need with want."

Spiritual Preparation

Spiritual preparation may be the most important precursor to a fast because this is the part of us so many of us tend to ignore, and the part that is likely to expand and become central in our awareness during a fast. If we aren't ready for this inner spiritual shift, we may become uncomfortable with it and break the fast in order to regain the temporary dulled consciousness that follows overindulgence just because it feels so comfortable and familiar.

To get spiritually prepared for short periods of not eating, it might help to consider your fast from a Zen perspective.

> **Fasting Wisdom**
>
> Our breath is the bridge from our body to our mind, the element which reconciles our body and mind and which makes possible oneness of body and mind. Breath is aligned to both body and mind and it alone is the tool which can bring them both together, illuminating both and bringing both peace and calm.
>
> —Thich Nhat Hanh, from *The Miracle of Mindfulness* (Beacon Press, 1987)

Let's just admit right now that you are attached to the pleasurable feeling of eating, and attachment to sensual pleasures is difficult to deny. We know, because we are, too.

Sensory impressions serve an important function. Food smells and tastes good, so you eat it in order to nourish yourself, or on the other hand, food smells bad so you don't eat it and avoid becoming sick. Your other sense impressions help to keep you safe and well, too: You hear a car screeching around a corner so you jump out of the way, you see a sharp object so you don't touch it, you touch a burning stove and you pull your hand away.

Aside from survival, our sense impressions make life more enjoyable, and that's great. But, just like too much available food can result in overindulgence, too many available sense impressions can result in sensory overindulgence. This, like overeating, throws equilibrium out of whack. You become unbalanced if you live to please your senses at the expense of the great expanse of awareness that has nothing to do with sensory impressions.

The Zen perspective is that sensory impressions, indeed everything we see around us in the world, is temporary, illusory, and soon to fade away. The only thing that is infinite and real is what is within us, far below sensory impressions. If we let our senses get in the way of perceiving this deep, inner, infinite self, we lose out on self-awareness and true happiness. We are, in a sense (pardon the pun), trading a shallow, fleeting, impermanent happiness for a deep, infinite, everlasting happiness.

Only in putting our sensory impressions in their proper place can we rebalance the whole self in order to perceive our own inner truth, which, according to Zen, is also universal truth. True self-awareness means recognizing and fully understanding that self and other, other and world, world and universe are all one and the same thing.

And that cheeseburger or piece of pie? They aren't the source of lasting happiness. They are distractions. Temptations, if you want to look at it that way. The pleasure you get from eating something lasts only a few moments, and the guilt that may follow overeating is equally distracting and perhaps even more destructive to liberated consciousness.

Fast Facts

According to a five-year study of medical care utilization statistics on 2,000 people throughout the United States who meditate on a regular basis, the rate of hospitalization was 56 percent lower for the meditating group than for the general population. The meditating group also had fewer hospital admissions in all disease categories, including 87 percent fewer hospitalizations for cardiovascular disease; 55 percent fewer for cancer; 87 percent fewer for diseases of the nervous system; and 73 percent fewer for nose, throat, and lung problems.

But the only way to see this—to really see and comprehend and understand this way of thinking for yourself in a way that can actually help you to grow—is to internalize it by thinking about it, mulling it over, making it your own. That's why we recommend meditation before a fast.

Meditation (see Chapter 5, "Fasting and Meditation") helps to calm your body, mind, and spirit as you focus on a single objective. Sit in meditation once or twice for five to fifteen minutes the day before a fast and consider how you view food, how attached you are to sensual pleasures, and how your spirit might benefit, grow, and balance itself in the temporary absence of solid food.

On the day of your fast, meditate as often as possible to fully develop your thinking about attachment to material pleasures and to help you look more closely at your own inner light. When you fulfill your spirit, you won't feel an emotionally charged, non-hunger-based, obsessive need to overfill your stomach.

What to Expect During a Short Fast

Knowing what kinds of things will happen to your body, mind, and spirit during a short fast will also help you to be prepared. Nothing will surprise you if you know what's ahead. During a short fast, you may experience any or all of the following, most of which are related to the purging of impurities from your system and adjustments in the body from fueling through food to fueling through inner resources:

- Hunger pangs
- A keen interest in what other people are eating
- Less need for sleep
- Bad breath, strong-smelling sweat
- Feeling cold, chills
- Irritability, euphoria, or quick swings from one to the other
- No hunger later in the day, which may completely reverse at the sight or smell of food
- Thirst
- Light-headedness, dizziness
- Headache
- Nausea
- Itchy skin, mild rash
- Elimination of excess mucus (from the nose, through coughing, or, for women, through vaginal discharge)

> **Fasting Wisdom**
>
> The disciples of Eastern mysticism embrace fasting with fervor. Yogis fast in the hope of achieving new mystical revelations. In Japan the disciples of Buddha fast as an exercise in asceticism. Dr. Imamura Motoo, who has supervised many fasts, wrote: 'Religious ascetics, who led their lives abstaining from food, came to the conclusion that fasting improved not only their spiritual state, but also their physical condition, and through fasting many diseases could be cured.'
> —Allan Cott, M.D., from *Fasting: The Ultimate Diet* (Hastings House, 1997)

What to Expect During a Longer Fast

During a longer fast—which, again, we don't recommend you undertake unless under direct medical supervision—you will experience the same things you experience during the first day or two of a short fast. After that, you will notice a few additional changes:

- ◆ A white, coated tongue
- ◆ Dark or cloudy urine which then clears at some point during the fast
- ◆ Relief of aches, pains, and other symptoms of previous chronic conditions
- ◆ Elated mood
- ◆ Clearing of skin conditions such as rashes and acne; healing of sores
- ◆ Bright, clear eyes
- ◆ Weight loss, especially loss of excess water weight/reduction of bloating
- ◆ Dry skin and hair
- ◆ At the end of the fast, the return of real hunger

Once you have ended a fast, one of the most pleasant aftereffects will be that food—that first bite of fruit—tastes better than food has ever tasted to you before. You'll recapture the joy of eating, a joy that has probably become dull after years of overindulgence or mindless eating.

But, unlike the kind of obsessive, addictive sensual pleasure you might get from eating food that is less than healthful, a post-fast fruit meal is practically a spiritual experience. Each bite is so delicious, but in a soul-satisfying, balanced way. The pleasure of this one event may be enough in itself to keep you on a fasting plan for the rest of your life.

Finer Fasting

For your first post-fast meal, don't eat more than one kind of fruit. An apple or two, a pear or two, a few slices of watermelon, but not a fruit salad. Your body needs simple, easily digestible foods at first and if you give it only one thing to digest, it will move back into its normal digestive process more easily.

The Importance of Mind-Body Transitions

The point of this chapter is that sudden, drastic changes are harder on our bodies, minds, and spirits, than gradual changes. Transitions are key to successful fasting, both for maximum effect and for your perception of how pleasant and easy it was to fast.

If you go from a huge meal to no food at all for two weeks to another huge meal "because you deserve it," your body will have difficulty adjusting. You'll be much hungrier, you'll feel less in control, and your body won't get the maximum benefit from the fast. In fact, you could seriously compromise your health, your metabolism, your muscle mass, your nutritional stores, your energy, even your immunity. Instead, a slow, gradual transition into and out of a fast will help your body, mind, and spirit to ready itself, heal itself, and recover itself.

Finer Fasting

Eventually, you may find that the kinds of foods you eat on the days before and after a fast are the kinds of foods you want to eat every day. Many people who make fasting a regular part of life gradually, with little effort, transition into a vegetarian lifestyle and never miss the meat that used to dominate their diets.

This theory extends to any aspect of life. Sudden, shocking change can, on occasion, be fun. A spontaneous vacation, an unexpected financial windfall, love at first sight—these precipitous events are exciting and make life more interesting.

But, when it comes to your health and the way you treat your body, moderation, routine, and gradual transitions are usually best. Once you are accustomed to fasting one day every week, for instance, your body will establish an equilibrium that works and will be best able to reap the full benefits of this healthy practice. Let your mind, body, and spirit know what to expect, and short fasts can soon become a regular, pleasurable, highly rewarding part of your life plan.

The Least You Need to Know

◆ You will be more likely to enjoy fasting success if you are fully prepared for your fast.

◆ Physical preparation for a fast includes sticking to a plant-based diet of fruits, vegetables, and complex carbohydrates the day before and after a short fast, as well as gradually reducing portion sizes before a fast and gradually increasing portion sizes after a fast.

◆ Mental preparation for a fast includes periodic positive self-talk to keep you mentally focused on your goals before a fast.

◆ Spiritual preparation for a fast includes meditation to stay centered on and to explore your commitment to balance your whole self by lessening your attachment to sensual pleasures in favor of spiritual development.

◆ During a fast, you can expect certain uncomfortable side effects related to the body's purging of impurities, such as headache, irritability, and nausea. You can also expect positive side effects such as elevated mood and loss of excess water weight.

◆ Rather than switching drastically from eating to fasting to eating, remember the importance of gradual transitions from one state to another for both mind and body.

The Biweekly 16-Hour Fast

In This Chapter

◆ What is the biweekly 16-hour fast?

◆ Your fasting schedule

◆ Your menu and shopping list

◆ Your calendar and fasting journal

◆ Inspiration to boost your resolve

The best way to start fasting is to start small, and we love the biweekly 16-hour fast for beginners. It's even great for experienced fasting practitioners who want to maintain good health with minimum effort.

In this chapter, we'll walk you step by step through the biweekly 16-hour fast so you know exactly what to do and how to do it. The 16-hour fast is a great way to start your fasting practice.

Your Biweekly 16-Hour Fast

For some people, especially beginners, even one day without any solid food is too much. A whole day of fasting is actually pretty difficult, but a 16-hour fast is, by comparison, relatively effortless. A 16-hour fast means that you simply tack on another eight hours of fasting to the eight hours of sleeping during which you are already fasting.

For example, you might fast after 3:00 P.M. until the next morning's breakfast, or you might eat dinner at 7:00 P.M. then fast until the next day's lunch. Because this fast is easy and short, you can do it twice a week instead of the weekly limit on a full-day fast.

Finer Fasting

Don't practice more than three 16-hour fasts each week. One or two 16-hour fasts each week are better for your health and will go a long way toward giving you all the benefits of regular fasting. More than three 16-hour fasts each week could compromise your nutritional stores over the long term.

Most people can handle this kind of fast, especially if they aren't feeling very well. When your body is struggling to recover from a cold, allergies, or any other minor health complaint and you feel the need to give your body some downtime, you probably won't be very hungry anyway and will welcome a break.

While we recommend juice during a longer fast, you don't need to drink anything other than water and, if you like it, herbal tea during a 16-hour fast. This will give your body the best chance at cleansing and resting during this short period. However, you can choose to make your 16-hour fast a juice fast, if you like.

You're Already Almost There

The great thing about the 16-hour fast is that with a long night of sleep, you are already almost there. All you have to do is fast through one meal, either dinner the night before or breakfast the day after. What could be easier?

You can prepare yourself mentally by reminding yourself that any healthy person can skip a single meal with no danger of any health consequences. People are less likely to criticize you for a 16-hour fast than for a longer fast, and most people probably won't even know you are fasting unless you tell them.

Because the 16-hour fast is so short, you don't have to worry quite so much about transitions. Your meals before and after should be moderate to small in size, and should be primarily plant based, but if they contain some animal products, it's not going to affect your body the way it would if you were fasting for a whole day or two.

The Best Way to Start

The best way to ease into a 16-hour fast is to have a light "last meal." If you plan to fast through dinner, let lunch be of moderate to small size and primarily based on plant foods.

When it comes time for the meal through which you are fasting, have a large glass of water with a slice of lemon (if you like it that way) or a steaming cup of herbal tea. Sit down and as you sip, think about your fast and how good it will feel and what a wonderful thing you are doing for your body, mind, and spirit.

Meditate, breathe deeply, or simply relax. Focus on letting your mind be calm and still. Enjoy yourself. Be mindful of your surroundings. Make the most of your short fast. By tomorrow, you're going to be feeling great.

Your Hour-by-Hour Schedule

Here's what to do and to expect hour by hour during your 16-hour fast. For the purpose of this schedule, we'll assume you're doing a 3 P.M.-to-morning fast, but you can easily adapt this schedule if you decide to do a 7:00 P.M.-to-noon fast instead.

3:00 P.M.: Eat your "last meal." Choose something plant based and light but nourishing and satisfying, like a hearty soup and a lightly dressed salad.

4:00 P.M. to 5:00 P.M.: You'll be digesting your meal and feeling fine, but this is the time to begin mentally preparing for the dinner hour. Keep talking to yourself and reminding yourself that you can do this fast and that it is for your own good health.

 Finer Fasting ⎯⎯⎯⎯⎯⎯⎯⎯⎯⎯⎯⎯⎯⎯⎯⎯⎯⎯⎯⎯⎯

Getting the urge to break your fast? Here are five things you can do instead of eating, to distract you:

1. Do as many sit-ups as you can.
2. Read an entire newspaper or magazine article, start to finish.
3. Write a letter to someone you haven't been in contact with for a long time.
4. Ego-surf! Search your own name on the Internet and see what comes up.
5. Pick one drawer, closet, or cabinet and take everything out, clean it, reorganize the contents, and purge clutter.

6:00 P.M.: If you normally eat dinner around this time, have a large glass of water and, in addition, if you like it, a cup of herbal tea. Focus on relaxation and stress reduction techniques such as deep breathing and visualization.

7:00 P.M.: By now you may be missing your dinner. This is the time to stay focused on something else. Take a brisk walk in the fresh air, preferably with a friend, or call a friend and chat. Catch up on your correspondence, clean something, pay some bills. If you do something productive that you've been putting off, you'll feel even better about how you spent your time.

8:00 P.M.: If this is the time when you normally turn on the TV and snack, keep the television off! If you think you can watch with a glass of water or some tea, however, then go ahead. Or, read a good book.

9:00 P.M.: As bedtime approaches, you may be feeling some hunger pangs and your stomach may be growling and gurgling. Let these feelings and sounds fill you with pride in your willpower and the strength of your accomplishment. Do something to reward yourself such as basking in a hot bubble bath or playing a game with a friend or family members.

10:00 P.M.: Finish up your daily routine, prepare yourself for whatever you need to do tomorrow, and plan your breakfast. Make sure it contains some fruit and isn't too heavy. Then, don't waste time pining for a late-night snack. Go to sleep.

11:00 P.M.: If you find getting to sleep is difficult because you are hungry or because you have too much energy, get up and have a cup of chamomile tea and read a good book or do a crossword puzzle, or try anything else that generally makes you sleepy.

> **Fast Facts**
>
> According to the National Sleep Foundation's 2001 Sleep in America poll, 63 percent of Americans reported getting fewer than the recommended eight hours of sleep each night, and 31 percent report getting fewer than seven hours of sleep on weeknights.

6:00 A.M.: Get up whenever you normally do and if possible, before you eat breakfast, take a long shower and gently scrub your skin all over to help release any impurities and waste your body has flushed through your skin during the night. Relax and enjoy. You probably won't be very hungry anyway, and your energy should be high.

7:00 A.M.: Have a slow, leisurely, portion-controlled breakfast of fresh fruit and whole grains such as oatmeal or cream of wheat.

Your 16-Hour Menu Planner

Here's what to plan for your eating and fasting before, during, and after a 16-hour fast. Adapt this menu to your own needs.

Your last meal:

> Vegetable soup
> Salad

Evening:

> 2 to 4 cups purified water
>
> 1 lemon cut in wedges (optional)
>
> 2 cups chamomile or fruit herbal tea (optional)

Your after-fast breakfast:

> 1 organic apple
>
> 1 cup oatmeal or cream of wheat

Your Shopping List

Here's what to buy at the market before you begin your 16-hour fast. Adapt this list to your own needs:

Ingredients for vegetable soup

Ingredients for salad

1 quart purified water

1 lemon

Chamomile or other herbal tea bags

1 organic apple

1 cup oatmeal or cream of wheat

Fasting Wisdom

To live a pure unselfish life, one must count nothing as one's own in the midst of abundance.
—Buddha

Your Calendar

When can you fit in your biweekly 16-hour fasts for this month? Fill in the following calendar template for the month during which you want to plan your fasts and mark them in. Or, mark them on your own calendar. Planning ahead will help you to be prepared, so you can schedule events—evenings out, dinner dates, and so on—around your fast.

MONTH:

Sunday	Monday	Tuesday	Wednesday	Thursday	Friday	Saturday

Your Fasting Journal

Whenever you fast, you may find it is very helpful to keep a fasting journal. Record how you feel and what your physical, mental, and spiritual challenges are. Keep track of the facts of the day as well as your own reactions to those facts. Over time, you'll be able to see your progress as you look back—a now experienced faster—on those journal entries from your very first fasting efforts.

You don't need to limit your fasting journal to an accounting of your day. Express your hopes, fears, wishes, and plans for the ultimate you. Or, express your creativity, which tends to blossom during a fast. Try your hand at poetry, fiction, or even drawing.

Use this journal in whatever way suits you. Photocopy the following page to use again and again for subsequent 16-hour fasts, or write in a notebook of your own.

My 16-Hour Fast Journal Entry

Date:_____

Just for You: Inspiration to Keep You Going

If your emotional hunger rears up during a 16-hour fast and tries to get you to rush to the kitchen in search of a snack, notice the feeling, see it for what it is, and gently push it out of your consciousness. If it returns, push it away again. Do your best to remain still, tranquil, and relaxed, especially during the time when you would have been eating a meal.

Remind yourself that you'll be eating again at the very next meal, but that for this time right now, eating is not necessary for your body. You are concentrating on mind and spirit right now.

The Least You Need to Know

- A 16-hour fast is the simplest form of a fast and best for beginners.
- The 16-hour fast involves fasting through only a single meal, either dinner or breakfast. This fast doesn't require juice and can be a water-only fast, although juice is an option.
- Plan your schedule, make your menu and shopping list, mark your calendar, and keep a journal during your fast.
- If you become tempted to eat during a 16-hour fast, remind yourself that your emotional hunger is probably seeking something other than food, and that you don't need to eat until the following meal.

Chapter 20

The Weekly 36-Hour Fast

In This Chapter

♦ What is the weekly 36-hour fast?

♦ Your fasting schedule

♦ Your menu and shopping list

♦ Your calendar and fasting journal

♦ Inspiration to boost your resolve

Maybe you've tried the 16-hour fast in the previous chapter and feel ready to try something a little more ambitious, or maybe you want to make a full-day fast your first fast. Either way, the 36-hour fast is also appropriate for those new to fasting. In fact, this fast is an ideal length for regular health maintenance and the slow but steady rebalancing of the body, mind, and spirit for quicker healing and correction of minor chronic complaints.

In this chapter, we'll walk you step by step through the weekly 36-hour fast so you know exactly what to do and how to do it.

Your Weekly 36-Hour Fast

One day may not seem like much, but for the person new to fasting, it can seem like an eternity without food. Yet, the more often you practice a one-day fast, the easier it gets, and the better, healthier, more energetic, and more balanced you will feel.

The one-day or 36-hour fast extends from dinner of one day to breakfast of the next. For example, if you chose Monday as your fasting day, your last pre-fast meal might be dinner on Sunday night and your first post-fast meal would be breakfast on Tuesday morning. The short length of this fast makes it ideal for practicing on a weekly basis.

Finer Fasting

Don't practice more than one 36-hour fast each week. While a 36-hour break from food is perfectly healthy for most people once a week, more than one such weekly fast could compromise your health.

Many people fast on nothing but water during a one-day fast, but we think fresh juice and vegetable broth work fine for this length of fast in addition to water and herbal tea. Fresh juice and vegetable broth give you energy and help to flush out your system while keeping you supplied with extra fluid, vitamins, minerals, and electrolytes. You'll have more energy but your body won't have to digest solid food.

The Next Step

The 36-hour fast is the logical second step once a 16-hour fast is mastered, but you needn't feel as if you must continue to work your way up to longer fasting lengths. Weekly one-day fasts, or even monthly one-day fasts, go a long way toward boosting your health and balancing your whole self. If you never fast for longer than one day, you'll still reap all the benefits of fasting without taking on any of the risks associated with longer fasts.

Because the 36-hour fast is short, you don't have to transition in and out of the fasting period for several days. Instead, a single transitional meal consisting primarily of plant-based foods before and after the fast should be sufficient for easing your body in and out of the fast.

The Best Way to Start

The best way to ease into a 36-hour fast is to have a light "last meal." If you plan to fast through dinner, let lunch be of moderate to small size and primarily based on plant foods.

When it comes time for the meal through which you are fasting, have a large glass of water with a slice of lemon (if you like it that way) or a steaming cup of herbal tea. Sit down and as you sip, think about your fast and how good it will feel and what a wonderful thing you are doing for your body, mind, and spirit.

Meditate, breathe deeply, or simply relax. Focus on letting your mind be calm and still. Enjoy yourself. Be mindful of your surroundings. Make the most of your short fast. By tomorrow, you're going to be feeling great.

Your Hour-by-Hour Schedule

Here's what to do and to expect hour by hour during your 36-hour fast. For the purpose of this schedule, we'll assume you're doing a dinner-to-breakfast fast, but you can easily adapt this schedule if you want to do a breakfast-to-dinner fast instead.

3:00 P.M.: Eat your final pre-fast meal. Choose something plant-based and light but nourishing and satisfying, such as a hearty soup and a lightly dressed salad.

4:00 P.M. to 5:00 P.M.: You'll be digesting your meal and feeling fine, but this is the time to begin mentally preparing for the following day. Get your supplies ready: juicer, produce, fasting journal, meditation area, and so on.

Finer Fasting

Getting the urge to break your fast? Here are five more things you can do instead of eating, to distract you:

1. Try a new kind of herbal tea you've never tried before.
2. Go to the park and swing or climb the jungle gym. Take a friend or a child with you if you are too embarrassed to do it alone.
3. Research a current issue on the Internet facing your local lawmakers and write a letter expressing your views as a constituent.
4. Draw a self-portrait. It doesn't have to be good. Just have fun with it.
5. Take an old toothbrush and scrub around the faucets of your bathroom sink. Did you know all that gunk was there?

6:00 P.M.: If you normally eat dinner around this time, have 8 ounces of water and, in addition, if you like it, a cup of herbal tea. Focus on relaxation and stress reduction techniques such as deep breathing and visualization.

7:00 P.M.: By now you may be missing your dinner. This is the time to stay focused on something else. Take a brisk walk in the fresh air, preferably with a friend, or call a friend and chat. Catch up on your correspondence, clean something, pay some bills. If you do something productive you've been putting off, you'll feel even better about how you spent your time.

8:00 P.M.: If this is the time when you normally turn on the TV and snack, for goodness sake, keep the television off! If you think you can watch with a glass of water or some tea, however, then go ahead. Or, read a good book. Either way, be sure to drink 8 to 16 ounces of water.

9:00 P.M.: As bedtime approaches, you may be feeling some hunger pangs and your stomach may be growling and gurgling. Let these feelings and sounds fill you with pride in your willpower and the strength of your accomplishment. Do something to reward yourself such as basking in a hot bubble bath or playing a game with a friend or family members.

> **Fast Facts**
>
> According to the National Sleep Foundation's 2001 Sleep in America poll, over one-third of Americans say they get less sleep now than they did five years ago.

10:00 P.M.: Finish up your daily routine, prepare yourself for whatever you need to do tomorrow, and plan your breakfast. Make sure it contains some fruit and isn't too heavy. Then, don't waste time pining for a late-night snack. Go to sleep.

11:00 P.M.: If you find getting to sleep is difficult because you are hungry or because you have too much energy, get up and have a cup of chamomile tea and read a good book or do a crossword puzzle, or try anything else that generally makes you sleepy.

6:00 A.M.: Get up whenever you normally do and if possible, take a long shower and gently scrub your skin all over to help release any impurities and waste your body has flushed through your skin during the night. Relax and enjoy. You probably won't be very hungry anyway, and your energy should be high.

7:00 A.M.: Have a slow, leisurely breakfast of fresh juice and herbal tea. Sip slowly and savor the liquid. As you do, think about the day ahead. Remind yourself of your resolve. Remember to use positive self-talk. Take deep, slow, relaxing breaths and get ready for the day.

8:00 A.M.: Begin your day (at whatever time it normally begins) and proceed through your day normally. Whatever you normally do, continue to do it. Just keep a big bottle or glass of purified water nearby for frequent sipping.

9:00 A.M.: Even though you probably aren't hungry, you may begin to miss your typical breakfast or midmorning snack. Have a glass of juice and 8 ounces of water.

10:00 A.M.: Stay focused on whatever work or job you are doing.

11:00 A.M. Have 8 to 16 ounces of water.

> **Finer Fasting**
>
> During a 36-hour fast, it is extremely important to stay hydrated. If you are well-hydrated, you will probably notice very few unpleasant side effects and fasting will seem relatively easy.

12:00 noon: Lunchtime for most. For you, juice time! Have another 8 ounces of fresh juice and another 8 ounces of water. Keep drinking and you'll stay full. If possible, avoid joining others who are eating. Even if you aren't hungry, the smell and sight of food will tempt you and could cause strong cravings.

1:00 P.M.: You should be feeling high on energy right now, but some of the energy may be negative. You may be feeling euphoric or irritable. Have a cup of herbal tea to help you feel calm.

2:00 P.M.: Time for another 8 to 16 ounces of water.

3:00 P.M.: Whether you are at home or at work, 3:00 is a good time to take an afternoon exercise break. Take a brisk walk, in the fresh air if possible. Afterwards, have another glass of fresh juice.

4:00 P.M.: You may be feeling as if you are on the home stretch. So close to dinner, the last mealtime of your fasting day. Spend some time in meditation to mull over how the day has gone. Breathe deeply.

5:00 P.M.: Slowly and mindfully chop some onions, celery, and garlic. Put them in a saucepan or stockpot with about 4 cups of water and put them over medium-high heat. Allow to simmer for about an hour. While the broth is cooking, have a final 8 ounces of fresh juice.

6:00 P.M.: Time to sit down and savor a big bowl of vegetable broth (strain out the vegetables and sip the liquid). Sip it with a spoon or from a mug. Enjoy the subtle taste. Follow it with another 8- to 16-ounce glass of water.

7:00 P.M.: Time to start winding down. Finish up chores around the house and get some things accomplished: file, sign permission slips, pay bills, balance your checkbook, or do those sit-ups.

8:00 P.M.: If this is the time when you normally turn on the TV and snack, keep the television off! If you think you can watch with a glass of water or some tea, however, then go ahead. Or, read a good book. Either way, be sure to drink 8 to 16 ounces of water.

9:00 P.M.: As bedtime approaches, you may be feeling some emotional hunger but chances are, your feelings of triumph will outweigh them. You made it through the first day! If you do feel tempted to blow it now, don't! Nighttime is the worst time to eat, and uncontrolled eating will destroy all the hard work you've accomplished today, not to mention how hard it will be to suddenly begin digesting again. Wait until morning, which will be here soon. Breakfast is just a few hours away.

10:00 P.M.: Finish up your daily routine, prepare yourself for whatever you need to do tomorrow, and plan what kind of fruit to have for breakfast, then go to sleep.

11:00 P.M.: If you find getting to sleep is difficult because you are too energized, get up and have a cup of chamomile tea and read a good book or do a crossword puzzle, or try anything else that generally makes you sleepy.

6:00 A.M.: Get up whenever you normally do and if possible, take another long shower and gently scrub your skin all over to help release any impurities and waste your body has flushed through your skin during the night. Relax and enjoy.

Finer Fasting

The best post-fast breakfast after a 36-hour fast consists entirely of fresh organic fruit, but avoid citrus fruits because they can be too acidic and might hurt your stomach. An apple and/or a pear are good choices.

7:00 A.M.: At last, time for your first post-fast meal. Have a slow, leisurely breakfast of fresh fruit, preferably an apple and/or a pear, and a glass of juice. Congratulate yourself on a great achievement—your first 36-hour fast! Reward yourself with something unrelated to food, but equally nourishing to the soul—call a friend or schedule some time off. And then get on with your day. It's sure to be a good one!

Your 36-Hour Menu Planner

Here's what to plan for your eating and fasting before, during, and after a 36-hour fast. Adapt this menu to your own needs.

Your last meal:

> Vegetable soup
>
> Salad

That evening:

> 8 ounces purified water
>
> 1 cup herbal tea

Your fasting day:

> 1 to 2 quarts purified water
>
> 32 ounces fresh juice
>
> 2 to 4 cups herbal tea
>
> 4 cups homemade vegetable broth

Your after-fast breakfast:

> 1 organic apple and/or pear
>
> 8 ounces of fresh juice

Your Shopping List

Here's what to buy at the market before you begin your 36-hour fast. Adapt this list to your own needs:

> Ingredients for vegetable soup
>
> Ingredients for salad
>
> 2 to 3 quarts purified water

herbal tea bags for 2 to 5 cups herbal tea (optional)

40 ounces fresh juice

1 onion

2 stalks celery

1 clove garlic

4 cups purified water for vegetable broth

1 organic apple and/or organic pear

Your Calendar

When can you fit in your weekly 36-hour fasts for this month? Fill in the following calendar template for the month during which you want to plan your fasts and mark them in. Or, mark them on your own calendar. Planning ahead will help you to be prepared, so you can schedule events—evenings out, dinner dates, and so on—around your fast.

MONTH:

Sunday	Monday	Tuesday	Wednesday	Thursday	Friday	Saturday

Your Fasting Journal

Whenever you fast, you may find it is very helpful to keep a fasting journal. Record how you feel and what your physical, mental, and spiritual challenges are. Keep track of the facts of the day as well as your own reactions to those facts. Over time, you'll be able to see your progress as you look back—a now experienced faster—on those journal entries from your very first fasting efforts.

> **Finer Fasting**
>
> According to the ancient Chinese art of placement, called feng shui, the center of your home is representative of your personal health. Look at what is in the center of your home. Make sure it stays clean and clutter free, and hang a crystal or place a symbol of good health such as a flourishing houseplant or even a picture of a beautiful flower. According to feng shui, these actions will help your health to thrive.

Use this journal in whatever way suits you. Photocopy the following pages to use again and again for subsequent 36-hour fasts, or write in a notebook of your own.

My 36-Hour Fast Journal Entry

Date of the First Evening:_____

_____

_____

_____

_____

_____

_____

_____

_____

_____

_____

_____

_____

_____

_____

_____

_____

_____

_____

_____

_____

_____

_____

_____

_____

_____

_____

_____

_____

Date of the Fast Day:_____

_____

_____

_____

_____

_____

_____

_____

_____

_____

_____

_____

_____

_____

_____

_____

_____

_____

_____

_____

_____

_____

_____

_____

_____

_____

_____

Just for You: Inspiration to Keep You Going

One day. It's only one day. It's only one day, you may chant to yourself as you head inexorably toward the refrigerator. Stop! Step back. Take a deep breath.

It's easy to become so immersed in the strange feeling of not eating that you think a day will last forever, but almost everyone in good health can go for a full day without food without any negative physical consequences.

Remember this, as you struggle to get through the evening before and the first part of your fasting day: Your cravings are largely emotional. You are attached to food. Your physical side is craving sensory pleasure, but your mind and spirit need equal time. Let them breathe. Give them room to grow. Give them some time to shine. The refrigerator will still be there, full of food, tomorrow. Today, you have better things to do.

The Least You Need to Know

- A 36-hour fast is a short but highly effective fast perfect for beginners and experienced fasters alike.
- We prefer a juice fast to a water fast for fasts lasting 36 hours. Juice makes the fast easier on your body and helps give you energy without activating your digestion.
- Plan your schedule, make your menu and shopping list, mark your calendar, and keep a journal during your fast.
- If you become tempted to eat during a 36-hour fast, remind yourself that you have made a commitment to give your mind and spirit equal time, and that your cravings for sensory pleasures can wait.

Chapter 21

The Lunar Two-Day Fast

In This Chapter

- What is the lunar two-day fast?
- Your fasting schedule
- Your menu and shopping list
- Your calendar and fasting journal
- Inspiration to boost your resolve

The lunar two-day fast is a more difficult fast for people who have become very comfortable with the weekly 36-hour fast that we discussed in the previous chapter. Fasting for two days still may not seem like much if you consider that some people fast for 40 days. But for the beginner, it's more than enough, and for the faster with some experience, it's just about right.

In this chapter, we'll walk you step by step through the lunar two-day fast so you know exactly what to do and how to do it.

Your Lunar Two-Day Fast

Fasting for two days is still safe for anyone who is healthy, and on the second day, you probably won't be hungry, but you will be more likely to experience some of the typical side effects of fasting, such as bad breath and the discharge of impurities from the skin, the nose and mouth, and elsewhere.

Finer Fasting _____

Don't practice more than one two-day fast each month. A two-day fast is more strenuous for your entire self, even as it balances and cleanses you. All that purging puts a temporary strain on the body as impurities have to make their way back out of the system.

You'll also notice a more extreme balancing effect, which means that your emotional and spiritual sides will probably come out more strongly. This could result in emotional highs and lows as well as spiritual insights and even some intense spiritual experiences—all more common the longer you fast, but perfectly likely to happen during a two-day fast.

We recommend that you drink juice during a lunar fast rather than only water. This will give your body the energy it needs to make it through two days without solid food. Fruit juice raises your blood sugar very fast, while vegetable juices do not. You may want to avoid citrus, because of its high acid content.

Fasting by the Moon

As its name implies, the lunar two-day fast should coincide with either the full or the new moon. If you fast during the full moon, fast the day of the full moon and the day after, as it begins to wane. If you fast during the new moon, fast the day before the new moon, and the day of the new moon.

There are benefits to both methods. Fasting with the full moon is good for repairing recent indulgences, because the full moon waning symbolizes the natural cycle that follows fullness. However, don't fast the day after eating or drinking too much. Give yourself a couple of days of healthy eating first. Because the lunar two-day fast is longer than a single half day or full day, transitional eating is more important. The entire day before and after a fast should consist of nothing but small portions of plant foods. This will give your body the best chance to ease into and out of the fast with the least stress and will keep your digestive system and metabolism working and transitioning smoothly.

Fasting with the new moon is perfect for health maintenance when you have been taking good care of yourself. Some people like to adjust their natural rhythms and energies in accordance with the lunar cycle. As the moon is in its least lit aspect, you can mirror that aspect with downtime, meditation, relaxation, extra sleep, and fasting. As the moon begins to wax again, you can gradually re-energize your life by increasing your activity level and eating more healthy food.

The Best Way to Start

The best way to ease into a two-day fast is to spend the entire day before eating small portions of plant foods only. Skip the meat and dairy, just for the pre-fast day.

When it comes time for the fast day, spend as much time as possible meditating on the moon, the stars, the universe, and your place in the scheme of things. Keeping your mind focused on higher (literally!) things will help you to stay strong in your resolve and will give you the best chance of fasting success.

Your Hour-by-Hour Schedule

Here's what to do and to expect hour by hour during your two-day fast. For the purpose of this schedule, we'll assume you're doing a new moon fast, which we prefer because we feel that the new moon energy and symbolism is most conducive to fasting. However, you can adjust this schedule to coincide with the full moon. In this case, the day before your fast would be the day before the full moon. The fast itself would be the day of the full moon and the day after.

Two days before the new moon: Eat small portions of plant foods only, with no meat or dairy products. Stick to vegetables, fruit, whole grains, nuts, and beans. Make dinner your lightest meal.

The day before the new moon: Begin your fast.

6:00 A.M.: Get up whenever you normally do and if possible, take a long shower as you contemplate the days ahead. You should feel good after your day of light eating yesterday.

7:00 A.M.: Have a slow, leisurely breakfast of fresh juice and herbal tea. Sip slowly and savor the liquid. As you do, contemplate the moon. Think about how it influences the tides and think about how much of your body is made of water. Remind yourself of your resolve and remember to use positive self-talk. Take deep, slow, relaxing breaths and get ready for the day.

8:00 A.M.: Begin your day (at whatever time it normally begins) and proceed through your day normally. Whatever you normally do, continue to do it. Just keep a big bottle or glass of purified water nearby for frequent sipping. Every time you take a sip, think about how the moon moves the water of the earth in a rhythm.

Finer Fasting

Water is crucial during the lunar fast, particularly due to the influence of the moon on the water of the earth. During a two-day fast, it is extremely important both symbolically and for your health to stay hydrated. If you are well hydrated, you will probably notice very few unpleasant side effects and fasting will seem relatively easy. Don't forget to drink at least 32 ounces of juice each day in addition to lots of water—at least 2 quarts of water daily during a lunar fast.

9:00 A.M.: Even though you probably aren't physically hungry, you may begin to miss your typical breakfast or midmorning snack. Have a glass of juice and 8 ounces of water.

10:00 A.M.: Stay focused on whatever work or job you are doing.

11:00 A.M. Have 8 to 16 ounces of water.

12:00 noon: Lunchtime for most. For you, juice time! Have another 8 ounces of fresh juice and another 8 ounces of water. Keep drinking and you'll stay full. If possible, avoid joining others who are eating. Even if you aren't hungry, the smell and sight of food will tempt you and could cause strong cravings.

1:00 P.M.: You should be feeling high on energy right now, but some of the energy may be negative. You may be feeling euphoric or irritable. Have a cup of herbal tea to help you feel calm.

2:00 P.M.: Time for another 8 to 16 ounces of water.

3:00 P.M.: Whether you are at home or at work, 3:00 is a good time to take an afternoon exercise break. Take a brisk walk, in the fresh air if possible. Afterwards, have another glass of fresh juice.

4:00 P.M.: So close to dinner, and to the close of your first day of fasting. You can do it! Stay strong and keep drinking water. This is a good time to meditate and consider how your first day has gone. Breathe deeply and stay focused on the moon. Meditate on the sky. Even though it is still daylight and you can't see the moon, think about how you know it is up there.

5:00 P.M.: Slowly and mindfully chop some onions, celery, and garlic. Put them in a saucepan or stockpot with about 4 cups of water and put them over medium-high heat. Allow to simmer for about an hour. While the broth is cooking, have a final 8 ounces of fresh juice.

6:00 P.M.: Time to sit down and savor a big bowl of vegetable broth (strain the vegetables from the broth and sip the broth). Enjoy the subtle taste. Follow it with another 8- to 16- ounce glass of water.

7:00 P.M.: Time to start winding down. Finish up chores around the house and get some things accomplished: file, sign permission slips, pay bills, balance your checkbook, or do those sit-ups.

8:00 P.M.: If this is the time when you normally turn on the TV and snack, for goodness sake, keep the television off! If you think you can watch with a glass of water or some tea, however, then go ahead. Or, read a good book. Either way, be sure to drink 8 to 16 ounces of water.

9:00 P.M.: As bedtime approaches, you may be feeling some hunger pangs and your stomach may be growling and gurgling. Let these feelings and sounds fill you with pride in your willpower and the strength of your accomplishment. Do something to reward yourself such as soaking in a warm bubble bath or playing a game with a friend or family members.

10:00 P.M.: Finish up your daily routine, prepare yourself for whatever you need to do tomorrow, and plan your breakfast. Set out the fruit you intend to use to make juice, if you're juicing your own. Fruit at room temperature juices better than cold fruit. Then, don't waste time pining for a late-night snack. Go to sleep.

11:00 P.M.: If you find getting to sleep is difficult because you are hungry or because you have too much energy, get up and have a cup of chamomile tea and read a good book or do a crossword puzzle, or try anything else that generally makes you sleepy.

> **Fast Facts**
>
> According to a recent Harris Poll, 6 million Americans (and millions more elsewhere) logged onto the Internet last year seeking advice about sleep. Sleep is now one of the top 10 health concerns on the Web.

6:00 A.M.: Get up whenever you normally do and if possible, take a long shower and gently scrub your skin all over to help release any impurities and waste your body has flushed through your skin during the night. Relax and enjoy. You probably won't be very hungry anyway, and your energy level should be high.

7:00 A.M.: Have a slow, leisurely breakfast of fresh juice and herbal tea. Sip slowly and savor the liquid. As you do, think about the day ahead and how well you did yesterday. Remind yourself again of your resolve. Remember to use positive self-talk. Take deep, slow, relaxing breaths and get ready for the day as you contemplate the day's new moon.

8:00 A.M.: Begin your day (at whatever time it normally begins) and proceed through your day normally. Whatever you normally do, continue to do it. Just keep a big bottle or glass of purified water nearby for frequent sipping.

9:00 A.M.: Even though you probably aren't physically hungry, you may begin to miss your typical breakfast or midmorning snack. Have a glass of juice and 8 ounces of water.

10:00 A.M.: Stay focused on whatever work or job you are doing.

11:00 A.M. Have 8 to 16 ounces of water.

12:00 noon: Lunchtime for most. For you, juice time! Have another 8 ounces of fresh juice and another 8 ounces of water. Keep drinking and you'll stay full. If possible, avoid joining others who are eating. Even if you aren't hungry, the smell and sight of food will tempt you and could cause strong cravings.

1:00 P.M.: You should be feeling energetic, not hungry, but possibly as if you are in a slightly altered state of consciousness. That second-day fasting feeling means your whole self, previously so physically focused, is coming into balance, and it may feel strange. Concentrate on your emotional and spiritual sides this afternoon. Have a cup of herbal tea to help you feel calm.

2:00 P.M.: Time for another 8 to 16 ounces of water.

3:00 P.M.: Whether you are at home or at work, 3:00 is a good time to take an afternoon exercise break. Take a brisk walk, in the fresh air if possible, and concentrate on the sky and thoughts of the new moon. Afterwards, have another glass of fresh juice.

4:00 P.M.: You may be feeling as if you are on the home stretch. So close to dinner, the last mealtime of your fasting day. Spend some time in meditation to mull over how the day has gone. Breathe deeply. Feel the new moon energy.

5:00 P.M.: Slowly and mindfully chop some onions, celery, and garlic. Put them in a saucepan or stockpot with about 4 cups of water and put them over medium-high heat. Allow to simmer for about an hour. While the broth is cooking, have a final 8 ounces of fresh juice.

6:00 P.M.: Time to sit down and savor a big bowl of vegetable broth. Sip it with a spoon or from a mug. Enjoy the subtle taste. Follow it with another 8- to 16-ounce glass of water.

7:00 P.M.: Time to start winding down. Finish up chores around the house and get some things accomplished: file, sign permission slips, pay bills, balance your checkbook, or do those sit-ups.

8:00 P.M.: If this is the time when you normally turn on the TV and snack, for goodness sake, keep the television off! If you think you can watch with a glass of water or some tea, however, then go ahead. Or, read a good book. Either way, be sure to drink 8 to 16 ounces of water.

9:00 P.M.: As bedtime approaches, you may be feeling some emotional hunger but chances are, your feelings of triumph will outweigh them. You made it through the second day! If you do feel tempted to blow it now, don't! Nighttime is the worst time to eat, and uncontrolled eating will destroy all the hard work you've accomplished today, not to mention how hard it will be to suddenly begin digesting again. Wait until morning, which will be here soon. Breakfast is just a few hours away.

Finer Fasting

Celebrate the new moon on its day by spending extra time in relaxation and meditation. Go to bed one hour earlier tonight.

10:00 P.M.: Finish up your daily routine, prepare yourself for whatever you need to do tomorrow, and plan what kind of fruit to have for breakfast, then go to sleep.

11:00 P.M.: If you find getting to sleep is difficult because you are too energized, get up and have a cup of chamomile tea and read a good book or do a crossword puzzle, or try anything else that generally makes you sleepy.

6:00 A.M.: Get up whenever you normally do and if possible, take another long shower and gently scrub your skin all over to help release any impurities and waste your body has flushed through your skin during the night. Relax and enjoy.

7:00 A.M.: At last, time for your first post-fast meal. Have a slow, leisurely breakfast of fresh fruit, preferably an apple or a pear, and a glass of juice. Eat very slowly and don't eat too much.

Finer Fasting

The best post-fast breakfast after a lunar two-day fast consists entirely of fresh organic fruit, but avoid citrus fruits, as they can be too acidic and might hurt your stomach. An apple and/or a pear are good choices.

Chew your food well to give your digestive system a chance to reactivate. Congratulate yourself on a great achievement—your first two-day fast! Resolve to do it again next month. And then, get on with your day. It's sure to be a good one!

Your Two-Day Menu Planner

Here's what to plan for your eating and fasting before, during, and after a lunar two-day fast. Adapt this menu to your own needs.

Your last meal:

>   Vegetable soup
>   Salad

During each day of the fast:

>   2 quarts purified water (minimum)
>   2 to 4 cups herbal tea
>   32 ounces fresh juice
>   4 cups homemade vegetable broth

Your after-fast breakfast:

>   1 organic apple or pear

Your Shopping List

Here's what to buy at the market before you begin your two-day fast. Adapt this list to your own needs:

Ingredients for vegetable soup

Ingredients for salad

4 quarts purified water (minimum)

herbal tea bags for 4 to 8 cups herbal tea (optional)

64 ounces fresh juice

2 onions

4 stalks celery

2 cloves garlic

8 cups purified water for vegetable broth

1 organic apple and/or organic pear

Your Calendar

When can you fit in your monthly lunar two-day fast for this month? Fill in the following calendar template for the month during which you want to plan your fasts and mark them in. Or, mark them on your own calendar. Planning ahead will help you to be prepared, so you can schedule events—evenings out, dinner dates, and so on—around your fast.

MONTH:

Sunday	Monday	Tuesday	Wednesday	Thursday	Friday	Saturday

Your Fasting Journal

Whenever you fast, you may find it is very helpful to keep a fasting journal. Record how you feel and what your physical, mental, and spiritual challenges are. Keep track of the facts of the day as well as your own reactions to those facts. Over time, you'll be able to see your progress as you look back—a now experienced faster—on those journal entries from your very first fasting efforts.

Finer Fasting

Try this moon meditation during your lunar fast: Relax in the evening facing a window and look at the sky. If you can see the moon, all the better. If you can't, just look at the night sky. Breathe deeply, then slowly think or say out loud to yourself:

The earth and the moon move through space together. The water of the earth moves with the rhythm of the moon. I move with the rhythm of the moon. The moon, the earth, the water of the earth, and I are one.

Repeat several times, until you feel very relaxed and focused.

Use the following journal in whatever way suits you. Photocopy the pages to use again and again for subsequent two-day fasts, or write in a notebook of your own.

My Lunar Two-Day Fast Journal Entry

Date of the First Fast Day:_____

Date of the Second Fast Day:_____

_____

_____

_____

_____

_____

_____

_____

_____

_____

_____

_____

_____

_____

_____

_____

_____

_____

_____

_____

_____

_____

_____

_____

_____

_____

_____

Just for You: Inspiration to Keep You Going

The great thing about a lunar fast is that you have a ready-made symbol up there in the sky to hold your focus and keep you inspired. Lunar fasts are great for those who want to fast for spiritual development. Concentrating on and contemplating the moon will help your spiritual side to flourish. We are part of the living earth and are influenced by the moon—by admiring it, using its reflected light, and noticing how it waxes and wanes. Perhaps we are even influenced by its gravitational pull ourselves.

Here are five fascinating facts about the moon to think about during your lunar two-day fast:

1. The moon and the earth are probably the same age: about 4.6 billion years old. However, some sources claim that the moon is much older than the earth.

2. The moon keeps one side permanently turned toward earth.

3. There is no water on the moon, but the gravitational forces between the earth and the moon affect the level of the ocean tides on earth, causing the earth to have two high tides per day.

4. The moon is the only extraterrestrial body humans have visited. The first moon landing was made by Apollo 11, on July 20, 1969. Neil Armstrong and Buzz Aldrin were the first human beings to walk on an extraterrestrial body.

5. All kinds of strange information about the moon—from speculation that the moon is hollow to supposed photographs of huge artificially constructed objects—is reported on the Internet.

Let the moon be your point of reference as you contemplate how you are part of an immense and intricate set of living and energy-rich interactions between different elements of our solar system. You are just one small person, yet every element on the earth, on the moon, in the universe is part of that great whole. The universe wouldn't be the same without you. Let yourself see this, feel it, live it.

The Least You Need to Know

◆ A two-day fast is still relatively short but should be practiced only by people who are experienced with a one-day fast. We prefer a juice fast to a water fast for fasts lasting two days.

◆ Fasting in conjunction with the rhythm of the moon provides a focus, symbolism, and a sense of unity with the natural world.

◆ Plan your schedule, make your menu and shopping list, mark your calendar, and keep a journal during your fast.

◆ If you find a two-day fast difficult, keep your perspective focused on your spiritual growth and your part in the grand natural scheme of the universe.

Chapter 22

The Seasonal Three-Day Fast

In This Chapter

- ◆ What is the seasonal three-day fast?
- ◆ Guidelines for fasting with the seasons
- ◆ Your menu and shopping list
- ◆ Your seasonal timetable and fasting journal
- ◆ Inspiration to boost your resolve

The seasonal three-day fast is more of an event that requires more preparation and occurs, as the name suggests, only once each season. For a three-day fast, we recommend a modified fast. Many wouldn't even call it a fast. For our seasonal three-day fast, we have set out an eating plan. You might even call the foods we recommend for each season "fast foods"!

When you fast by eating—a seeming contradiction—you are still limiting the strain of normal digestion on your body. Even if your only food is one you really love, you'll be surprised how little you'll find yourself eating. Your first meal of fruit or porridge or soup might be hearty, and that's fine. But after a full day of nothing but one type of food, your body won't crave large amounts. You'll find your portions become smaller. Modified fasting is, in this way, self-regulating, helping the body to resist overeating in a natural way.

In this chapter, we'll walk you step by step through the seasonal three-day fast so you know exactly what to do and how to do it.

Your Seasonal Three-Day Fast

Each season has a certain character and energy. Winter is a time for hibernation, contemplation, re-evaluation, and the casting off of old ways. Spring is a time of renewal and rebirth. Summer is a time for growth and fruition. Fall is a time for maturation and reflection.

All the world religions contain messages for the spirit about the preservation of, sacred nature of, or responsibility to the natural world. Earth-based religions in particular, such as neopaganism, put a special emphasis on the cycles, seasons, and evolution of the natural world.

Finer Fasting

We don't recommend fasting without solid food for three days without medical supervision, and we strongly advise you to talk to your health care provider before undertaking a fast that doesn't involve solid food for longer than two days.

Eating according to the season is a way to celebrate and welcome each new period of the year. Because a seasonal fast consists of eating only one or two different foods during the three-day period, it is an excellent way to help simplify life, become more humble, focus on something other than eating, and live in harmony with nature.

The seasonal three-day fast also gives the body a chance to synchronize with the natural cycle of the earth and the way the world around you is changing in the region you live.

Your Winter Solstice Fast

In the winter, the whole earth slows down with the cold. Deciduous trees stand bare, twigs hardened. The ground freezes and at last, snow blankets the earth. If you live in a warmer climate, you may continue to enjoy temperate weather in the winter, but you will also notice changes in the natural world around you. Colder evenings, variations in plant life, changes and migrations in local wildlife all characterize winter, no matter what the temperature. During the winter solstice, the sun is at its lowest point in the sky. This is the day with the least daylight all year long, also called the shortest day of the year.

For a winter solstice fast, begin your fast the day before the winter solstice and fast for three days so that the day after the solstice is your last day. During the winter, warmth is important and we think the season calls for a porridge fast. Choose your favorite type of porridge: oatmeal, cream of wheat, or rice porridge. You can eat the porridge with a little honey, if desired, and a small amount of low-fat milk or soy milk. Eat nothing but this porridge for three days. Then, gradually reintroduce other foods into your diet. The porridge fast is warming, comforting, and induces a contemplative and calm feeling perfect for reflecting on and appreciating the season. Plus, the winter solstice happens just before the holiday season, so it can help stem the temptation to overindulge during the holidays.

Your Vernal Equinox Fast

Spring is a time for renewal and rebirth. The earth begins to warm, and pale green buds emerge on the trees. Flowers begin to bloom, leaves unfurl, and hibernating animals slowly reemerge. We like a raw vegetable fast for spring. Eat nothing but baby lettuces, new peas, pencil-thin asparagus, wild dandelion leaves and whatever fresh, preferably locally grown vegetables you can find emerging and freshly plucked for spring. Organic, of course, is also best if you can get it.

Beginning the day before the vernal equinox and ending the day after, eat nothing but these tiny, new vegetables, uncooked. Contemplate on letting their life energy fill you with a new sense of your own rebirth. It's time to cast off the heavy slowness of winter and generate a new, fresh spring energy. Let your vernal equinox fast make it easy.

Your Summer Solstice Fast

In summer, growth is at its peak. The world is burgeoning with flowers and vegetables and big, full, succulent fruits warmed in the sun. Summer is the time to fully develop the evolving you. By now the changes generated in spring should be coming into fruition just like the vegetables and fruits growing in gardens and on the trees. The warmth of the sun generates energy from within and although the heat can wear us down, we can also feel in harmony with the summer world and filled with the intensity of solar energy. During the summer solstice, the sun is at its highest point in the sky, and this is the longest day of the year, or the day with the most daylight.

For summer, we love a fresh fruit fast. Beginning the day before the summer solstice and extending to the day after, eat nothing but fresh, preferably locally grown and organic fruits: peaches, apricots, nectarines, plums, blueberries, blackberries, raspberries, or melons. Fruit in season is always the least expensive, so have fun looking for bargains. Whatever is available and fresh will work.

> **Fasting Wisdom**
>
> The flower is the poetry of reproduction. It is an example of the eternal seductiveness of life.
>
> —Jean Giraudoux, from *The Enchanted*, 1933

Your Autumnal Equinox Fast

Autumn is a time of winding down. Even the leaves age in color, turning a mature gold, orange, or red. Fruits and vegetables drop from the vines and are harvested. Now is the time to enjoy the fruits of your labor, bask in the full maturation of your year's growth, and prepare for the cold by stocking up. Fill your pantry for winter and fill your soul, too, to get you through the long months of cold ahead.

For thousands of years, humans have grown and harvested grapes to make wine, and eaten the apples that are at their ripest in the fall. For fall, we like a grape fast or an apple fast. Choose whichever of these fruits you enjoy best—both of which mature in the fall—and beginning the day before the autumnal equinox and ending the day after, eat nothing but grapes (red grapes are better than green grapes because they contain additional phytonutrients) and grape juice or apples and apple juice.

Eating only fruit and juice is actually easier than a juice fast because of the fiber in the whole fruit, which helps to keep you feeling full. You'll soon get tired of the taste and you'll eat less and less of the food over the course of three days, but your body will continue to derive energy and bulk from what you do eat, and the fruit and juice together have a similar cleansing effect as opposed to juice alone. Fruit is relatively easy to digest compared to many vegetables and especially animal products such as meat and dairy foods, so your body remains unstrained, nicely full, and pleasantly clean feeling.

The Best Way to Start

Because you will be eating food during your seasonal three-day fast, you don't need to worry about a long transition before and after, but you should nevertheless stick to plant foods the day before and the day after the fast to prepare your body for reduced consumption. The best way to ease into a three-day fast is to spend the entire day before eating small portions of plant foods only. Skip the meat and dairy, just for the pre-fast and post-fast days.

Finer Fasting

During any season when the weather is pleasant, take a long walk outside in the fresh air on fasting days. What better way to tune into the season than to be out in nature noticing how the world around you is changing?

When it comes time for the fast day, eat as much of the porridge, fruits, or vegetables you've decided on for your fast, and drink lots of water and herbal tea. Drink juice made only from the fruits or vegetables of your fast, or in the case of a winter fast (the porridge fast), drink apple juice or white grape juice only. Apple and white grape juice are easier on your digestion than red grape juice, and because you are focusing on porridge for your winter fast, you want to keep things simple for your body.

Spend as much time as possible meditating on the season you are entering. Think about what the season will mean for you, in practice and symbolically. Let your spirit surface during the time of seasonal transition and let the event be a ceremony, a ritual, something that becomes an important part of your existence.

Your Seasonal Fast Guidelines

For the seasonal fast, we won't provide an hour-by-hour schedule, but keep a few things in mind. First of all, when you are involved in a modified fast, remember to eat only the fruit, vegetable, or grain set forth in your fast, but eat as much of it as you want. Don't get obsessive about it, but if you are hungry, eat. When you no longer want any more grapes or porridge or vegetables, you will learn to recognize the meaning: You aren't hungry anymore!

Again, the good thing about modified fasts is that when you eat only one kind of food, you tire of it *very* quickly and your body won't feel like overeating. If you were doing a cookie-only fast, maybe you would overeat because of the refined carbohydrates, but natural, healthy foods such as fruit and oatmeal help your body to regain its natural sense of appetite and help you to recognize signals of real hunger and true satisfaction of appetite.

Also, because fasting involves an element of discipline and self-restraint, it makes sense to keep portion sizes reasonable; however, your real discipline will be to stick to the single food and not venture back into regular meals before your fast is over. Because modified fasting is self-regulating, overeating will probably be much less of an issue and a challenge than the temptation to stray to other foods. Don't get caught in that trap: "Well, it's oatmeal. I can have some toast, too. And then I might as well have some eggs. Oh heck, pass the doughnuts!"

Here are a few additional things to remember:

♦ Drink at least 2 quarts of water each day. Water is crucial during the seasonal fast. Even though your food will contain water, you won't be eating as much as you normally do and you'll need to compensate with extra water to keep your body well lubricated and running smoothly, and to help flush out impurities. So drink up!

♦ Drink as much herbal tea as you wish.

♦ For fruit fasts, also drink at least 32 ounces of your chosen fruit in juice form, such as apple juice for an apple fast, grape juice for a grape fast, any summer fruit juice for a summer fruit fast such as melon juice or peach juice. Having your own juicer becomes very handy for a summer juice fast because you can have great fun experimenting with different kinds of juices.

♦ For a vegetable fast, also drink at least 32 ounces of spring vegetables, juiced. Again, a juicer is very handy.

◆ Spend lots of time during a seasonal fast meditating and contemplating the meaning and changes associated with the season.

During the winter when the weather is chilly, you may find it difficult to get outside very often. Instead, try gentle, contemplative indoor exercises such as yoga. During the summer when the weather is nice, you can focus more on brisk walks outside on fasting days.

Your Seasonal Three-Day Menu Planner

Here's what to plan for your eating and fasting before, during, and after a seasonal three-day fast. Adapt these menus to your own needs. Don't feel limited by the seasonal suggestions we give you. Regions vary dramatically in terms of what produce is locally available during what season. Tailor your seasonal fasts to the rhythms and growth seasons in your own region.

Your Winter Menu and Shopping List

Each day, be sure to consume …

◆ At least 2 quarts of water.

◆ As much herbal tea as you want (cinnamon is especially good for winter).

◆ As much oatmeal, cream of wheat, or rice porridge as you want (but stick to one kind) with honey and small amounts of low-fat milk or soy milk if desired.

◆ At least 32 ounces of apple or white grape juice (easier on the digestion during a porridge fast than red grape juice, which is best reserved for fruit-centered fasts).

Shopping list:

6 quarts of purified water (minimum)

Tea bags for 6 to 12 cups of herbal tea (optional)

Enough oatmeal, cream of wheat, or rice porridge to make 18 to 20 bowls

Low-fat milk, soy milk, honey (if desired)

96 ounces apple or white grape juice (minimum)

Your Spring Menu and Shopping List

Each day, be sure to consume …

◆ At least 2 quarts of water.

◆ As much herbal tea as you want.

◆ As many raw spring vegetables as you want, such as baby peas, baby lettuce, thin green beans, thin asparagus, and whatever else is fresh at the market or in your garden (dress the vegetables with a small amount of extra virgin olive oil and vinegar, if desired).

◆ At least 32 ounces of vegetable juice.

Shopping list:

6 quarts of water (minimum)

Tea bags for 6 to 12 cups of herbal tea (optional)

About 8 to 10 pounds of raw spring vegetables, preferably locally grown and organic

Extra virgin olive oil, vinegar (optional)

96 ounces vegetable juice (minimum)

Your Summer Menu and Shopping List

Each day, be sure to consume …

◆ At least 2 quarts of water.

◆ As much herbal tea as you want.

◆ As much fresh, raw summer fruit as you want, such as peaches, nectarines, apricots, plums, and berries of all kinds (whatever is ripe and fresh at the market is good). If you live in an agricultural area, visit a local orchard or berry farm. Most will let you pick your own. Take some friends and make it a ritual event.

◆ At least 32 ounces of fresh juice made from summer fruits.

Shopping list:

6 quarts of water (minimum)

Tea bags for 6 to 12 cups of herbal tea (optional)

About 8 to 10 pounds of fresh raw summer fruit, preferably locally grown and organic

96 ounces fresh juice (minimum)

Your Fall Menu and Shopping List

Each day, be sure to consume …

◆ At least 2 quarts of water.

◆ As much herbal tea as you want.

◆ As many grapes or apples (choose one or the other, not both) as you want. Remember to choose red over green grapes when possible during a fruit fast, since red grapes contain more cancer-fighting phytochemicals than green grapes.

◆ At least 32 ounces of apple juice for an apple fast or red or white grape juice for a grape fast.

Shopping list:

6 quarts of water (minimum)

Tea bags for 6 to 12 cups of herbal tea (optional)

About 8 to 10 pounds of fresh red grapes or apples, preferably locally grown and organic

96 ounces fresh grape or apple juice (minimum)

> **Fasting Wisdom**
>
> Knowledge of the self is the mother of all knowledge. So it is incumbent on me to know my self, to know it completely, to know its minutiae, its characteristics, its subtleties, and its very atoms.
>
> —Kahlil Gibran, "The Philosophy of Logic"

A Timetable for the Turning of the Seasons

The seasons turn on or about the 21st of December, March, June, and September. Wondering when to fast in the next few years?

For the year 2002:

◆ Winter solstice: December 22

◆ Vernal equinox: March 20

◆ Summer solstice: June 21

◆ Autumnal equinox: September 23

For the year 2003:

◆ Winter solstice: December 22

◆ Vernal equinox: March 20

◆ Summer solstice: June 21

◆ Autumnal equinox: September 23

> **Fast Facts**
>
> For a fun and informative calendar of celestial events through the year 2004, check out www.seasky.org/astronomy/sky1e.html.

For the year 2004:

◆ Winter solstice: December 21

◆ Vernal equinox: March 20

◆ Summer solstice: June 20

◆ Autumnal equinox: September 22

Your Fasting Journal

Whenever you fast, you may find it is very helpful to keep a fasting journal. Record how you feel and what your physical, mental, and spiritual challenges are. Keep track of the facts of the day as well as your own reactions to those facts, your meditations, feelings, and creative efforts. Over time, you'll be able to see your progress as you look back—a now experienced faster—on those journal entries from your very first fasting efforts.

Use the following journal in whatever way suits you. Photocopy the pages to use again and again for subsequent three-day fasts, or write in a notebook of your own.

My Seasonal Three-Day Fast Journal Entry

Date of the First Fast Day:_____

_____

_____

_____

_____

_____

_____

_____

_____

_____

_____

_____

_____

_____

_____

_____

_____

_____

_____

_____

_____

_____

_____

_____

_____

_____

_____

_____

_____

Date of the Second Fast Day:_____

Date of the Third Fast Day:_____

_____

_____

_____

_____

_____

_____

_____

_____

_____

_____

_____

_____

_____

_____

_____

_____

_____

_____

_____

_____

_____

_____

_____

_____

_____

_____

Just for You: Inspiration to Keep You Going

Thinking, living, eating, and noticing the changes of the seasons will help you to feel a special spiritual link to the natural world that may have been missing from your life before. Even when you aren't fasting, we recommend eating according to what is locally available during any given season. However, fasting with the seasons by limiting your food intake to a few seasonal items helps to cleanse your body and give your digestive system less to do while it allows your spirit room to expand and synchronize with the earth's cycles.

Meditate on each season. In your fasting journal, write down how you feel about that season's symbolism, place in the natural cycle, and meaning for you. Talk about it with friends. You are a part of the natural world, just as the changing trees and blooming flowers and sleeping animals are a part of the natural world. Long ago, your ancestors had no choice but to live according to the season, and while survival was much less sure in earlier times, the human participation in the natural world was a given. Now that we can eat whatever we want shipped from anywhere and go anywhere in our climate-controlled vehicles, from one climate-controlled enclosure to another, it becomes so easy to forget ….

You can begin to reclaim that link to the natural world and reclaim your place in it by being mindful of the change of seasons, particularly when you practice a seasonal fast. You are part of the earth. The earth is part of you. Let your spirit help you find your place again. All you need to do is remember, and then you can take your place in the cycle of life.

The Least You Need to Know

- A seasonal three-day fast in our book is a modified fast during which you eat only a specific type of food appropriate for the season and spend time reflecting on the change of season and what it means for you, your life cycle, and your personal development.

- We suggest fasting on porridge for a winter fast, raw spring vegetables for a spring fast, ripe summer fruits for a summer fast, and either grapes or apples for an autumn fast.

- Plan your schedule, make your menu and shopping list, mark your calendar, and keep a journal during your fast.

- Let the symbolism and cycles of nature be your inspiration during a seasonal fast.

Chapter 23

Not-Quite-Fasting Variations

In This Chapter

- ◆ How to fast without actually fasting
- ◆ A new kind of fast food
- ◆ Fast foods tailored to different needs
- ◆ Fasting from spending, media, talking, and other addictions

As you may have discerned from the previous chapter, we use the term "fasting" pretty loosely. For us, fasting is a form of self-restraint, an exercise in willpower, and a way to increase the body's self-cleansing efforts. For us, fasting can mean drinking juice or water instead of solid food, and sometimes, it can mean eating limited amounts or types of foods.

In this chapter, we'll expand a little more on our alternative view of fasting, giving you lots of ideas to incorporate modified fasts into your life.

Fasting: An Alternative View

Let's talk fast food. No, not the grease-laden kind you pick up at the local drive-thru, but the kind of food you eat while fasting.

We can think of lots of reasons to fast without actually fasting. Limiting the amount and/or type of food you eat for short periods of time can help the body to cleanse itself in much the same way a total water or juice fast encourages cleansing, especially if the foods you limit yourself to are uncooked plant foods and/or fiber-rich foods.

Fast Facts
It is not length of life but depth of life. —Ralph Waldo Emerson, U.S. essayist and poet (1803–82)

Modified fasts do more than help the body cleanse and rest the digestive system, however. A modified fast can also be an exercise in self-discipline, an experiment in doing without, a suppression of sensory pleasures in favor of spiritual ones, the foundation of a vision quest, a response or protest to a world event, an attempt to find the rhythm of the natural world, or part of a spiritual practice.

In other words, a modified fast can serve any of the same purposes a regular fast accomplishes, but because you are eating, you can sustain a modified fast for a day or two longer than a complete fast.

People practice modified fasts for many reasons, but the best reason we can think of is because your inner guide tells you it's time. The more self-aware you become, the more mindfully you live your life, the more you'll be able to hear your own body when it asks something of you.

After too much food, too much fat, too much sugar, too much alcohol, too much caffeine, too little sleep, too little relaxation, too little conversation, we begin to wear down. When you hit a low cycle, you can learn to recognize it and respond appropriately. This is the best time for a modified fast. Stick to something very simple—fresh fruit, raw foods, or rice, for example—until your energy returns.

In this chapter, we'll go through some different types of modified fasts and explain how to do them. We don't recommend doing any modified fast for more than three days, however, unless we specifically say so when discussing that fast. For instance, we think you can live carefully on raw foods for longer than three days, but not solely on, say, potatoes.

Maybe you can think of a modified fast you'd like to do that isn't listed here. As long as the food is a plant food that is low in fat and high in fiber, you should be fine, but use your common sense.

And don't skip the end of this chapter where we talk about fasts from other things besides food. Taking a break from spending money, media exposure, even talking, are all alternative forms of fasting that can offer immense spiritual benefits.

Finer Fasting

It's easy to get in the habit of eating things that aren't very good for you. As a kind of fasting variation on eating one single healthful food for a day or two, try going for a full day or two *without* a type of food that isn't so healthful. For example, see if you can go for a full day without sugar, or chocolate, or fried foods, or diet soda. One day can expand to two, three, a week, a month ....

The Fresh Fruit Fast

The fresh fruit fast is a lot like the summer solstice fast described in the last chapter. Eating nothing but fresh fruit offers your body nutritional variety, energy, and fiber, but because fruit is easy to digest and passes quickly through the body, it also has an excellent cleansing effect.

A fresh fruit fast is perfect for whenever you think you are coming down with a cold, are feeling low on energy, or simply feel a little blue. Fruit has a revitalizing effect and the phytonutrients in fruit may boost immunity to help you fight off that cold.

For a fresh fruit fast, drink plenty of water, herbal tea if desired, and fresh fruit juice. Also eat as much fresh, preferably locally produced and organic fresh fruit as you like. You can practice a fresh fruit fast for up to five days if you eat lots of different kinds of fruits. If you stick to a single fruit, such as grapes or apples (as in the autumnal equinox fast in the last chapter), don't fast for more than three days.

Always come into and out of a fresh fruit fast by eating only plant foods, mostly uncooked for a day or two before and after the fast. The longer your fresh fruit fast, the longer your transitions should be.

The Bread Fast

For a bread fast, don't think you can do well with a couple of loaves of soft white bread slices from the supermarket. For a truly healthy bread fast, stick to dark, high-fiber, whole-grain bread or sprouted-grain bread. Making your own bread is best, but many bakeries, especially those in natural foods stores, make excellent bread, too. If you like, you can drizzle your bread with a small amount of extra virgin olive oil, which is highly digestible in small amounts and good for you, too. However, don't exceed two tablespoons of olive oil in a day, and please avoid butter, cream cheese, or jam during a bread fast. Butter and cream cheese are dairy products that are high in fat and difficult to digest. Jam is full of sugar, which can also be hard to digest. The point is to rest your system with the bread alone.

For a bread fast, drink at least two quarts of water each day and as much herbal tea as you want. Also eat as much bread as you want, but take small bites, chew them well, and don't eat too much at one time. You can nibble all day long, though.

Finer Fasting

If you love homemade bread, consider investing in a bread machine, which whips up homemade loaves with hardly any effort. Keep it next to your juicer!

A bread fast is especially good if you have indigestion, heartburn, or other digestive problems and need something mild in your stomach. It nourishes you, the fiber keeps your system moving along, but it doesn't stress or overtax your digestive system. You can fast on bread for up to three days.

Always come into and out of a bread fast by eating very mild, gentle foods such as cooked cereals and soups before and after the fast.

The Rice Fast

Like a bread fast, a rice fast is good in the case of digestive problems. Brown rice is best because it contains whole grain and fiber. Rice is very easy on digestion and doesn't cause gas. Avoid processed rice products, rice "dinners" with added ingredients, and instant rice. You can, however, add fresh herbs to your rice, and if you don't have digestive problems, you can add very finely diced tomatoes, carrots, and/or celery. Try mixing your rice with a little applesauce and cinnamon in the morning.

For a rice fast, drink at least two quarts of water each day and as much herbal tea as you want. Also eat as much rice as you want, but take small bites, chew them well, and don't eat more than one cup of cooked rice in one sitting so as not to overstrain your digestion, as well as to practice self-restraint. Wait an hour between cups of rice. You can fast on rice for up to three days. And like any other modified fast, after a very short time, you'll soon tire of rice and won't feel compelled to overeat it.

Always come into and out of a rice fast by eating very mild, gentle foods such as cooked cereals and soups before and after the fast.

The Oatmeal Fast

An oatmeal fast is essentially the same as the winter solstice fast discussed in the last chapter. This fast is good for cold weather, for comfort during low periods, to nurture the spirit, and also to soothe digestion.

During an oatmeal fast, drink at least two quarts of water each day and as much herbal tea as you want. You can also drink apple juice if you like. You can add small amounts of low-fat milk or soy milk and honey to your oatmeal if you like it that way, or a little applesauce and cinnamon. Eat as much oatmeal as you want, but eat it slowly and don't eat more than one cup of oatmeal in one sitting. Wait an hour between cups. You can fast on oatmeal for up to three days.

Always come into and out of an oatmeal fast by eating very mild, gentle foods like soups and fruit before and after the fast.

> **Fast Facts**
>
> Steel-cut oats are less processed than "old-fashioned" oats, which are in turn less processed than instant oats. The less processed the oats you use to make your oatmeal, the better and more nutritious the oatmeal will be.

The Potato Fast

A potato fast is also good for an acid stomach, or in the case of high stress, nervousness, and anxiety. Boil or bake white, yellow, or sweet potatoes and eat the insides mixed with fresh herbs and diced steamed vegetables drizzled with a little olive oil, but don't exceed 2 tablespoons of olive oil in a day. For your potato fast, skip the butter, sour cream, or other animal products, please.

During a potato fast, drink at least two quarts of water each day, as much herbal tea as you want, and 32 ounces of apple juice. Eat up to six potatoes in a day, slowly savoring them. Don't eat any green areas or "eyes" on the potato skins. You can fast on potatoes for up to three days—five if you add vegetables and apple juice.

The Raw Foods Fast

Some people eat primarily raw foods all the time, and you can live on raw foods if you get enough protein, vitamins, and minerals. Raw foods are high in fiber, enzymes, and some say, life energy. They are extremely refreshing and revitalizing, although they are more difficult to tolerate as the sole dietary element when the weather is cold.

But for a few days, or up to a week, a raw food fast is an excellent way to rejuvenate, cleanse, and restore the body, mind, and spirit. Eat any uncooked plant food, emphasizing fresh greens such as lettuces, spinach, and other greens, and brightly colored fresh vegetables and fruits such as carrots, tomatoes, red peppers, broccoli, peaches,

> **Fasting Wisdom**
>
> Once you're ready to eat your fresh fruits and vegetables, handle them properly. The most important thing you can do is wash all fruits and vegetables in clean drinking water before eating. This applies to all fruits and vegetables, even if you don't eat the rind or skin (such as melons and oranges). Remember to wash produce just before you use it, not when you put it away.
>
> —aboutproduce.com

plums, watermelon, and cantaloupe, plus cabbage, cauliflower, onions, garlic, radishes, celery, and mushrooms.

The possible variety of a raw food diet is practically endless. Fresh peas, beans, soybeans, and raw nuts and seeds provide protein, and the broader your variety, the more nutrients you'll receive. We love the raw food diet for its great nutrition, high fiber, and disease prevention. We think you'll love it, too, for how great it makes you feel.

You can stay on a raw food diet indefinitely, as long as you drink at least two quarts of water every day and get sufficient nutrients. See a registered dietitian if you are unsure about getting the nutrients you need from a raw food diet, to help you work out a solid plan.

Nonfood Fasts

The last category of fasts we want to tell you about are fasts that have nothing at all to do with eating and drinking. But, this category does have everything to do with overindulgence.

Food isn't the only thing we have a surfeit of in our society. It is easy to become addicted to any of the pleasurable excesses of modern life. And, just as with food, our minds, bodies, and spirits (not to mention our wallets) can derive great relief, tranquility, and balance by "fasting" from these excesses.

Money, noise, communication, media—television, the Internet, even radio—not to mention substances like tobacco, alcohol, and other drugs, can easily become addictive. Sometimes the only way to stop the drastic downward spiral of excessive consumption is to quite literally stop for a short period of time. That is what the nonfood fast is all about.

Fasting from Spending Money

We are an intensely consumerist culture and our economy is heavily based on where we spend or money. Big business makes it a business to try to influence us to spend our money on their products rather than someone else's.

And spending money is fun—even addictive. How many people do you know who shop incessantly, especially when they are feeling depressed or dispirited? What about all of you who shop obsessively, then return everything you bought in a fit of guilt? We think of this as a sort of spending bulimia, and certainly a disorder. The shopping is often out of control, the returning an act of contrition and shame.

Yes, we understand you have bills to pay, necessary expenses. But why not try going for one full day—a day when no bills are due—without spending one single cent?

Once you've tried a day of fasting from spending money, you may feel so freed by the power of saying no to consumerism that you decide to fast from spending for longer periods.

Longer no-spending fasts really only work if they themselves are modified. That means you can pay bills that have to be paid and address any emergencies, but other than that, you do everything within your creative power to not spend any money on anything that isn't necessary. This can be fun and challenging. And you may be amazed at how much money you are able to save when you stop nickel-and-diming yourself to death.

> **Fast Facts**
>
> Ninety-three percent of school-age girls in the United States say one of their favorite activities is "store hopping."

Fasting from Media

Media is such an integral part of modern life that it's hard to imagine going without it, even for one day. Instead of starting with an all-out media ban, limit your media fasts to one thing. The first thing that comes to mind? Try a television fast.

Horror of horrors—how would you get through a day without the TV? If you aren't sure how, then chances are good that you could really use a television fast.

Television is incredibly addictive. It numbs the mind, makes us apathetic, and is a major factor in mindless overeating. You know how it goes: grab a bag of snacks, plop down in front of the tube, and boom—four hours later, you find yourself stuffed and snoozing.

Fasting from television can help you to regain your ability to think quickly, not to mention think for yourself. Try going for one day at first. A TV-free week every month could change your life.

You might also consider an Internet fast. Internet surfing, e-mailing, instant messaging, chat rooms, discussion boards, and more surfing eat up countless hours of the day for many people in the twenty-first century. And what about music? Music (and commercials!) from the radio or even all-day music coming from five-disk CD changers in our homes and cars, may not be an obvious addiction. Music can be quite nice, but it can also easily become a source of constant loud noise all day long and a substitute for quiet inner contemplation.

> **Fast Facts**
>
> According to several different studies on television viewing in America, by the age of 65, the average American will have spent nine years of life watching television, and most children spend more time watching TV than they spend in school. What's more, 66 percent of Americans eat dinner while watching television.

Fasting from Talking

Talking. Communication. That's good, right? Sometimes, if the talking is mutual. But what about those people who get addicted to talking—incessant, constant talking without any obvious ability to listen? You don't have to be a monk in a monastery to take a vow of silence. Some people like to fast from talking for a full day every now and then, and some people even go for longer periods—a week, a month, a year.

When you stop talking, you will certainly be occasionally inconvenienced. You might also find yourself incredibly enlightened. When you can't talk, you are forced to listen, and learning how to really listen can completely overhaul and renew your relationships with others.

Talking is more than face-to-face communication. A fast from talking could include no more telephones, cell phones, even e-mail and instant messages. You can read them, you can listen, but you can't send. Let yourself be quiet for awhile. You might be amazed at what you hear.

Fasting Away Your Bad Habits

Any bad habit, obsession, addiction, or overindulgence you have is a good thing to try fasting from, whether it is a chemical substance such as alcohol or tobacco; a pleasurable activity that occupies too much of your time and thoughts, such as eating chocolate or having sex; or a behavior such as being sarcastic or insulting people.

Examine your life. Examine who you are. What are the things you would like to change about yourself? What are the things on which you put a little too much emphasis? What preoccupies you, obsesses you? This is the place to look for the "fasts" that can turn your life around.

Loving the Integrated You

Here's the bottom line: Fasting is a way to make yourself into a better version of yourself—a more evolved, actualized, realized human being. Throughout this book, we've spent a lot of time emphasizing that you are more than just a body, just a mind, or just a spirit. You are even more than your body plus your mind plus your spirit.

There is nobody more interesting than you. There is nobody more worth spending time on than you. There is nobody who deserves whole-self health more than you. There is nobody whose spirit is bigger, better, or more beautiful than yours is.

Fasting is simply a method of balancing your whole self so that the fully integrated, multi-faceted you can be what it was intended to be: happy, healthy, wise. Let fasting lead you back to the path of moderation in a world of excess. Let it reintroduce you to yourself. Let it help you to see exactly what you need to be who you really are. Fasting is powerful, but it is only a tool. The real power lies within you.

We know you can reclaim it—your inner power, your true self, the you of your dreams. We hope you enjoy every moment of the journey toward yourself, and we most sincerely wish you a long life ahead filled with healthy eating, healthy fasting, vibrant energy, and a most joyful integration.

The Least You Need to Know

◆ Modified fasts mean eating only a few limited things, such as fresh fruit, raw foods, bread, oatmeal, rice, or potatoes.

◆ You can fast from anything in which you tend to overindulge. Common overindulgences of the modern world that make good activities for fasts include spending money, watching TV, and talking.

◆ You can subvert many bad habits by temporarily fasting from them.

◆ You are an amazing, complex, interesting person who deserves to be happy, to take care of yourself, and to thrive, fully integrated, by living a well-balanced, healthy life.

Appendix

How to Feast Beyond Your Fast

Most of the time, you won't be fasting, and what you eat when you aren't fasting is extremely influential on your physical as well as your emotional and spiritual well-being.

The week's worth of plant-based meal plans for breakfasts, lunches, dinners, and snacks that we present here work in any combination to equal healthy eating. Use this menu plan whenever you need some fresh ideas or just want some guidance about what to eat for your next meal. Or, try this menu for a whole week and bask in good health.

After the week of meal plans, we've also included suggestions for additions to your own homemade vegetable soup or vegetable salad. Because soup and salad make the perfect, light, plant-based, high fiber, low-fat meal for just before and just after a day of fasting, you may find yourself enjoying these foods again and again.

Happy eating!

One Week of Vegetarian Eating for Good Health

Each day of meals and snacks equals 1,800 calories for the day with from 25 to 50 grams of fiber, less than 30 percent of calories from fat, and between 60 and 80 grams of protein.

DAY ONE:

Breakfast

>   Whole-wheat toast with peanut butter
>   Whole naval orange
>   Vanilla yogurt

Snack

>   Hummus on rye crackers

Lunch

>   Boiled black beans
>   Herbed carrots
>   Whole-wheat tortillas
>   Vegetable juice

Snack

>   Roasted soy nuts

Dinner

>   Spinach quiche
>   Summer squash
>   Tropical fruit salad
>   Sour cherries with whipped cream

DAY TWO:

Breakfast

> Raisin bran cereal with soy or low-fat milk
>
> Banana slices

Snack

> Whole-wheat bagel
>
> Cream cheese

Lunch

> Mixed bean soup with vegetables
>
> Falafel sandwich on whole-wheat pita

Snack

> Fresh whole apple
>
> Whole-wheat crackers with cheddar cheese

Dinner

> Walnut pesto on spinach rotelle noodles
>
> Fresh tomato slices

DAY THREE:

Breakfast

> One-egg vegetable fritata
>
> Bran muffin
>
> Orange juice

Snack

> Rice cake with peanut butter

Lunch

> Tabbouleh salad with feta cheese
>
> Watermelon wedges
>
> Light-rye roll

Snack

> Strawberry banana smoothie

Dinner

> Stir-fried garden vegetables with tofu
>
> Brown rice
>
> Fresh citrus salad

DAY FOUR:

Breakfast

> Hot oatmeal with dried fruit
>
> Fresh blueberries

Snack

> Whole-wheat toast with one ounce low-fat cheese

Lunch

> Lentil curry
>
> Baked acorn squash with raisins
>
> Dilled cucumbers with yogurt
>
> Whole-wheat bread
>
> Pears with cinnamon

Snack

> Carrot muffin
>
> Brewed tea

Dinner

> Mixed grain pilaf
>
> Tofu loaf
>
> Steamed broccoli
>
> Apricot halves

DAY FIVE:

Breakfast

> Tofu scramble
>
> Cubed potatoes with onions and peppers
>
> Whole-wheat toast
>
> Fresh strawberries

Snack

> Whole-wheat raisin scones

Lunch

> Italian vegetable soup
>
> Cornbread
>
> Melon slice

Snack

> Toasted sunflower kernels

Dinner

> Red beans and rice
>
> Cauliflower with cheese sauce
>
> Asparagus spears

DAY SIX:

Breakfast

> Fresh citrus fruit salad
> Cottage cheese with granola topping

Snack

> Fresh apple

Lunch

> Three-bean salad with grated carrots
> Whole-wheat roll

Snack

> Cranberry juice and roasted peanuts

Dinner

> Soybean and eggplant casserole
> Grape leaves with feta cheese
> French bread with herbed dipping oil

DAY SEVEN:

Breakfast

> Breakfast burrito with scrambled eggs and fresh salsa
> Refried beans
> Whole-wheat tortillas

Snack

> Grapefruit half

Lunch

> Grated vegetables with sesame oil dressing
> Whole-wheat roll

Snack

> Chilled buttermilk or low-fat yogurt

Dinner

> Tempeh barbecue with crushed tomatoes
> Tossed salad with poppyseed dressing

Vegetable Soup Suggestions

We love homemade vegetable soup. It tastes fresh and is filled with nutritious, immune-boosting vegetables and herbs. It's also very comforting, especially when the weather gets chilly. If possible, use organic produce and/or locally grown produce.

When making your own vegetable soup, use whatever vegetables are in season. Zucchini is more available in the summer and early fall, while butternut and acorn squash are more available in the fall and winter, for example. Make up your own recipe that you can change every time you cook it. Think of it as a lesson in nutritious creativity!

Here are some of the ingredients you might consider using in your vegetable soup:

> Onion
> Garlic
> Red bell pepper
> Portabella or shiitake mushrooms

Celery (including leaves)

Carrots

Spinach and/or other greens like collard, mustard, or kale

Zucchini

Butternut or acorn squash

Green chilies

Brown rice, barley, or oatmeal for thickening

Lentils, split peas, red beans, white beans, or other legumes

Potatoes—red, white, yellow, or sweet

Red pepper flakes for spice

Fresh ginger

Fresh chopped herbs, such as cilantro, parsley, Italian parsley, basil, oregano, tarragon, rosemary, or dill

Vegetable Salad Suggestions

Vegetable salad is another of our favorites. It's fresh, crisp, cooling, and revitalizing; the ultimate raw-food meal, full of fiber, protein, vitamins, minerals, and phytonutrients. It's also very refreshing when the weather gets warm. If possible, use organic produce and/or locally grown produce.

Like vegetable soup, vegetable salad is infinitely adaptable. Use your imagination and whatever is in season. Here are a few suggestions for what to put in your vegetable salad (and don't forget to top your salad with a dressing low in fat or based on extra-virgin olive oil, lightly drizzled):

Mixed greens (many supermarkets sell packaged or bulk organic mixed salad greens of all kinds)

Carrots

Celery

Red, white, or yellow onion

Red, yellow, orange, or green bell pepper

Green or red cabbage

Broccoli

Cauliflower

Cooked white beans (optional—not a raw food)

Garlic

Other nonraw but yummy flavoring ideas to use in small amounts (most are high in sodium):

Olives

Capers

Pickles

Marinated artichoke hearts

Baby corn

Pimentos

Fasting Resources

Looking for more information? You might find this list of websites and books interesting. Enjoy browsing. (We did!)

Interesting Websites Related to Fasting and Holistic Health

www.aapn.org/vegstats.html
Earth Save's sobering set of statistics about world hunger, the depletion of natural resources, and vegetarianism, a part of the Asian Animal Protection Network site.

www.alt-med-ed.com/mainforum
Alternatives for Healthy Living Chat Forums on subjects from fasting to weight control.

www.arthritis.org
The Arthritis Foundation's site offers help, resources, and support to people who suffer from either rheumatoid arthritis or osteoarthritis.

www.beliefnet.com
The source for spirituality. This excellent, comprehensive site provides detailed information about many different religions, religious support, international prayer chains, guided meditations, inspiration, events, opportunities for charity, relevant news, columns, prayer circles, questions and answers about religion, and a completely nondiscriminatory focus on religion as a

whole, whether Buddhism, evangelical Christianity, Judaism, Islam, Taoism, Paganism, or Scientology. A must for your bookmark page!

www.cdc.gov
Centers for Disease Control in Atlanta, Georgia. One of the definitive resources for health information in the United States.

www.cdc.gov/nccdphp/index.htm.
The National Center for Chronic Disease Prevention and Health Promotion, a subdivision of the Centers for Disease Control, is devoted to preventing chronic disease through the dissemination of health information to the public.

www.counterbalance.org
The Counter Balance Foundation, a nonprofit organization, is dedicated to the dissemination of scientific knowledge and the integration of the "seemingly opposing worlds of science and religion." It has a huge glossary of scientific terms and explanations of scientific theories made accessible for the general public. Containing videos, interviews, articles, and discussion forums on everything from bioethics to Steven Hawking's views of God, this is another site you could spend hours browsing if you like this sort of thing. We find it fascinating!

www.drweil.com
Health guru Dr. Andrew Weil's comprehensive and user-friendly website that offers a holistic but realistic view of health trends and sound health advice. Dr. Weil puts fads into perspective, and his approach to good health is infused with common sense and rationality while still being holistic. You can also sign up for his free online newsletter through this website.

www.eatveg.com
True, this website sells juicers and water distillers. However, it is also a comprehensive source of information about famous people who are vegetarians, some of whom also practice fasting, and lots of other interesting vegetarian and vegan information. Hours of good reading for practicing or prospective vegetarians and vegans.

www.geocities.com/socialism_2000/pages/genetic.html
This is one of many sites devoted to the pro-genetically modified foods perspective.

www.goodsleep.com
An interesting interactive website about sleep problems with quizzes and good advice about how to get more and higher quality sleep.

www.healthy.net/asp/templates/article.asp?PageType=article&ID=1996
The Nutritional Program for Fasting site, which is part of Health World Online's network of health-related websites, contains a long and interesting excerpt about fasting from Dr. Elson M. Haas's book entitled *Staying Healthy with Nutrition*.

www.living-foods.com
This site describes itself as "the largest community on the Internet dedicated to educating the world about the power of living and raw foods."

www.lupus.org
This Lupus Foundation of America website contains definitions, symptoms, treatments, and other lupus information as well as support resources for people who have lupus.

www.menshealthnetwork.org/library/mhn_links.htm
A comprehensive website covering hundreds of health-related issues relevant to men.

www.naturesstandard.com/bioaccum.html
This interesting page, which is actually part of a website that sells water purification systems, explains the process through which chemicals, from helpful vitamins to toxic pesticides, gradually accumulate within the body.

news.bbc.co.uk/hi/english/special_report/1999/02/99/food_under_the_microscope/ newsid_280000/280868.stm
BBC News Q&A on genetically modified food. A good, relatively unbiased informational site.

www.niddk.nih.gov/health/nutrit/pubs/statobes.htm
The Statistics Related to Overweight and Obesity is part of the National Institute of Diabetes and Digestive and Kidney Diseases, which is itself a division of the National Institutes of Health. This site is full of helpful information and tools for calculating your body mas index (BMI) and determining whether you might be overweight or obese.

www.nimh.nih.gov/publicat/eatingdisorder.cfm.
This National Institutes of Mental Health Eating Disorder Fact Sheet informational page describes the three most common eating disorders, including symptoms and typical treatments.

www.nmss.org
The National Multiple Sclerosis Society website is user-friendly and full of information about multiple sclerosis: resources, support, and detailed discussion of symptoms and treatment.

www.purefood.org
This site of the Organic Consumers Association, an anti-genetically modified foods group, is one of many sites devoted to the anti-GM foods perspective.

www.simpleliving.net/default.asp
A comprehensive site on how to live more simply. Inspirational.

www.vivavegie.org/vv101
"101 Reasons Why I'm a Vegetarian" essay. A comprehensive and convincing list of reasons to go vegetarian. Inspirational (and disturbing!) for vegetarians and those trying to make the switch.

Books Related to Fasting or Holistic Health

Airola, Paavo O. *How to Keep Slim, Healthy, and Young with Juice Fasting*. Sherwood, OR.: Health Plus Publishers, 1971.

Bragg, Paul C., N.D., Ph.D., and Patricia Bragg, N.D., Ph.D. *The Miracle of Fasting: Proven Throughout History for Physical, Mental, and Spiritual Rejuvenation*, 48th edition. Santa Barbara, CA.: Health Science, 1999.

Budilovsky, Joan, and Eve Adamson. *The Complete Idiot's Guide to Yoga*, 2nd edition. Indianapolis, IN.: Alpha Books, 2001.

____. *The Complete Idiot's Guide to Meditation*. Indianapolis, IN.: Alpha Books, 1999.

____. *The Complete Idiot's Guide to Massage*. Indianapolis, IN.: Alpha Books, 1998.

Cameron, Julia. *The Artist's Way*. New York: Jeremy P. Tarcher/Putnam, 1992.

Carter, Karen Rauch. *Move Your Stuff, Change Your Life*. New York: Fireside, 2000.

Chopra, Deepak, M.D. *Ageless Body, Timeless Mind*. New York: Harmony Books, 1993.

____. *Creating Health*, Revised Edition. Boston: Houghton Mifflin Company, 1991.

____. *Perfect Health*. New York: Harmony Books, 1991.

Cott, Allan, M.D. *Fasting: The Ultimate Diet*. Norwalk, CT.: Hastings House, 1997.

Davich, Victor N. *The Best Guide to Meditation*. Los Angeles, CA.: Renaissance Books, 1998.

Dominguez, Joe, and Vicki Robin. *Your Money or Your Life*, new ed. New York: Penguin Books, 1992.

Elgin, Duane. *Voluntary Simplicity*, rev. ed. New York: Quill, 1993.

Epstein, Mark, M.D. *Going to Pieces Without Falling Apart*. New York: Broadway Books, 1998.

Farhi, Donna. *The Breathing Book*. New York: Henry Holt & Company, 1996.

Fuhrman, Joel, M.D. *Fasting and Eating for Health: A Medical Doctor's Program for Conquering Disease*. New York: St. Martin's Griffin, 1995.

Goleman, Daniel, Ph.D., and Joel Gurin (eds.). *Mind-Body Medicine*. Yonkers, N.Y.: Consumer Reports Books, 1993.

Hanh, Thich Nhat. *Peace Is Every Step*. New York: Bantam Books, 1992.

Harrar, Sari, and Sara Altshul O'Donnell. *Woman's Book of Healing Herbs*. Emmaus, PA.: Rodale Press, Inc., 1999.

Hellmiss, Margot, and Norbert Kriegisch, M.D. *Healthy Fasting*. New York: Sterling Publishing Co., Inc., 1999.

Kabat-Zinn, Jon, Ph.D. *Wherever You Go, There You Are*. New York: Hyperion, 1994.

_____. *Full Catastrophe Living: Using the Wisdom of Your Body and Mind to Face Stress, Pain, and Illness*. New York: Delta, 1990.

Klauser, Henriette Anne. *Write It Down, Make It Happen*. New York: Scribner, 2000.

LeVert, Suzanne, and Gary McClain, Ph.D. *The Complete Idiot's Guide to Breaking Bad Habits*. Indianapolis, IN.: Alpha Books, 1998.

Linn, Denise. *Quest: A Guide for Creating Your Own Vision Quest*. New York: Ballantine Books, 1997.

Meyerowitz, Steve. *Juice Fasting and Detoxification*. Great Barrington, MA.: Sproutman Publications, 1999.

Monro, Robin, R. Nagaranthna, and H. R. Nagendra. *Yoga for Common Ailments*. New York: Simon & Schuster, Inc., 1990.

St. James, Elaine. *The Simplicity Reader*. New York: Smithmark, 1998.

Schiffman, Erich. *Yoga: The Spirit and Practice of Moving into Stillness*. New York: Pocket Books, 1996.

Takoma, Geo, and Eve Adamson. *The Complete Idiot's Guide to Power Yoga.* Indianapolis, IN: Alpha Books, 1999.

Weil, Andrew, M.D. *Eight Weeks to Optimum Health.* New York: Alfred A. Knopf, 1998.

_____. *Spontaneous Healing.* New York: Alfred A. Knopf, 1995.

Whitaker, Julian, M.D., and Carol Colman. *Shed 10 Years in 10 Weeks.* New York: Simon & Schuster, 1997.

Fasting Glossary

agni   The Sanskrit word for gastric fire, the source of elimination energy in the body that burns energy and fuels the body.

aura   The electromagnetic energy given off by the body. Auras change colors according to the quality or state of the body's energy at any given time, and it can reveal through dark or light spots physical problems and strengths.

autoimmune diseases   Diseases that cause the immune system to attack the body, or self, rather than foreign substances such as viruses and bacteria. Autoimmune diseases are not contagious and may be heritable. Some common autoimmune diseases are multiple sclerosis, rheumatoid arthritis, systemic lupus, Type 1 diabetes, psoriasis, and inflammatory bowel disease.

ayurveda   An ancient system of health designed to maximize longevity and optimize the body and mind through purification practices such as fasting, eating pure foods, and internal and external cleansing techniques.

body mass index (BMI)   A number many health professionals use to determine whether someone is overweight or obese. BMI is calculated by dividing weight in kilograms by height in meters squared, or multiplying weight by 705 then dividing the answer by height in inches twice. A BMI between 18.5 and 25 is generally considered a healthy weight. A BMI between 25 and 29.9 is considered overweight, and a BMI of 30 or more is considered obese.

chi   *See* life-force energy.

fasting   The practice of abstaining from food for the purpose of improving physical, mental, and/or spiritual health. There are many different kinds of fasts but the most common kinds are water fasts and juice fasts.

fruitarians   People who eat only raw plant foods because of their belief that cooking destroys valuable enzymes in plant foods and/or the plant's life-force energy.

holistic health care   One of many names—alternative medicine and complementary medicine are others—for a form of health care that considers the whole person, including lifestyle, habits, attitudes, and personality, in the diagnosis and treatment of disease.

homeopathy   A holistic health therapy developed by Samuel Hahnemann (1755–1843), a German physician who discovered that quinine induced the symptoms of malaria in a healthy person. Hahnemann developed the theory of homeopathy, based on the idea that "like cures like." Homeopathic remedies are highly diluted substances that treat the symptoms they would induce in someone without those symptoms. Homeopathy is considered a very safe therapy because the remedies are so diluted.

immune system   A function of the tonsils and adenoids, lymph nodes, thymus gland, bone marrow, white blood cells, spleen, appendix, and intestinal lymphoid tissue. These organs and tissues destroy foreign or harmful substances in the body such as viruses, bacteria, and tumor cells. Emotional, mental, and spiritual states also contribute to immune system effectiveness.

Kirlian photography   A photographic technique developed by Russian scientist Semyon Kirlian in 1939. This technique reveals a colored halo around photographed subjects (from people to leaves). While skeptics claim the process doesn't actually reveal auras, many believe the process is good evidence for the existence of electromagnetic fields around all living things.

Koran (Q'ran)   The sacred book of the Islamic people and according to the Islamic religion, contains the revelations Allah or God bestowed upon the prophet Mohammed. The Koran is also the final authority on Islamic beliefs.

Lent   The 40 weekdays or eight weeks between Ash Wednesday and Easter Sunday traditionally observed by Christians as a time of penance. Fasting is a common practice during Lent.

life-force energy   Also called chi, ki, and prana, life-force energy is the immeasurable energy that animates the body and all other life on earth. It also flows in pathways over the earth, through inanimate objects, and throughout the universe. Acupuncture, Chinese medicine, and Shiatsu massage all focus on freeing and balancing this energy in the human body. The ancient Chinese art of placement, called feng shui, frees and balances chi in the environment. In Hinduism and yoga, this energy is taken into the body through breathing exercises.

prana   *See* life-force energy.

Ramadan   The ninth month in the Islamic calendar and a time during which Muslims fast from sunrise to sunset.

vegans   People who don't eat any animal products at all, including milk, yogurt, and cheese. Their diets are entirely plant based.

vegetarians   People who don't eat animal flesh, including poultry and fish. Some eat eggs and some eat dairy products such as milk, yogurt, and cheese. Some vegetarians stay away from cheese containing rennet, which is made from the stomach lining of cows.

whole foods   Foods that are in the same form as when they were originally harvested. Fresh, unprocessed fruits, vegetables, and whole grains are whole foods. Grain products with parts of the grain removed are not whole foods.

yoga   An ancient method of health preservation with the goal of ultimate mind-body synthesis. It has many branches, and its practices include certain physical exercises or poses, specific breath control techniques, and meditation.

Yom Kippur   Also called the Day of Atonement, this holiday is considered the most important of all the Jewish holidays. Yom Kippur occurs on the tenth day of the seventh month of the Jewish calendar (usually sometime in mid to late September) and is a day for asking for forgiveness.

Index

Q-R

A Little Knowledge Goes a Long Way ...

Check Out These Best-Selling COMPLETE IDIOT'S GUIDES®

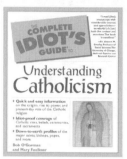

Understanding Catholicism

0-02-863639-2
$16.95

Learning Spanish on Your Own
SECOND EDITION

0-02-862743-1
$16.95

The Bible

0-02-862728-8
$16.95

Feng Shui

0-02-863105-6
$18.95

Playing the Guitar
SECOND EDITION

0-02-864244-9
$21.95 w/CD-ROM

Personal Finance in Your 20s & 30s

0-02-862415-7
$18.95

Creating a Web Page
Fourth Edition

0-7897-2256-9
$19.99 w/CD-ROM

Digital Photography
SECOND EDITION

0-02-864235-X
$24.95 w/CD-ROM

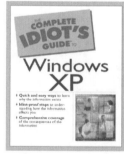

Windows XP

0-02-864232-5
$19.95

More than *400 titles* in *26 different categories*
Available at booksellers everywhere

ALPHA